# Lagunatics

# Lagunatics

Stories from the Beach

*Robert Heylmun*

***Lagunatics*** Stories from the Beach
© 2024 by Robert Heylmun

All rights reserved. No part of this publication may be reproduced, distributed, or transmitted in any form or by any means, including photocopying, recording, or other electronic or mechanical methods, without the prior written permission of the copyright owner and the publisher, except in the case of brief quotations embodied in critical reviews and certain other noncommercial uses permitted by copyright law.

ISBN: 979-8-89021-235-1 Paperback
ISBN: 979-8-89021-236-8 Hardback
ISBN: 979-8-89021-234-4 eBook

Printed in the United States of America.

Reviews for *The House on Shadow Lane*, prequel to *Lagunatics*

*Reading "The House on Shadow Lane" was like enjoying a year of friendship with a lively, intelligent group of men. I loved having brunch with Hal and Simon and the boys (I could practically taste the quiche!); I loved the melodrama in the restaurant where Hal worked; I loved the whole Laguna Beach scene. The story seemed very real, and so did the people. The love scenes were beautifully written. As a straight woman, I haven't read much gay fiction and I wasn't sure what it would be like to read gay love scenes. As it turned out, it was very much like reading any love scene. What struck me was not so much the anatomical specifics as the love between the partners and their mutual enjoyment. The scenes are essential; they give the story a deeper level of warmth and texture. And they are beautifully woven into the tale. I recommend this book to anyone who yearns for home and happy endings, and to anyone who enjoys a long, lazy meal with good friends. Salud!*

—Catherine Thiemann

*I bought this book after seeing it advertised in "The Gay and Lesbian Review". I thought the title sounded interesting. I was completely taken in by this book and its cast of characters. I could not put it down having read it in two days. I could not wait to find out what was going to happen to each character. Mr. Heylmun is a superb author and his writing style leaves you begging for more. I loved all of the gay characters and the love stories behind them. This is just a great story filled with surprises and begging for a sequel.*

—T. Vanetten

*Peopled with such interesting and varied characters, the plot of* The House on Shadow Lane *required a skillful hand to keep events moving at its almost frantic pace while remaining believable. As Heylmun weaves the lives of his characters into the nap of his plot, their connections produce the complicated, even twisted, events that make the novel so intriguing. How, the reader wonders, will the romance developing between Hal and Simon survive the challenges they face? How will Carl, who is "in love two people of different genders" decide? While readers have likely never known such characters or situations, the author's ingenious interplay cements the reader's interest. As a result, Heylmun's readers will likely share on finishing* The House on Shadow Lane, *a "joyful sense of loss" that paradoxically occurs whenever I finish a novel I have much enjoyed. Good stories like this leave the reader to ponder what will happen next to those characters. I knew I would like this book.*

—Michael Dryden

## *for Bob*

*He was my North, my South, my East and West,*
*My working week and my Sunday rest,*
*My noon, my midnight, my talk, my song;*
*I thought that love would last for ever: I was wrong.*

—W. H. Auden

# Contents

| | |
|---|---|
| Acknowledgements | xiii |
| Lagunatics | xv |
| Chapter 1 Hilltop Clouds | 1 |
| Chapter 2 A Brief Introduction | 7 |
| Chapter 3 Paradise Almost Regained | 10 |
| Chapter 4 Art For the Sake of Art | 15 |
| Chapter 5 Breakfast Among the Stars | 25 |
| Chapter 6 New Arrangements | 38 |
| Chapter 7 Reading the Sunday Comics | 41 |
| Chapter 8 All the News That's Fit to Print | 54 |
| Chapter 9 Around the Neighborhood | 57 |
| Chapter 10 There's No Business Like Show Business | 63 |
| Chapter 11 How sharper thana serpent's tooth | 68 |
| Chapter 12 Dalliance, Delicious Joy | 74 |
| Chapter 13 A Bloodless Revolution | 78 |
| Chapter 14 The cares that infest the day | 83 |
| Chapter 15 The Oasis | 86 |
| Chapter 16 Paying the Piper | 90 |
| Chapter 17 Desert Adventures | 95 |
| Chapter 18 Land Ho! | 103 |
| Chapter 19 More Sunday Comics | 109 |
| Chapter 20 All In a Day's Work | 114 |

| | |
|---|---|
| Chapter 21 Sotto Voce No More | 121 |
| Chapter 22 Lofty Neighbors | 127 |
| Chapter 23 More Rain on the Dark Tower | 132 |
| Chapter 24 Mirrors and Ghosts | 137 |
| Chapter 25 Hard Days at Tara | 143 |
| Chapter 26 The Unexamined Life | 149 |
| Chapter 27 Another World of Nouvelle Cuisine | 158 |
| Chapter 28 Gin and Moonlight | 163 |
| Chapter 29 Hear Ye, Hear Ye! | 166 |
| Chapter 30 In Vino Veritas | 171 |
| Chapter 31 Gaudeamus Igitur | 175 |
| Chapter 32 The Kindness of Strangers | 179 |
| Chapter 33 Pageantry and High Art | 183 |
| Chapter 34 Where the Heart Is | 190 |
| Chapter 35 Party Conversations | 200 |
| Chapter 36 Aftershocks and Aftermaths | 214 |
| Chapter 37 Heavenly Treasures | 224 |
| Chapter 38 Once to every man and nation | 228 |
| Chapter 39 Comes the moment to decide | 233 |
| Chapter 40 For the good or evil side | 240 |
| Chapter 41 Duty and Action | 246 |
| Chapter 42 By the light of burning martyrs | 250 |
| Chapter 43 It's Always Something | 256 |
| Chapter 44 Family Values | 261 |

# Acknowledgements

Thanks to all who read *The House on Shadow Lane* and asked for a sequel to that novel. For those of you who urged me on and pestered me about when the next book would be finished, I am very beholden to you. You kept me writing and thinking about how to evolve the characters you said you came to know in the first novel. I am grateful to Linda J. Patterson who kindly edited the text very thoroughly. Although she claims not to be a professional editor, she should be. Her notes and suggestions were immensely valuable. Alice Cowan and Horace Gibson read the very early pages in Florence last fall. As always their advice and counsel helped me a great deal.

# Lagunatics

Now who thought of that? Of course, no one knows, but nearly everyone in town identified with the name. Laguna Beach was a harbor, not for ships but for her people who were happy to be called Lagunatics; owners and renters and even visitors who came to town often enough to feel they belonged there. The envious outsiders made the word sound as if it came from 'lunatic' and liked to defined the residents of the seaside town as fulfilling the notion from even farther away that California was the land of fruits and nuts. By the time of our story, being a Lagunatic had taken on a sense of pride, a badge of honor. Most Lagunatics were anything but nuts, although a few, gay, straight, and in between, make their eccentric appearances in these pages. Nuts or not, they sought to lead their lives while adding to the color, sound, sense, and love of the song that sang in their heads, the paean to that special place in that special time, the poem that captivated them, and that was their home.

The year is 1978.

# CHAPTER 1
## *Hilltop Clouds*

"Dammit! Whose car is this?" Hal stormed out loud to himself as he negotiated the narrow slot between cars parked on either side of his carport. As usual, their street was entirely lined with parked cars. "Next thing they'll just park in the carport," he said, exasperated and fatigued from a day at school, topped off by a stop at the grocery. He managed to edge in, just barely missing one of the offending cars that extended itself a good two feet across the carport entrance. Just one more annoyance that he had not been able to get used to up here on the hill.

Theirs was a house like many others along the street: built on long, thin lots that allowed for views out their front windows toward the ocean, lots that required a closeness to neighboring houses that bothered Hal. Between their house and the neighbor's was a narrow passage that hardly provided room to walk. Two doors from their carport gave access to the house, one to the living room and one to the kitchen.

Unlocking his trunk, he removed three bags of groceries, put them in his arms, and while slamming the lid down, felt one bag slip away. It hit the pavement and exploded apples, grapefruit, oranges, lemons, and canned goods everywhere. He gingerly lowered the other two bags and tried to collect his errant groceries as many of them merrily rolled out of the carport and down the constricted walkway, some making it into the neighbor's backyard. He did the best he could to stow what he picked up in the other two bags, locked his car, and angrily stomped toward the kitchen door. He knew that the irritation of the intruding cars had nothing to do with his grocery accident, but the two incidents went hand in hand to darken his mood. His normally placid face took on a scowl.

Simon heard him coming, and also saw the tempest brewing on his lover's face as he opened the door and helped with the bags. Uh oh, this looks bad, he thought. "Got any idea whose cars those are? They might as well just park in our driveway. It gets harder all the time to pull in here," Simon consoled, setting the groceries down.

"Yeah, I just said the same thing loudly to the wind," Hal said as he reached over to give Simon a kiss. "Too bad nobody who owns those damned cars heard me." The parking problem was one of a list of things that had begun to accumulate into Hal's growing annoyance with living high up on the hill. Too far to a market, too little parking, too isolated; at least, that's how Hal felt. Despite the neighbors' houses proximity to each other, he and Simon had not made friends among the young and upwardly mobile set who had bought up the row houses on their street. While it was true that many people down in the village, often referred to as the flats, envied the ocean views and the relative quiet that living on the hills provided, it was a solitude that Hal thought could just as easily have been obtained by confinement in prison; the house turned out not to be the ideal aerie that he and Simon had imagined it would be.

They had thought about calling the parking police, but they also knew that doing so would not remedy the situation in the long run, and would more than likely mark them as cranky neighbors. "Look Hal, why don't we put the place on the market and move back down to the flats. I know you haven't liked it up here for a long time," Simon was smoothing down some raised hackles. This topic had come up several times of late.

"Oh Simon, it's just a bad day. The talk in the lunchroom got pretty heated. You'd be surprised at how many of my esteemed colleagues favor that filthy Briggs Initiative that's going on the ballot. Not everybody, but enough. OK, I won't get started on that, I promise."

"Go ahead, you've got every right to be anxious. Grab two beers and come sit down and let me rub your head," Simon said.

"But don't you miss the house on Shadow Lane? I know that we couldn't have afforded to fix it up and buy it, but . . ." Hal said as he was calming down, and moving into one of his ritual chants, he opened a beer. "It's not only the parking up here, or lack of it; it's just that I miss everyone coming and going as they did down there in the old days. I miss the boys, although, speaking of them, now that they've graduated from the university, we don't see much of them." He had felt secure down there on Shadow Lane, the secluded street where stood the house in which his gay family had been born and had flourished.

"I don't see why we can't move. This is 1978, after all, the economic slump is over, and the real estate market is booming. This place would sell in no time. Just look at this view," Simon said wistfully; he loved the view of the ocean and of the town nestled along the shoreline that their front windows gave them. Hal watched him look out over the vista of blue sky and sea, watched Simon's handsome features as they took on a faraway look while he gazed out over the majestic vista.

"Just like that, huh? And you could give up living here? You can't get enough of this view and you know it. I couldn't expect you to hand over the keys to somebody else and march back down to the flats just for me," he said, settling down on the sofa.

"It's not just for you, and it's not as if we'd be leaving town, you know. We can always go to Frank's and enjoy the view. Besides, I miss being able to walk down to the beach. I miss being close to the sea."

"Come on, you're coddling me at the expense of what you want. Look, I'm just being a crank. We'll be OK here; at least, I've got the kitchen the way I want it, and God knows it's a better one than that antique we had on Shadow Lane was. Feel like putting up with a grump?" Hal said, relaxing his mood and smiling. He reached up to touch Simon's hair. Simon plopped down beside him and curled up under his arm. "Let's just wait a while, talk about it some more, see how things go," Hal whispered into Simon's neck, breathing in the intoxicating aroma that smelled slightly of lemons mixed with some herb that he could never identify until he finally had decided long ago that it just was essential Simon. Sniffing led to nuzzling which led to much more rigorous activities; so, their conversation on the topic of houses was shelved for the moment.

Later as they lay in bed, Hal said, "Did you hear what Norman told somebody at the Labor Day party when he didn't think I overheard? That he parked blocks away, walked up Alta Vista around that dangerous curve to get here," picking up the house topic again. Fewer friends visited than previously, and that bothered Hal a great deal. Their house on Shadow Lane had for years been gay central, a warm and loving place where everyone considered themselves welcome, where they felt as if they could drop in, particularly during one of Hal's breakfasts, to chat, have coffee, catch up on everyone else's lives, and generally just hang out. That had been the essential charm of that house, its accessibility aided by genuine hospitality. By contrast this house up on the hill seemed like an almost unassailable fortress in Hal's mind, and he reminisced about those days around the big dining room table on Shadow Lane.

The "boys" Hal had mentioned earlier were Mike and Tom, the two guys whom he felt he had almost adopted back in 1973. Time and circumstances had separated them; one lived in San Francisco, the other in San Diego. They had found new lovers, and had established new lives. "Interesting that they all get along, huh?" Hal mused. "I mean, when the four of them were all here over Labor Day, you'd have thought they were brothers."

"That's because they were all here to see their Mommy," Simon teased, earning him an attempt at being tickled, something he always avoided if he could. "It was great having them here, wasn't it? Lucky we have all this room to put them up. Never could have done it on Shadow Lane."

"But that's all they talked about, you may remember, those days we spent together down there," Hal said as he went to the bookcase to find a photo album.

More than the house problem loomed in Hal's mind. The clouds of hatred against gays had begun to gather and were no longer on the distant horizon. Just last year Anita Bryant had moved her bigotry campaign into the public arena in Florida where she managed to get the voters of that far-thinking state to overturn statutes against gay discrimination. She then led another hate campaign against gay teachers that bled into California in the form of the Briggs Initiative. As a gay teacher, Hal was more than a little concerned about how voters in California might turn against him and thousands like him. The talk about the issue predominated the faculty lunchroom at his school; Hal listened but stayed out of the general discussion. Instead, he fretted, wondering exactly where he stood, or might stand, among his colleagues once they knew about him.

He thought back to that happy day when his school principal phoned to confirm that he'd been hired. That September, those golden days of new adventures, new kids, and finally being where he wanted to be, in the classroom. He acquired a reputation for being a hard worker, for being a fair teacher, and a good colleague. So went nearly four years of unmolested peace in which he and Simon shared a deeper commitment to their relationship, bought a house of their own, and looked forward to years of happiness.

But now the uncertain political climate fed the smoldering embers of fear in his mind, an apprehension that he usually managed to sublimate. He taught his classes, stayed concerned about his students, and did his job without attracting attention from anyone in the administration. But probably for the first time, the sense that his future might be in jeopardy, that his life with Simon that they had meticulously built together could end, or at least be seriously altered, produced both an anger over having to abide the presence of evil, as well as a penchant toward venting bouts of temper aimed at more inconsequential things.

Simon saw what was going on and identified Hal's moods for what they were, recognizing as he always had, when exterior forces plagued his lover. It had been Simon who had buoyed up Hal's diminished self-esteem in the early days of their relationship by merely loving him, showing that he was unwavering in that love, until Hal came to believe in its power and majesty as well as its transforming balm. Simon listened, consoled, encouraged, but did not succumb to any angry outbursts that Hal from time to time displayed. He knew that the anger was not aimed at him, that the demons inside Hal's mind were at fault, and that Hal's occasional rants were a kind of exorcism of them. It was Simon who came up with calmer and more logical ideas for Hal's troubles.

Together they felt safe, away from the world's assaults, secure in the family of friends they had cemented into their lives, a family that they wanted to reinforce against the coming hurricane of gay bigotry, and they longed for the days on Shadow Lane in that falling down house where they had first evolved into a family. The photo album that Hal was looking through showed dozens of pictures of dinners, parties, celebrations, and gettogethers in the house on Shadow Lane, and only a scant few taken in this hilltop house whose only attribute seemed to be its view of the distant sea. "See what I mean? We might as well install a moat to keep people out," Hal said.

Their huge Labor Day bash last year had been their first big party since moving up on the hill. With two or three exceptions, the party list included everyone who had been to an unforgettable Christmas party on Shadow Lane a few years before. Norman Stands had arrived bedecked and bedizened with his usual assortment of Navajo turquoise jewelry and a youngish man in tow; George came with his partner Marty (aka Martha) whose penchant for making everything he said into a question had grown even more annoying; Dan, who apologized for not having brought any of his suspicious culinary creations (his apology was more than graciously accepted); Frank Binder, and about thirty or so other acquaintances and friends. And of course, Edward the regal Siamese cat greeted everyone.

There had been something wrong with that party; no one openly complained, but word got back to them that a number of invitees besides Norman had parked far away. Quite a diminished number finally arrived, and many left early. Things just weren't the same as they had been on Shadow Lane. Wistfulness and nostalgia for the old days and the possibility of reliving them in a more hospitable home had begun to seep into Hal's mind, creating a mood that was becoming more and more solidified into a genuine and purposeful desire to move, to recapture some of the old magic down on the flats. The truth was that as much as Simon liked the ocean view, he had begun to take it for granted, and like Hal, was beginning to feel that they had lived long enough up on the hill.

Christmas magnified their increasing unease with living on the hill; it had come and gone without the old joy and fun that had been its hallmark at the house on Shadow Lane, and although Hal and Simon managed to have a few small dinners for friends, nothing seemed to elevate their mood to holiday heights. Bleak January set in, and the ocean view began to pall. So did the allure of Hal's terrific kitchen. "A house is more than a kitchen, Hal," Simon said after a number of discussions had begun to make up their minds about moving. Finally, the search was on for just the right house back down on the flats, and the house on the hill, view and all, went on the market.

Oblivious to this decision, Edward proceeded to find his usual spot on his own cushion in front of the west windows where the setting sun still warmed him into a late afternoon nap.

# CHAPTER 2
# A Brief Introduction

To say that Edward was merely a cat would be to minimize the force, the spirit, and the prevailing attitude that he embodied when he came to live with Hal and Simon. His royalty sprang from his blue-point Siamese pedigree, and he felt a certain noblesse oblige to uphold a dignified attitude among the humans from whom he deigned to accept meals and lodging. This attitude often took the form of draping himself gracefully on various of the softest furnishings in the house, generally in the center of sofa cushions, but sometimes on the top of the stereo unit whose inner electronics provided a constant source of just the right amount of heat for his comfort. His humans humored him, outdoing each other to provide him with delicacies such as boneless chicken breast, his favorite repast.

He became the center of attention at any gathering among other humans—he had no tolerance of others of his own kind on the premises—and everyone greeted him with caresses and chat, often before they greeted Hal or Simon. He accepted these greetings as his due, responding with the amount of deference and regard owed the visitors who offered such compliments according to what he considered to be their pitiably lesser station in life as a human, so inferior to his own as a cat. For a special treat to the humans foregathered around the coffee table as they had drinks, Edward would from time to time delight one and all by sitting amid the glassware while meticulously cleaning his underwear. Such a display was reserved for special occasions and for favored guests; he never bothered when only Hal and Simon were home alone.

But his was not an altogether indolent life, far from it. He had duties that took him ranging over his territory on a daily basis. The house overlooked a canyon and that meant that any number of animals populated the area that surrounded Edward's domain. He made friends with a particularly amiable family of raccoons whom he once invited to lunch inside the house and whom Hal discovered upon returning from school one afternoon, all of the masked guests very comfortably nibbling cat food in the kitchen. Once these were run off—no mean feat to dislodge raccoons from one's kitchen —a sign went up over Edward's dishes that read **NO GUESTS**. That seemed to have worked; at least, if the raccoons did return for free lunches, Hal never knew about their forays into the house nor of Edward's willing complicity in their care and feeding.

Not all of the animals of the canyon were treated with such courtesy and regard however. From time to time, the carcass of a dispatched mouse (once even a rat) would be displayed on the doorstep, the results of Edward's nascent skills as a successful hunter. He felt duty-bound to maintain this expertise as well, to demonstrate to his humans that his ancient lineage had bequeathed him more than merely elegant looks and an affinity for adding to household décor. While these trophies of the hunt were exhibited and subsequently praised by his humans, Edward never deigned to eat any of his quarry, preferring to keep his diet on the more aristocratic level provided by his humans.

His arrival at their house had been the result of his no longer being wanted at his previous place of residence, a fact that never diminished his own vision of his entitlements and privileges. His former human (did Edward ever have an owner?) had been a young man who was moving to Berkeley to attend the university there, and despite the advanced toleration of nearly everything and everyone at Cal, that tolerance had not extended to blue-point Siamese, no matter how nobly they carried themselves, for inclusion in the dorm rooms at that august center of higher learning. Thus, a new home had to be found for Edward, and unbeknownst to him that he was taken in at the point of being homeless, he very easily accustomed himself to his new domain with not one but two doting humans who served his every whim. In the prime of his young life of less than two human years, Edward assumed the throne and reigned with dignity and a stateliness acquiesced to by one and all.

The name given him by his former human—who could possibly know what his real and regal Siamese name might have been—was Gainsborough, the English artist who painted *The Blue Boy*. Since Edward was a blue-point Siamese, that had seemed an appropriate name, but it didn't seem so to Hal who was working on an essay involving the gay king of England, Edward

III; he therefore bestowed on his new and regal companion a better and less hokey name. Thus it was that Gainsborough became Edward, a name change that made very little difference to him although he came to recognize the name as his own. He would, if he were in the mood and not otherwise employed in feline activities, occasionally respond to it.

"How do you think he would get along in a new place? He has so many friends here," Simon joked as he scratched Edward's ears.

"If he has a yard to patrol, he'll be fine," Hal said. "He's fine everywhere he lives. It took him exactly two days to figure out that he had arrived in a palace with two slaves to wait on him when he condescended to live with us."

Although it is commonly supposed that cats do not like change, preferring instead to inhabit familiar surroundings, it must also be noted that Edward was anything but common. If he sensed that change was in the air, he displayed no outward signs of distress, confident that his humans would comfortably provide for him in the fashion to which he had long assumed was his due. And of course, he was right.

# CHAPTER 3
# Paradise Almost Regained

"We're driving the realtor nuts," Simon said as they waited outside the house on Myrtle Street. "This is the fourth time we've got him over here."

"Hey, it's his job. Besides, if we buy this place, he should take us out for a celebratory dinner in gratitude. Ah, here he comes."

Desmond Downs had been selling real estate in Laguna Beach for thirty years. His arrival in a new Mercedes proclaimed his successful career, but he was starting to burn out these days and thought constantly about retiring. As he slowly made his way toward the house, it was clear that he would have preferred getting this over with and returning home. This had better be the last time I have to show this place to these two, he thought, as he pasted on his plastic, but what he considered winning, smile to greet his clients. "Well, gentlemen, here we are again. Do you have more questions?" he said, displaying his gleaming array of dental crowns and caps.

"Simon wanted to look at the electrical circuits in the place, but all I want to know is how soon we could move in."

"How does forty-five days sound?" Desmond grinned. He and Hal talked on about paperwork and finances while Simon went off to look at circuit breakers. Desmond guided them once more into the kitchen, knowing very well where Hal's interests lay.

"What do you think, Doc?" Hal asked the returning Simon.

"No problems that I can see," he replied. "The place has been recently rewired and it all looks good. Want to do it?"

And it was done. They signed the papers then and there. The doubts and fears that sat brooding in the back of Hal's mind dissipated in light of the joy of having bought this new home, and their life suddenly seemed less vulnerable. The house emitted an instant aura of safety, its old style whispering quietly of permanence and stability. Here he felt that they could both weather whatever storms might come their way, and also restore the larger family of friends they had on Shadow Lane. Both of them saw those possibilities in each other's eyes as Desmond Downs stowed the contract and then lumbered down the front walk toward his car.

It had everything they wanted and more. In some ways it resembled the house on Shadow Lane, sitting back from the street as it did, but behind a somewhat smaller front yard. One story, rambling across the lot with an easy grace and style. It differed in that the paint was new, the original windows had been replaced with modern ones, both bedrooms were in the back, and the garage and parking spaces were accessible from the alley. This house also sported a separate guest cottage at the back of the lot, across a nicely arranged garden from the main house. "It's got everything but a pool," Hal had said when they first viewed the house. "And who needs one of those? Oh Simon, it's a terrific house, don't you think?"

"We'd need to redo the master bathroom, keep that in mind," Simon had said with his usual cautionary view of things while going over the photos and notes they had taken which were spread out on the coffee table. "It won't be cheap, either."

Discussions of costs, sales, finances, loans, and escrows had consumed their days, generally led by the practical Simon, and by and large boring Hal who simply wanted to move. At last, they had found a buyer for the house on the hill, a couple named Initson, and things began to go forward quickly. They sat on the front deck and looked at their view for one of the last times. "You know, it really is beautiful up here, but I won't miss it. It's like watching from afar someplace you can't visit. We'll soon be close to the sea again," Simon said. "Mrs. Initson really loved the kitchen, Hal. You were right to have it remodeled when we bought here. I think that's what sold the house."

"Maybe. *He* certainly didn't look very enthusiastic until we pointed out that extra space under the living room floor that's big enough for a hot tub. Have you seen him anywhere before? He looked familiar to me somehow."

"Market? A restaurant? On the beach? Who knows? It's a small town," Simon suggested. But Hal pondered that face for a while, and tried to index where it fit into the array of men he might have met over the years of living in Laguna, famously known as a "fishy little sleeping village".

"It will come to me. Meantime, we have forty-five days to get out of here and into the new house. Think we can do it?" Simon agreed that they could, and Edward added his usual "pffft" as he sauntered off toward a sunlit chair.

By mid-March they had more or less moved into the house on Myrtle Street. Another week of living out of cartons and bags, and finally something like order was restored; life looked as if it might resume a more comfortable routine as they sank down onto the sofa for the first time in their new living room.

Suddenly, "What the hell is that?" Hal exclaimed, springing up. "It sounds like somebody in horrible pain."

"Oh, didn't I mention it? When I was here two days ago, I discovered that we live next door to none other than the celebrated Bertrand Lebland, star of stage and The Blue Cove. That's him vocalizing."

"Vocalizing? My God! Does he do that all the time, do you think? You'd expect to hear the sound of a crash after screeching like that."

"Unfortunately, but I don't think he does it at night, if that's any consolation," Simon said. "Look at Edward." His nibs showed signs of extreme discomfort by twitching his tail and hissing as he crept around the room as if he were being stalked.

"Hey! Who's coming up the front walk?" Hal said.

All they could see at first was an unidentifiable pair of legs, and arms carrying two stacked boxes. What was exposed of the arms gave away the visitor's identity. Each was bedecked with silver and turquoise bracelets, the fingers of both hands equally decorated with Navajo rings. It could only be Norman Stands. "Come take this top box, one of you. My God, it weighs a ton!" he said, jingling his way toward the door.

Simon rushed out to help Norman with the carton. "What's in here anyway? A piano?"

"Just some things I thought you two might use here in your new palace," he said, collapsing into a chair. "Open it up and let's see if you like them." Inside was a complete tableware service for twelve in silver. "Not just silver, my dears, but sterling silver. This had belonged to my aunt. I never use it and you might as well have it. You get to polish the stuff. I obviously have enough silver of my own to polish, and I certainly can't wear knives and forks. Now, do you have a drink for this tired old lady?"

"Norman! It's beautiful! But are you sure you want to give this away? It must be worth a fortune," Hal said, glowing over such a wonderful present and pleased that the design was not florid and baroque. In fact, the pattern looked very art nouveau, clean and simple. Simon handed Norman a vodka tonic and Hal a scotch and soda.

"It's yours. Consider it a housewarming and belated wedding present. Invite me over from time to time to dine and I'll be happy. Have I told you that I'm reviewing the new dinner theater? The star, if that's what you can call him, is none other than your neighbor, Bertrand Lebland, singing most of the male songs from *Oklahoma!*"

"You didn't have to tell us, Norman. Hear that noise? We've been hearing him rehearse through these very windows," Hal moaned. "Are there any good notes in the actual production? We've heard all of the ear damaging ones."

"No, not many I'm told, but he has great presence, you have to hand him that. I take it that you haven't met the great Bertrand; it's hard to believe that you haven't seen him around. He's a looker, and I can remember not many years ago when he swept into town and wowed all those old queens at The Cove into a rare five minutes of awed silence. You'll see what I mean. Well, I'm off. I can get you free tickets if you want," Norman teased. "Thanks for the drink, dears."

"I think we'll pass," Simon said. "But I'm looking forward to your review." And Norman was gone, clanking his usual collection of Navajo jewelry through the door on the way out.

"Maybe after the show closes, we can get some peace," Hal said, sinking into a chair. "Just maybe . . ."

Edward began producing his throaty howl now that he was within earshot of Bertrand's practice session. This particular wail had heretofore been reserved for any occasion when Edward was forced to ride in a car, an ordeal he hated, thinking that he was headed for some unpleasantness at the vet's. It was a sound that was at once pitiable and eerie. Passersby must have thought that something dreadful and life-threatening was in progress, perhaps a poor animal being gutted alive, if they happened to hear Edward's response to the operatic exertions from the next-door neighbor. In tandem, the combination was unendurable. Hal did his best to move Edward out of earshot, and therefore out of harm's way while Bertrand trilled out his scales and arpeggios, very audible through his open windows. "He's really convinced that everyone is enjoying this, isn't he?" Hal said, tightly closing the windows on that side of the house. "It's like having someone ten feet away whose hobby is playing with fire sirens."

"And he's tireless, a true devotee to his uh . . . art," Simon remarked. "How were we to know that this would be going on when we bought the place? It certainly wasn't part of the real estate ad. But what can we do?"

"It goes a long way to explain why it took so little time to close the deal on the house with the Schenleys, and Mr. Schenley is deaf. They couldn't get out of here fast enough."

They sat in abject misery as the vocalizing continued. "Oh God! It's already been over an hour since he started and he shows no sign of quitting. We've got to think of something. A firebomb? No, too close to our place. Hired assassin? No, we'd get caught. Besides, he probably isn't a bad person. It's just that he can't sing."

"We'll come up with something, we *have* to come up with something," Simon moaned as Bertrand hit a particularly ungodly high pitch (more or less), and Edward echoed it from the bedroom. "I'm beginning to understand the origin of the phrase 'That was a hell of a note.'" They decided to take a walk to the beach and allow the dueling singers to have it out with each other.

* * * *

*"Thinks he got away from us, huh? Moved to another house in Fagtown, but we got him. He and that faggot doctor he's got living with him. This'll be fun getting that queer fired from his teaching job. We gotta protect our kids from queers like him. When can you help me take some pictures of the two fags? Hey, Willie! Look at this! A little house back there. Perfect, man. We can keep an eye on the queers from right in there. Bet we can get in there through the back wall by the fence. Help me with this loose board, will ya? Keep quiet!"*

# CHAPTER 4
## *Art For the Sake of Art*

Perhaps it was because Laguna Beach had for decades been home to the annual Pageant of the Masters, a summer extravaganza which consisted of a series of *tableau vivant* copies of famous works of art, that configured it also as ground zero for the stage-struck among its citizenry whose inner longings for a stage career thrust them toward dreams of stardom. Perhaps it was simply that the village seemed to support various forms of artistic endeavor, good and not so good, and tolerated a wide range of attempts at gaining a reputation among the locals that propelled the likes of Bertrand Lebland into the circle of whatever spotlight would have him. His talent, if that is the word, was as a tenor, insomuch as he had a voice roughly in that vocal range, and an imagined ability that he felt that fate had unjustly ignored, fate having sent him instead into a career as a teller in a bank. As one might expect from an ego that presumes to unite with the luminaries of the stage, Bertrand always announced that he was 'a banker' when asked about his nine-to-five job. In fact, nearly everything about Bertrand's life came across as larger than its reality, but regardless of how he described it, the bank provided him sufficient income to indulge his real passion, astonishing an audience.

Bertrand was possessed of the kind of singing voice that one wants to hear very little of, a tinny tenor which might have served better by being buried deep within a chorus. His solo high notes caused serious concern for one's hearing, particularly if he decided, assisted by a microphone, to favor his audience with what he believed emulated operatic greats such as Caruso, and more recently, Pavarotti. Reaching such musical heights via an ascending scale and sustaining them once he got there often took more singing skill than Bertrand truly had, but reach them he did (usually), and he attempted them at every opportunity, convinced that his audience was in awe of them. It often was. At the cessation of such notes, a look of consummate pride invariably seated itself on his flushed face as he waited for the acclamations of his listeners to help him generate the very studied and rehearsed smile that was meant to show his audience just the appropriate amount of gratitude, tempered with a slender touch of star quality condescension.

Bertrand's star had risen several years ago, thanks to a certain reviewer.

There had been a production of a locally composed opera, presumably derived from the style of Verdi (or was it Puccini?), called *The Plains of Windy Troy*, written by Maestro Gaston Plimpton, and produced on the local stage through the financial backing of several wealthy patrons of the Laguna Light Opera, particularly of one Mrs. Ethel Declamber, these days living in widowhood on the largesse of the late Mr. Declamber, in a house of vast proportions. Her late husband had shown no penchant for the opera in any form, and Ethel felt it her duty to make up for his shortsightedness during his life by patronizing struggling musicians after his death, an arrangement that would have suited Mr. Delcamber perfectly. In this case, it was Maestro Plimpton who found himself installed in one of the many bedroom suites in her mansion overlooking the sea.

"So inspirational, don't you think?" Ethel had cooed to her new resident who spent about an hour or so altogether during any given day working on his 'magnum opus', once he rose in the morning (often closer to noon) after a night of carousing in various local bars, most notably The Blue Cove, in pursuit, he said, of more backers for the upcoming production of his opera. Meanwhile, his patroness got quite a lot of mileage out of his majestic presence in her house among her friends by crowing about having a living, breathing (not to say eating, drinking, and spending) composer living under her roof. "But Gaston, my dear, you needn't bother trying to find more backers. If the opera needs more financial help, you have only to is ask," Ethel purred. "There's no need for you to exhaust yourself by being out every night this way. It's so much more comfortable here, don't you think?"

"Ah, my dear Ethel, you have already been so very generous, and it's time that others contribute as well. I'm writing this great work for the fame of the city, for the sake of opera here. It will be a hallmark, composed right here by the sea and in your home. Pray let others join in on making it all possible."

Mrs. Declamber was only partly mollified, her interests in Maestro Plimpton having moved from art for the sake of art toward much more permanent, matrimonial hopes. She dreamed of future operas pouring forth from what she supposed to be the prolific pen of the great maestro, and visions of her playing Clara Schumann to Plimpton's Robert filled her with utter bliss. She envisioned endless days of shared breakfasts and lunches before the maestro made his way to his studio to produce wonderful art, days and days of togetherness and a steadfast devotion to each other, all wrapped in an elegance that only the creation of beautiful music, and her sizeable fortune, could bring into existence.

The musical extravaganza that he was writing was, to paraphrase Dr. Samuel Johnson, both good and original. Unfortunately the part that was good was not original, and the brief part that was original was not good as it borrowed liberally from almost every extant 19th century opera. Maestro Plimpton contrived a plot involving most, if not all, of the major Olympian gods and goddesses as they dabbled in the dubiously interesting affairs of mortals encamped before the walls of Troy. Very little of the *Iliad* was used; in fact, a completely new and heretofore unheard of set of mortal Greeks and Trojans took the stage to do vocal battle, to be armed with clanking swords, armor, and other authentic noises associated with ancient warfare, as well as incomprehensible singing. In the interest of verisimilitude, the combatants were encouraged to grunt, groan, moan, and even scream warlike epithets as they advanced whatever skirmish had been called for in the opera's libretto.

The important thing was that the work was finished—not polished, but finished as far as Maestro Plimpton was concerned, and just in time after the unfortunate discovery by the smitten Mrs. Declamber of the maestro and her pool boy in bed together one afternoon. Disappointment of her dashed hopes that had begun to sprout a more permanent dream for her and the maestro ensconced in her mansion immediately catapulted her to similarly dizzying heights of fury, the outcome of which was the insistence that the perfidious maestro leave her house at once. Having been kicked out of similar situations in his murky past, Maestro Plimpton had taken the precaution of fortifying himself with quite a lot of spending money while Mrs. Declamber was still in his pocket, romantically speaking, and he was in hers in every other sense. He decamped to the rooftop penthouse of the hotel across the street from The Blue Cove, installing the pool boy, similarly discharged from Mansion Declamber, in his rooms as his valet. He had also taken the precaution of placing Mrs. Declamber's considerable contribution to the opera in a bank account on which he was the sole signer.

The task of putting on the opera began despite Mrs. Declamber's increasingly vocal and widespread rants concerning the composer's character. The project took enormous resources beyond money; dozens of singers were needed from the town's supply of vocalists. If any of them had had any sense of loyalty and duty to the scorned Mrs. Declamber, they managed to rise above those considerations with the higher calling of donating their talents to the grander realms of music.

Finally anyone who had so much as sung alto in a church choir was commandeered to be at least a chorus member in the production, and tryouts for the innumerable major roles, which seemed to feature more warriors than even Homer could have imagined, had winnowed out the chaff, somehow retaining Bertrand Lebland as a candidate for the role of Ares, Greek god of war. For one thing, he looked the part if indeed Ares had a warlike brow as Homer tells us he did. Bertrand's handsome features could also look fierce; he certainly sounded fierce to the casting director, and the next thing Bertrand knew, he was an opera star.

Hazel McKenna, a lady of indeterminate age, won the role of Ares' paramour, Aphrodite, not because she in any way resembled anyone's idea of the goddess of love, but because she had carefully maintained her strong mezzo soprano voice, some said by vying with the sea gulls that flocked to her house to squawk for handouts every day. But such an opinion was likely born of envy from the also-rans who were relegated to minor roles; in fact, the author of the remark became one of the lesser Pleiades whose brief sojourn across the crowded stage in Act II would scarcely be noticed. Hazel went to work on her role immediately after she had written a substantial check in support of this worthy and artistic cause. "Just make that out to Gaston Plimpton," the maestro smiled.

It is perhaps unfair to assert that such financial contributions exclusively fueled the maestro's decisions, but it is safe to take for granted that this was the sort of production in which someone with the fiscal resources of say, Florence Foster Jenkins, could have easily been called upon to be the leading diva.

Rehearsals were closed to the public of course, but news soon got out that the opera, written right there in Ethel Declamber's mansion by a known composer, would no doubt put the town on the map, bolstered by what had been overheard outside the rehearsal doors and from the Pageant stage itself. The excited opera company members could not help but discuss what was going on as they met with friends for drinks, and at The Blue Cove, every detail of how things were proceeding was greeted with increasing anticipation. Thus, the long awaited opening night saw a sold-out house at the Pageant of the Masters auditorium; no one in town wanted to miss this.

The first scene, unannounced by an overture, opened suddenly on the windy plains of Troy, made gusty indeed with the aid of huge fans that maintained a gale from stage right to stage left, competing with all but the loudest of singers. The battle was in progress as the curtain rose, with much clanking of swords, spears, and shields, and with various of the gods and mortals emerging from the fray from time to time, and coming to the front of the stage to tell the audience in high operatic style just what was going on, who was winning, who was losing, followed by something about the unfair advantage given the Trojans by a highly incensed Ares.

As all of this confusion and hubbub continued for quite a while, Maestro Plimpton supposed that his epic presentation of ancient battle would entertain the local bumpkins regardless of any musicality (or lack of it), but the audience began to grow restive. Giggling broke out, then outright laughter erupted from the audience as the combatants on stage wearied from repeated fake sword fights; uproarious guffaws exploded as the whole battle scene devolved, despite the director's and the composer's vision of a classic panorama, into something reminiscent of a Three Stooges skit. Finally, the curtain dropped on Scene One, and the orchestra abruptly moved from accompanying a battle scene to music that hoped to usher in a more amorous mood.

The curtain rose on Scene Two, displaying the palace on Mount Olympus where Ares and Aphrodite were found in amorous conversation that included her warnings against letting her husband, the ugly Vulcan (his Latin name was used for some reason), know about their tryst. Their competitive duet continued to reveal the librettist's skill:

ARES: Oh my love, immortal Aphrodite,
by the lyre of Orpheus,

APHRODITE: Oh mine Ares whose strength at arms,

Thy husband Vulcan, smelly and odorous,
Shall not, if we take care, be ware of us,
Or if he will find us thus amorous,
In flagrante delecto inglorious,
Shall we not show up notorious
Before all the gods?

Bestirs my heart and soul and harms
Mine own repute o'er towns and farms
Tho' danger all 'round ring loud alarms
From whose loins springs noted ardor
That moves mine ichor to dewy odor . . . .

And on and on it went. Not all of Aphrodite's part could be clearly heard, and therefore cannot be faithfully recorded here—the original libretto has been regrettably lost—but probably just as well.

At this point in the production, the audience, whose ability to suspend disbelief that the young, not to say effete Aries would be making love to an Aphrodite who was, despite the best efforts of the make-up crew, old enough to be his grandmother, had moved from laughter into open guffaws and not a few cat calls that included loud suggestions about taking the whole scene to a retirement home. Such remarks might have discouraged other stars of lesser magnitude, but Bertrand sang on as the amorous Ares, pursuing Hazel McKenna, the sought-after and coquettish Aphrodite around the stage, proclaiming his love as well as his sexual prowess, his blood fired to the boiling point by the heat of recent battle. His ardor was perhaps spreading the marmalade of artistic intention too thinly over the bread of possibility as their duet culminated on a kind of sofa with Bertrand all but lying on top of the pinioned Hazel who was having noticeable trouble breathing, and therefore, singing. His conquest complete, the curtain rang down on Act One to the intensifying noise (not all of it applause) from a highly amused audience.

Despite the unexpected hilarity produced in Act One, intermission saw about half the audience departing for various bars around town, congratulating themselves that they had paid very little for tickets to *The Plains of Windy Troy*. What they would miss out on was the final act in which a huge banquet was being set on Olympus around an enormous table, and it was discovered that the gods ate off of what had to be Melmac dinnerware, clacked down onto the wooden table by the Pleiades.

When the gods had assembled for dinner, the table bore the brunt of Ares' anger as he flung dishes around (obviously the reason for the indestructible Melmac), one of which rolled into the orchestra pit and struck the viola player in the back of the head. That unfortunate orchestra member calmly quit playing, and with a look on his face that communicated that he had had enough anyway, merely packed up his instrument and left.

These histrionics were of course accompanied by a very vigorous aria in which Ares (Bertrand) disclosed the real reason he supported the Trojans over the Greeks, a somewhat garbled libretto that nevertheless revealed his unrequited love for one Halitoses, a Greek soldier of unparalleled beauty described in detail by the angered and sexually frustrated Ares. Never mind the previous act in which the same Ares was all over Aphrodite like a cheap suit in his lengthy declamation of undying love for her eternal beauty. The gods, it seems, are fickle.

It is not likely that what was left of the audience took note of Ares' unusual lyrics nor of their prurient import, given the chaos that chiefly reigned on stage during Bertrand's delivery of them. Competing with the aria were the gods who had foregathered for the meal, and here Maestro Plimpton, taking a cue from Mozart, attempted the skill of having a number of things happen at once as incidental conversations were set to music, presumably to provide a chorus for Ares' rant.

Finally, the opera merely ended, and none too soon since it never seemed to have a plot or much of a story to begin with, and instead had a second act that concerned itself with looking in on Zeus and Hera's place to see what might be on the menu for dinner. It left the audience with many uncertainties about what the gods were doing about Troy, or how the Greeks had figured into their lives or what happened to any of the mortals or anything else, but it also left the audience laughing its way out of the theater. Clearly any reviewer would have his job cut out for him as he wrote up his notes on *The Plains of Windy Troy*.

The resulting review sustained Bertrand in the belief that he had missed his calling as an opera tenor. "As Ares, the god of war," the reviewer wrote, "Bertrand Lebland's performance was quite unearthly. One cannot fathom how the human voice could be capable of such sound." High praise indeed as far as Bertrand was concerned, and the reviewer's 'acclaim' became his mantra. It was on this meager crust of bread that Bertrand fed an exaggerated estimation of his vocal talent. It is not surprising that a man who, despite his exceptional good looks, desperately needed validation and assurance—neither of which he had received from his aloof and emotionally unavailable parents—should seize on any scrap of faint praise, ignore the possibility that it might have been rendered in a less generous spirit than the one he interpreted, and feed on it to grow his starved ego.

The opera had only the one performance; no one seemed interested in buying tickets for subsequent ones, despite the highly touted amusement value (Was it a spoof? Were they serious? Wasn't it the funniest thing ever?) that tongues wagged around town about what they had seen and heard. Maestro Gaston Plimpton disappeared after a stop at the bank to cash a final check, leaving behind both a large bar bill at the hotel as well as his pool boy; the sets came down, the cast dismissed, and that was the end of *The Plains of Windy Troy.*

During the ensuing years Bertrand had waited in vain to be called into the production of other operas, but there were no others that the deep pockets among the Laguna Beach Light Opera were willing to back unless the opera had been written by a tried and true composer, say Mozart or at least Mascagni. Their collective experiment into financing unknown itinerant composers like Gaston Plimpton had been nearly ruinous, and they retreated to safer musical, not to say fiduciary, ground. Certainly, the wounded heart of Mrs. Declamber had not healed sufficiently to allow her to do anything except to approve the opera company's new conservative stance.

Despite what might be called spurious approbation, Bertrand enjoyed a certain local notoriety, even a kind of stardom. While it was true that he languished without new operatic offers coming his way, and nothing that Mozart or Mascagni wrote seemed to have roles that suited his particular talents, he was not discouraged, and undaunted, he ensconced himself at the piano bar of The Blue Cove where he "kept his voice up" by deigning to sing a show tune or two after being begged and pleaded with to do so, pretending to acquiesce to popular demand only very reluctantly. Here various bar pianists turned over the mike to him as he let loose with something he deemed to be classic like "Danny Boy".

His was the bar stool at the side nearest the mike at the piano, and anyone who was a regular at The Blue Cove knew that Bertrand's entrance meant vacating that particular stool in deference to the great singer's appearance. Not all of the piano players hired there were avid fans of Bertrand's particular—some might say peculiar—style of musical rendition, and were therefore not always eager to share the entertainment spotlight with him. But one old veteran who always coddled Bertrand was the inimitable Vi Winters. She had been playing bar piano since one of the world wars (conjecture was rampant about exactly which) and she had played it all; that is, she had played everything for everybody, and frankly, she was played out. She therefore welcomed Bertrand for whom she merely had to accompany, only occasionally joining him in a duet.

These special treats were not as rare as many of the regular diners would have wanted, shrilly interrupting as they did most conversations over the dinner table. In the middle of one's steak sandwich, which was not as juicy as the gossip at the table, would come the unignorable vocals from the famous Bertrand, sumptuously accompanied by his willing collaborator, Vi Winters. Florence Foster Jenkins had her Cosme McMoon; Bertrand Lebland had his Vi Winters.

Regardless of Bertrand's questionable vocal abilities, his good looks sustained him over the disappointing years during which he was not recalled to the operatic stage. Over six feet tall, trim and well-proportioned, Bertrand had loyally visited a gymnasium where, as far as possible, he kept the ravages of time from invading the tone of his muscles without his efforts producing the vulgar look of a weight lifter. He had a good crop of light brown hair which nature had yet to tinge with grey, a face that people admired when he came into a room, and a regal bearing, and there were more than a few who attested to one other of Bertrand's generous physical attributes. He looked magnificent, and his handsome face and figure got the attention of the impresario who was assembling the cast for the new production of *Oklahoma!* It had been several years since Bertrand's debut as Ares, and the impresario, ignorant of that ill-fated production, saw only Bertrand's winning smile beaming in his direction. When the producer, at once struck by Bertrand's splendid appearance, learned that he was also a singer, he wasted no time in proposing that the role of Curly might suit Bertrand's talents.

It was rumored about The Blue Cove that the deal was consummated on the producer's casting couch, or more accurately, bed, a story that received more than a little credence owing to the speed with which Bertrand got the role, not to mention that nothing like a vocal audition seemed to have been part of the selection process. Whether the producer awoke to regret his hasty decision to cast Bertrand after he heard him sing, the deed was done, and a new Curly would shortly navigate the ditties written by Rogers and Hammerstein.

The show had opened on a Thursday evening to a desultory crowd of diners, and it was on the second night of its run that Norman Stands showed up to gather information for his newspaper's review of not only the food—this was Norman's usual topic—but of the show as well. The producer had put his hopes on the publicity the review would generate to keep the show going through a fairly long run, and it was with more than a little anxiety that everyone waited for Norman's widely-read article to appear.

The show's backers attended as well, watching every gesture that Norman made in an effort to ascertain whether or not his review might be a good one. Although Norman may have clinked his jewelry through dinner and the performance, his face was a study in stoicism, not betraying anything of what he intended to write. No one was therefore any wiser as Norman and his party left after the show. The review would appear in the Monday edition.

# CHAPTER 5

# *Breakfast Among the Stars*

The house on Myrtle Street had more going for it than did the house of sacred memory on Shadow Lane. Along with its bedrooms and guest cottage already mentioned, the new house's splendid kitchen was large enough for a breakfast nook. The dining room allowed for larger numbers of friends to come by and share meals. The kitchen windows, shaded by an arbor on which grew a happy trumpet vine, looked out onto the patio. Both sides of the back yard were flanked by raised flowerbeds, just coming into bloom with iris and early roses. The former owners had remodeled the kitchen, sparing no expense on the range and other appliances. The real estate ad had accurately described the house as a 'Laguna Beach charmer'. The kitchen won Hal's heart, and he wasted no time in putting it into action.

His work at Le Bleu had rendered him a fine cook, and during those days of slaving for the infamous Denise for the years during his graduate studies, he had learned how to put out fine food for large parties. The family breakfast gatherings that had characterized many mornings on Shadow Lane were fewer here on Myrtle Street, owing to everyone's work schedules, but Saturdays revived the tradition and found old friends gathered around once more for scones, eggs, ham, or almost anything anyone wanted for a weekend brunch. Hal was in his element.

It was to such a Saturday breakfast that the celebrated tenor from next door was persuaded to take time off from his vocal exercises and come eat with Hal and Simon. "I don't eat anything with milk in it, you know," Bertrand announced upon his arrival, "clogs up one's vocal cords. Oh, and if I could just have the eggs lightly poached, no butter on the bread. Oh, and tea. I never drink coffee. Much too stimulating. Is there very much sugar in the scones? No, I won't have any marmalade. Watching the waistline. Have either of you got tickets for the show yet? I can help you there, you know. Just let me know when you want to see it." His plate arrived. "Oh, the eggs are almost perfect!" Simon glanced at Hal and gave him a look that begged for charity and forbearance.

Norman is certainly right about one thing, Hal thought. Bertrand is strikingly handsome. This was Hal's first close look at his and Simon's neighbor, and as Bertrand was accustomed to people looking at him, he seemed utterly at ease as Hal studied his face. Bertrand's clear gray eyes complemented his straight and elegant nose, eyes that seemed never to rest on anything or anyone for long. Those restless eyes moved around the table to take in how his performance was being received, for it was clear that Bertrand always considered himself on stage, even among so small an audience that now sat down to breakfast. He had chosen a seat at the table that allowed the morning light to illuminate his left profile—he thought it the better one—as if always aware of how best to present himself.

Along with seemingly endless banter about how the show was staged, accompanied by various anecdotes of near disasters on stage ("She skied right off the set, slipped on whatever it was, singing her one high note all the while . . . tee hee hee"), breakfast was taking on an uneasy air as Hal wondered if they were not better off merely listening to Bertrand's vocalizations from across the fence after all. Bertrand was busy disguising his slight nervousness (was it stage fright?), knowing that Norman Stands had been in the audience the night before and was very likely writing up a review of *Oklahoma!* "I do believe that you know Mr. Stands, don't you?" he asked. "I think I saw him come by your house a few days ago. It would be so nice to know how he liked the show last night," he hinted.

"Yes, we know Norman quite well, and if there's one thing we know very well about him, it's that he never divulges the contents of his column ahead of time. Got him into trouble once, and so he never talks about work," Hal said, watching Bertrand mince through the remains of his breakfast as if he were looking for something poisonous in the eggs after all.

"Well, I'm sure he was pleased. Except for the dancing perhaps," Bertrand assured everyone as he sipped his tea and bit into another scone.

A fortunate interruption. Up the walkway came none other than Tom and his new partner Mark in town for the weekend. They arrived with very little baggage, but with two surfboards. "Hi Mommy!" Tom called to Hal, coming around the table to kiss him. Hal had indulged Tom and Mike's (Tom's former lover) calling him Mommy, although he was only ten years their senior, when they had lived on Shadow Lane. He liked what it meant to all of them, a sign of genuine affection. Mark planted a kiss on him too, and on Simon, and they both settled down long enough to be introduced to the distinguished tenor from next door. Hal, grateful for a break from the unlimited fountain of news from the world of the musical stage, took the cue and made an attempt to turn the conversation to how long their drive was, traffic conditions, and other items about their trip up from San Diego.

"You'll figure out which room is yours, or do you want the cottage out back? Just put your stuff down when you decide, and come back for some breakfast," Hal called after them as the two men headed for the hallway.

Bertrand had not only stopped talking; he was clearly in awe. "That can't be your son!" he gasped. "And who's that with him?"

"In a way, Tom's like a son. Lovely family we've got, huh?" Simon said, taking an unspoken signal from Hal to keep Bertrand in the dark for a while. Tom's dark good looks had always impressed more than a few anytime he came into a room. Mark, Mike's replacement in Tom's life, completed the ensemble.

"You'd better tell him about us before his wide-open mouth dries out entirely," Hal joked, heading for the kitchen.

Finally Simon gave the bedazzled Bertrand a brief history of their lives on Shadow Lane. "It's a little confusing. First it was Tom and Mike. Now Tom has a partner named Mark. Mike lives up north with *his* new partner John. Tom and Mike were really Hal's 'kids' and when I moved in, they saw me as something like another parent." Naturally, Bertrand's thoughts moved to the possibility of more than parental activities among all of the residents of the house. "And I know what you're thinking," Simon went on, "but it was nothing of the sort. We were a real family, and Hal credits them with bringing him out of the funk he was in at the time."

"Aren't you leaving out somebody else who helped do that?" Hal smiled at his lover. "Got to tell you, Bertrand, that this man saw more in me than I did, stayed around to make sure, and just gave me love. He still does."

"Most of the time, yeah," Simon kidded him back, "but he snores. You'll want to keep your windows closed on our side of the house. Want to hear how we met?"

"Oh God! Say you don't!" this from Tom who had returned from stowing their bags. "It's a story that will make you die of syrup poisoning, believe me. I was there and I know," he said, grinning at Hal and Simon.

"Well some other time when we don't have so many critics around, and by the way, I have a few snore stories of my own," Hal said. "Now how about coffee? And what else are you two having?"

"Eggs for both of us. What a great house!" Tom exclaimed. "Shadow Lane was home, but this place has it all over it, hands down. Love the cottage. How's Edward dealing with all this?"

"Have a look. He's begging for a petting session right now," Hal said. "You still like them scrambled?"

Just breakfast as usual at Hal and Simon's with Hal radiating as he went to the kitchen. It's all back, he thought as he got eggs out of the fridge. We're a family again and ready to invite the world in for meals and good times. God was this a good move back down here where friends can find us and be with us, or what? Wish Mike were here too. And look at my Simon, my beautiful lover and best friend, just sitting there being the lovely man he is. Why, we might even thaw out Bertrand after a while. Poor man, thinks he has a real life with his uh . . . singing career, but he doesn't have what we have, and look at him there, ogling Tom and Mark, and still wondering what we do behind closed curtains over here. Well, let him wonder. He'll get used to us. Will we get used to him is the question.

It was a rare occasion when Bertrand relinquished acting and became a mere mortal, but this was such an occasion. Still in awe of the two beautiful and natural men who had joined Hal and Simon's breakfast table, he suddenly felt upstaged, and even more strangely, didn't mind feeling that way. Something overwhelmed him, something that he could not identify, something comfortable and homey perhaps. He watched from the wings, as it were, studying the drama unfolding before him.

Gathered around the table with Edward taking the sixth chair, the family plus Bertrand listened to Tom who was full of news about a new teaching job he was offered in San Diego where Mark had been working as a computer type. "And that's a topic you won't want to ask about," Tom said. "Nobody knows what the handsome Mark does in these days of new computer technology, and if you ask him, he'll tell you and then you won't know after he tells you. Something about writing 'software' whatever that is. All you need to know is that he's smart and in demand, and that he knows computer languages that no one thought existed two years ago." Yes, in demand, thought Bertrand, in more ways than one.

The chat turned to Mike and his partner John who lived in San Jose. "They are coming down in the summer," Hal said. "Plenty of room here, so do you two think you could make plans to come up while they're here?"

"Absolutely," Tom said. Although he and Mike were obviously no longer lovers, they had remained close friends.

Bertrand was getting a better picture of how this all worked, of how things had been in the house on Shadow Lane. Like many gay men who had lived away from a family, he had forgotten what a family was like, but what revived in his consciousness was the long lost sense that he was watching one in action. The glow of warmth and affection around the breakfast table first elated him and then as quickly presented an unpleasant contrast to his own life, which he abruptly saw as solitary and spare. He sensed that he had missed something along the way, of his having imposed a kind of prissy rigor onto his days that took the place of what he was experiencing at Hal and Simon's. It wasn't just the lack of a partner, exactly; he'd had a couple of those over the years. No, it was something else, something he hadn't thought about for many years that produced in him a feeling of peace and even joy as he sat at their table. Silenced as the hubbub of eating and amiable chatting went on around him, and despite his not being the center of attention, he rose out of his momentary funk, and went back to enjoying himself. Like Scrooge on Christmas day at his nephew's house, he didn't want to leave, and he wondered if everyone who came to breakfast felt the way he did, that he could have happily spent the day simply drinking tea and nibbling food.

"We want to get some surfing in this morning, so we're off. Thanks for breakfast, Hal," Mark said, gathering dishes to take to the kitchen.

"Orders now being taken for tomorrow morning," Hal replied.

"French toast! French toast! You haven't lived until you've had Hal's French toast," Tom enthused. "You have to order it a day in advance. You'd better come back over tomorrow morning for this, Bertrand. It will make you sing like a canary."

Hal already thought that Bertrand sang like another, larger, blacker member of the avian species. "Yes, certainly come back around 9:00 tomorrow and we'll have Tom's favorite. It has to be early, though. We promised to meet George and Martha at The Cove for brunch later." "French toast as well as brunch?" Simon asked.

"We'll eat light," Hal replied. "I can't resist making French toast for Tom."

"I'll have to pass, Hal," Bertrand said, "but thanks for the invitation. Probably see you at The Cove tomorrow." He drained his teacup and rose to go. "What a wonderful time, Hal and Simon. So glad you're here in the neighborhood." And with that, he was gone. So were the boys, driving toward the ocean, surfboards loaded onto their car.

"You are a master at diplomatic suggestions, my love," Hal said, hugging Simon once they were alone. "That idea of his keeping his windows closed on our side of his house was a stroke of genius. I hope he'll take your advice since his music room seems to be right across the fence from our bedroom."

"We'll see. Maybe we should stage a general snoring session this afternoon once we hear the uh . . . music start up. We must be pretty formidable once we both get going."

"Hmm . . . I can think of a few things I'd like to do in there before the nap," he grinned, kissing Simon on the head.

They were settling down into a quiet Saturday of house chores, reading, and having no real agenda apart from dinner plans later. This was life as it should be as far as Hal was concerned, and once again he had that far away but very present feeling that he ought to be grateful to someone or something beyond himself, to . . . whom? He was not prepared to say it was God or anything like the old god of his youth, the angry and vengeful god. No, if it would be a god to whom he owed gratitude, it would have to be a different one, one who bestowed love instead of retribution. He would think about this possible god later, but for now he was conscious of a lightness and joy that he felt very happy to share with Simon and those whom he considered to be the rest of his family.

As he contemplated these weighty philosophical notions, Simon called to him from the living room. "Zero at 6 o'clock, coming right up the walkway." By the time he joined his partner, there was none other than the fabulously dressed Denise Lebouche carrying a bottle of something, and bearing down on the front door.

"Denise! What a surprise! It's been a very long time," Hal said, thinking that it hadn't been long enough. "Come in, come in." Nothing, not even the presence of the nefarious Denise had the power to dispel his good feelings, at least for the moment. "To what do we owe the honor of this visit?"

"Ay ave heard you bought zees place and Ay wanted to come to warm zee house wees you," she said in her improving but still very accented English. Her Belgian country French continued to predominate her linguistic output, but it was widely held that she purposefully clung to her thick accent, believing that it lent a certain authenticity to the French restaurant that she owned and governed like a supreme sovereign. When Hal had worked for her during his graduate school days, he had, like everyone else in her employ, become wary of her motives, particularly when they resembled anything like generosity. Her proffered gift of champagne on this occasion was especially suspect as she swept through Hal and Simon's doorway.

Over the years of knowing her, both men had become accustomed to Denise's extraordinary wardrobe and the various get-ups that it provided her. Today's ensemble was relatively subdued compared to some of her other astonishing ones, as she appeared like something out of a 19th century country picnic: large picture hat, frilly and flowered blouse, tight-waisted skirt (a definite mistake, given that she was shaped like an oversized ironing board), and boots that had to have been custom made to fit over her enormous feet. Not having seen Madame Lebouche for some time, both Simon and Hal merely gawked at her for a moment. "You look like springtime itself, Denise," Hal said once he had recovered from the initial survey of her dress, "Where do you keep finding your endlessly fascinating clothes?"

"Tonk you, but Ay find zees dress not in Paree as you might tink, but in Santa Ana. Zees boots Ay buy in Belgium. But Ay don't come to talk about dat. Let's drink some wine and Ay tell you what."

Hal's history with Denise had been anything but amiable, and had ended abruptly when he finished working for her more than four years ago. Oblivious to any possibility of bad blood between them that might have lingered over those intervening years, Denise always assumed that she was welcome wherever she went, and further believed that her presence was enough to grace any dwelling or gathering. The truth of course was that over the years she had garnered more than a few enemies who would have happily been on hand to sharpen a stake with which to impale her through the heart if they could have found it—her heart, that is. Hal had long ago put any old animosities behind him with regard to Denise; she had after all been abandoned by her husband who ran off with a male lover, and despite his giving her the business (in more ways than one), Hal thought that life had beaten her up enough without his adding his own ill will to the cosmic mix. Thus his mind was in neutral as he prepared to hear what she really came to call about.

She got right down to cases. "You know zat Carl zat my Eric get involved with?" Of course, Hal knew Carl, probably better and longer than anyone in town, their having been in the Navy together many years ago. "Well, Ay tink he stealing money from Eric." The irony of this statement was that Eric himself had tried to steal some $80,000 from investors a few years back, had turned himself in and returned the cash, thus avoiding a long prison sentence. "Why do Ay tink so? Because he not work except at Le Bleu and he spend money like crazy, zat's how."

"Is Eric complaining?" Hal wanted to know, pouring flutes of champagne.

"No, he don't complain but Ay see what goes on. Ay pay my Eric very good from Le Bleu, but Ay don't pay zat Carl so much. He live in my house, he eat my food, and he steal from Eric."

"Well if Eric isn't complaining, why are you? They have been partners for a couple of years and should have figured out how to get along with each other. Maybe that's the way Eric wants it," Simon suggested.

"No, zat Carl he got something on my Eric, maybe all zat business back zen. Ay don't know how to get rid of heem but Ay want heem to get out of our lives up dere in my house."

The reason for Denise's visit began to clarify. Denise and Eric, had they been similarly oriented sexually, would likely have been perfect for each other. As it was, Denise had fostered an unrequited—one might say sexually impossible—love for her protégé, and in the years when he had been in her good graces before he made a dash for financial independence with embezzled dollars and a great deal of Denise's art collection, the two of them were for all intents and purposes, a couple—in all ways but one. After Eric's return, an event that had coincided with her husband's defection, they took up with each other once more, but this time with the added ingredient of a love interest for Eric in the person of Carl Teal, all three of them living together in Denise's enormous house. The arrangement had at the time seemed ideal, all of them sharing a devious and suspicious nature, and living in gothic splendor, surrounded by Denise's gloomy décor. Apparently things on the tier of the Inferno where the house sat had got more hellish.

"Wouldn't that mean that Eric would leave too? We haven't seen them for a long time, but the last time we did, they seemed happy with each other."

"Zat's all made up to look good, zat's all. Zat Carl he lazy and he no good."

"OK, well, I'm not sure what you think we can do about it, Denise."

"Ay know you got zee leetle house in zee back of zees one. Ay tink you could rent it out to zat Carl." Hal and Simon stared at her.

How does she find out these things? Hal wondered. "First of all, Denise, we only have your story here for what you think about Carl and Eric. Has Carl said anything about wanting to leave Eric? Or do you really believe that they are ready to break up just because you want to break them up? And second, we do not intend to rent the guest cottage to anybody. We use it and we like it for ourselves. No, you will have to work this out on your own."

"You used to rent out zat room on Shadow Lane all zee time, even to zat rat my ex-husband Jean-Jacques and hees hoor boyfrien. Ay might have known you would not help me here," she spat, her whole put-on demeanor of well-wisher having evaporated, revealing her disingenuous motives. "After all Ay do for you over zee years. Ay geev you a good job back den when you need zee work, and now you do me zees way."

"As usual Denise, you are taking one of your favorite walks down convenient memory lane," Hal said as he began to heat up. "Let me turn up the lights on our history for a minute. First, I worked for you like everyone else does, like a slave, that is until Jean-Jacques hired me to cook there and you were forced to ease up. You bullied my boys, you tried to take away my tables, and you stole tips. You were and probably still are insufferable, and if your plans to get Eric for yourself haven't worked out, I am not surprised. Would you like some more champagne?"

My, my, my, thought Simon. Her English really has improved. I think that she understood every word of Hal's rapid speech. He used to be able to bamboozle her when he spoke in an English that she was unused to hearing, producing a dazed, sometimes frustrated expression on her pale Belgian countenance. But Simon was right; she understood every word. She took the refilled champagne flute and swigged down its contents, rose with all the dignity that her Essence of Springtime dress allowed, and made for the front door. "You see, Ay get rid of heem," she steamed as she clomped down the walkway to her car. Hal and Simon watched her roar off.

"What's that French saying about the more things change the more they stay the same?" Hal asked as he put his arm around Simon's waist. "She'll never change; she's one of the constants of the universe. What do you make of this campaign?"

"Even Denise can get lonely, I suppose. She's run out of friends; nobody trusts her, and she probably sees Eric as her last hope for keeping somebody in her life."

"Maybe, but that would mean that she's taken a look at her current state and found out what she is. That's giving her more credit for insight than I think she deserves. No, I'm guessing there's money behind this push to get rid of Carl somehow. That's what always inspires Denise to action. She is probably the only person I've ever met who is entirely devoid of being sorry for anything she does. Remember when we invited her to the Christmas party and she showed up with a case of champagne? We thought that maybe, just maybe, she was turning over a new leaf, becoming a human being. And then the next day, she was the same old grasping, greedy, underhanded Denise."

"Well, you've got to hand it to her, she's got colossal nerve. I wonder what she'll do next to get rid of Carl."

"No idea, but I'm going to butt in and talk to him, not that I think he doesn't know how she feels about him. Matching her nerve is her penchant for absolute direct action when it comes to somebody she hates. Remember how she treated Eric when he was on trial? She was ready to send her best friend up the river for an extended sentence just for attempting to steal some of her paintings that anyone with a modicum of taste would have been glad to see the last of."

"Is there any point trying to figure out why she is the way she is?"

"No, there isn't, but I'm sure of one thing. There's something else bothering her besides just Carl and Eric. So, how about that nap?"

---

Denise smoldered over Hal and Simon's flat refusal of her first plan to provide a rental for Carl, but it was not long before her mind moved to the grand scheme she was concocting. She was determined to rid her life, and Eric's as well, of Carl who had been in the way for the past few years; her resentment of his and Eric's love affair and the permanence of their relationship had begun to boil up into real hatred. Hal was right to surmise that something else troubled her.

There had been that Ned, the busboy she had hired a summer ago. Young, virile, and sexy, he had arrived with the kind of oversexed energy that no one could ignore, particularly the very needy Denise. Still determined to have a baby, she had systematically seduced horny Ned who, with the aid of just the right amount of alcohol and pot, managed to count about twenty naked push-ups into the receptive Denise, impregnating her. Once his duties in that regard were over, he was summarily dismissed from employment at the restaurant, an outcome that he preferred rather than reflect, in his sober moments, on what he had been called on to perform.

As before, Denise miscarried that time as well, but there was an added component, a hysterectomy that ended any further possibilities of child bearing. During a rare day of introspection, she came to the conclusion that if she were to have any sort of companionship, she had better settle on whatever compromise she might find now that the possibility of an heir was out of the question. She settled her sights on Eric, just as she had years ago. Things between them had not appreciably changed, she thought, and once she had reestablished him as the man of her life and house, she saw him as a substitute for the affection that she had thought to shower on a baby.

But Carl had to go. After that, she could once more have Eric to herself, just as she had before the 'trouble' over the money. She would again have his undivided interest, his total attention on her. She thought back on the ten years she had known him, and when they had first met. What a handsome man he was, and before she had the shocking news of his sexual orientation, her heart had swum in his beauty and in the plans she made for much more than friendship. One by one, her hopes had been dashed on the rocks of hard reality.

When Carl came into the picture, she had been willing to make him a part of their life together; after all, it was what pleased Eric and kept him living in her house. Carl provided Eric with the kind of sexual expression that she could not give him, and that's how she thought of Carl, as merely Eric's toy. But the toy had begun to wear on her, demanding more and more of Eric's time away from her wants and desires. Besides, she had detected a growing distance between her and Carl, and he was becoming difficult to manage and control.

She knew that getting rid of him would have to be done carefully, and although she wasn't sure how moving him to Hal and Simon's cottage might fit into her plans exactly, she thought to test the waters, just to see if there might be a place for him once she effected his expulsion from her house and hers and Eric's life together. No fear; there would be other apartments where he could go. She would have to show Eric once and for all how Carl could not be trusted and therefore had to be dispensed with.

She had hired a new gardener, having unceremoniously dumped the old and reliable Luis in favor of the new and fabulous-looking Miguel who, apart from helping his grandmother plant petunias, had only the dimmest notion about caring for a lawn, much less a garden. Such facts did not bother Denise whose neglected front yard horrified her neighbors and exhibited more brown and dying plants than green and living ones. What Luis had done all these years had more to do with raking and hauling than pruning and planting. Thus she was convinced that Miguel could do as well, and he came with the added allure of male sexiness. He was also instructed on how to clean the swimming pool, dressed appropriately in Speedos.

Miguel's arrival into The Dark Tower provided exactly the reaction that Denise had hoped it would. Miguel's taut muscles, well-developed shoulders and pecs, long and slightly hairy legs, and a significant bulge, which the Speedos did more to emphasize than to hide, immediately fascinated Carl. Miguel took hours to maintain the pool, and when done, sunned on a raft in it, keeping up the light copper and chocolate tone of his flawless skin. Denise congratulated herself that the seeds of sexual infidelity had been so successfully sown, and she made preparations for Eric's discovery of what she imagined would be Carl and Miguel in bed.

Weeks of Miguel's heady sexuality went by with Carl watching but keeping a respectful distance as far as Denise could see. Patience not being one of her strong points, she had upped the ante by raising Miguel's pay with the intimation that he might want to be friendlier to Carl whom she portrayed as shy and in need of friendship. Still nothing happened that she could point out to Eric.

Eric meanwhile noticed Carl's watching Miguel too, and was not surprised at his lover's interest in the new gardener. "When do you think you'll get him into bed," he asked Carl one afternoon while Miguel worked out with a makeshift set of weights.

"Hmm . . . could be any time. When should we plan the sandwich party? Tonight be OK?"

"He looks ready to be the pivot boy for us. Denise has given him a raise to get him to be friendlier to you, did you know that? You do know what she's up to, don't you?"

"Well, we wouldn't want to disappoint the mistress of the house, now would we?" Carl said, watching Miguel show off his sensational butt that strained his Speedos as he bent over. "Let's see what Madame's cash bought for us. Where is she anyway?"

"Downtown somewhere. I'm meeting her at the restaurant later," he said, kissing his lover and reaching down to grope the bulging front of his pants. "Think you can wait until tonight?"

"Hmmm . . . I can if he can," Carl said, wrapping his arms around Eric. "I'll call if I get into trouble. See you later, handsome."

# CHAPTER 6
## *New Arrangements*

When Bertrand left after breakfast that morning, his mind swam with the thrill of being in the presence of Tom and Mark, two of the most beautiful men he had ever seen. He returned to his quiet house and sat thinking about it all. It was the combination of beauty and genuine affection that Tom in particular had extended to Hal that made Bertrand's heart ache. He looked in the full-length mirror in his music studio and took stock of what he saw there. Not bad for a man of his undisclosed age (he was forty-five according to his passport); in fact, he thought he looked a good ten years younger. How to attract the likes of Tom occupied his mind, still laboring under the wrong assumption that sex was the basis for what he had just experienced at breakfast, and he tried to figure out how Hal and Simon had achieved what he so desired. Tom was obviously devoted to the older men, and Bertrand determined to find out how he could duplicate that kind of attentiveness and affection in his own life.

Perhaps, he thought, he needed to work harder at the gym. He looked more carefully at every area of his body, and determined that parts of it had been neglected and shouted out to everyone that he was aging, and to his critical eye, aging rapidly. That slight bulge in his lower abdomen would have to go, and so would that crepe-like skin under his arms, not that there was much of it. Yes, that was it! He simply wasn't sexy enough or good looking enough to attract someone like Tom or Mark, and that conclusion led him to greater plans for more rigorous workouts.

But, he thought, Hal is hardly what anyone would call a fine physical specimen of a man. How old is he anyway, maybe thirty-five or so? Simon looked good, but neither did he represent Bertrand's highest notions of masculine beauty although he did have a very fine butt. So there must be something else, something he'd missed that had occasioned the kind of affection from two young and very hot studs that he had met next door during breakfast.

He began looking slightly beyond his mirror and into the possibility that it no longer told him that he was the fairest of them all. How depressing to come to the slowly dawning news that he was forty-five, not as physically desirable as he had been seemingly only yesterday, and that some great ingredient was missing from his life, a life, reflected from what he had seen next door, that at the moment looked more and more empty and wasted. He took inventory of what he had: a nice house, thanks to an inheritance, where he lived alone, a decent income, more than passable looks, and he was a singer, a star in his own galaxy, something of a celebrity, and therefore well known. As he totted up these assets, he still came up short, and his mind devolved to that void, that missing something.

Opening the windows, he thought he would begin his daily vocal exercises. These always gave him great pleasure, and the concentration they demanded took away any cares and troubles he had on his mind. What greeted him was the distinct sound of snoring, not light snoring, but snoring from two earnest sleepers whose windows next door were similarly open. Hal and Simon. It had to be them, he thought. Their bedroom was directly across on the other side of a board fence, and they were indulging in an afternoon nap, a very noisy one. This would not do, he thought as he closed his windows, but could still hear his neighbors through the glass. He had to have quiet to work, to perfect his art, to keep his vocal cords in shape for the musical stage! Today he would move his practicing to his own bedroom on the other side of the house, and later, he would think what to do next.

"Did you hear that?" Simon said with one eye open, knowing full well that Hal was not asleep.

"Yes, he opened his windows but no sound came out. He must have heard us. Good job, by the way. Do you think we really do sound that loud when we're asleep?"

"God, I hope not. In fact, I know we don't. We would never get any sleep if we did. I wonder what he'll do."

"Don't know and I don't care. Let's have that nap, what do you say? Think we could have it naked?" Hal said, unbuttoning Simon's shirt.

"It's the only way to do it," Simon murmured into Hal's neck, his hand moving down Hal's front and finding exactly what he wanted to find there.

Hal nestled his face into Simon's chest hair and breathed in that intoxicating aroma that was so familiarly erotic to him, the lemony essence of Simon. "If he opens his window again right now, he'll figure out we aren't sleeping. Want to make some other noises, just for entertainment value?" Hal said as he mounted Simon.

"I wonder if we haven't entertained him already the last time we did this. And I can't help it if I make noise when you're inside me. Who wouldn't with that huge thing up there?" Simon grinned, moving to allow Hal to enter him. It was true; Simon couldn't stay quiet as Hal pumped into him. It wasn't that it was at all painful, quite the opposite. It was the most thrilling feeling Simon knew, and his vocal responses were something he neither could nor wanted to repress. Hal pushed fully inside him, and his cry of joy filled the room and went out through the open window toward Bertrand's closed one.

Long practice had honed their skills, and Hal was quite aware of when his partner was ready to climax. He also knew how to prolong their pleasure, when to slow down his rhythm, and when to find that spot that brought Simon to ejaculation so that they could arrive there together. They had reached that moment, and afterwards lay together locked into each other as they regained their breaths.

"Wow, that should have done it. It sure did it for us, wouldn't you say?" Hal nuzzled into Simon's neck.

"If he is still listening, my guess is that either he will never leave that room as he hopes for more, or he will change his studio to the other side of the house where he won't be distracted by his highly sexed neighbors," Simon sighed, holding his contented lover as they came down from their mutual high.

"Let's hope for the second," Hal said, drifting off into the promised nap and wrapping himself around his beautiful Simon.

Bertrand had indeed overheard the sounds of the activities next door and as exciting as those sounds were, he had no desire to compete with them by practicing vocal scales. He left the room and made plans to exchange his studio for his bedroom that very afternoon. He looked at the clock. All that would have to wait; he headed for the bathroom to get ready for the Saturday evening performance of *Oklahoma!*

# CHAPTER 7
# *Reading the Sunday Comics*

Sunday brunch at The Blue Cove, an every week occasion for the retailing of the weekend's events among the highly coifed and stylishly dressed of Laguna's gay men. The fashionable time to arrive was 1:00PM. The menu consisted of what nearly any brunch offered, and what to eat was far down the list of important items for those who had gathered for the afternoon. Heading the catalog of hot topics was who had gone home with whom, who was new to whose house, who was now being kept by whom, whose new Mercedes was that parked outside, and what damage had been done to whose relationships as a result of any of the answers to these burning questions.

Brunch was presided over by one Stockley Quinton, described and made famous in other chronicles, but who deserves a review of his more salient attributes. To the extent that Stockley possessed the genitalia (one supposed) that distinguished him from the feminine gender, and wore (generally) men's clothes, he was a male, but here anything like masculinity ended. Men's clothes they were, but only just. He was fond of beachcombers, popular years ago, pants that looked suspiciously like 1950style pedal pushers, pants that women of that bygone era favored, and ones that he had possibly come across in a thrift store and made a part of his inimitable style. To aid this mid-century look, he would from time to time tie the tails of his shirts together around the upper part of his midriff (do men have midriffs one might well ask?), looking for all the world like an escapee from an *I Love Lucy* episode. The only accessory such an ensemble lacked was a bandana.

Stockley had lived in town for an indeterminate number of years—some sarcastically said over 100—had never had much of a job that was apt to place him among the landed gentry, and as far as anyone could remember, or cared to, had resided in the same small apartment above a shop in the center of town since time immemorial. His circumstances, however lowly, did not interfere with the regal bearing which he took on as part of his position as maitre d' of the Sunday brunch at The Blue Cove. Here he was deferred to, cajoled into placing diners at good tables, and enjoyed an authority of which his life had otherwise deprived him. With a sense of noblesse oblige that was wonderful to behold, he was kindly and generally accommodating with just the right amount of haughtiness that customers felt gave them a sense of having been granted some privilege by an aristocrat.

"He is our cat Edward in bad clothes," Hal whispered as he and Simon arrived to put their names in for table seating.

"Except that Edward wouldn't be caught dead with those fingernails. It's not quite pink, is it? More a sort of enhanced flesh tone. He must spend all of Saturday doing those up. They shine like polished opals," Simon whispered back.

"Gentlemen. We would have a table for you within half an hour. Would you care for cocktails in the patio while you wait?" Stockley asked after a slight bow in their direction, carrying his usual cargo of menus. They instinctively bowed back; everyone impulsively did so when greeted by Stockley without even thinking about it, and they followed him to the outside area where they ordered drinks.

"They won't have your French toast on the menu," Simon smiled. "How many pieces did Tom actually eat?"

"Lost count, but it makes me feel good to watch him eat. Mark enjoyed it too, don't you think?"

"Who wouldn't. Hard to resist, but I skimped knowing that we were coming here for fairy fare. No sign of George and Martha yet."

At Sunday brunch, the patio enjoyed the radiant glow from the town's gay luminaries of every age and stripe, all done up in their finest, all drinking various stylish cocktails, and all perusing the rest of the crowd as if they were dowagers at a formal ball in Jane Austen's time. No one and nothing they wore escaped general notice and subsequent commentary. New arrivals to the patio more or less passed in review before this formidable congregation of harpies, some who hoped to be charitably judged worthy of further acquaintance among the old guard, and others like Hal and Simon who didn't give a damn, and thought the panel of judges as silly as Alice had found most of the denizens of Wonderland. Of course, it was their disdain of what the harpies thought of them that immediately produced favorable comments and a desire by many to know Hal and Simon on a more intimate basis.

"Ah! It is Hal and Simon come down from the lofty heights to grace us today!" this from a Blue Cove denizen known as Paulette, or La Pompadour by some, who came toward them with his bejeweled fingers (a ring and sometimes two on every one of them) extended in greeting. You got the feeling upon meeting him that if he had been able to get away with wearing a Louis XIV court wig, he would have. He assumed all of the grandeur of that century's French court, promoted French culture, presumed to speak the language (he didn't, but salted his discourse with the scant French phrases he had garnered), and adored Denise and her restaurant. He had been one of Hal's table customers in the days when Hal had worked at Le Bleu, and had been a pill, having brought his pretentious manners and condescension, not to mention his faulty pronouncements of French cuisine, with him on every visit. He was also a stingy tipper.

"I guess you haven't heard, Paulette (did anyone know his real name?), that we have moved from the hill to the north end. It all happened so fast that it apparently escaped even your news sources. We're on Myrtle Street now, so it wasn't a question of coming down from the heights today."

"Mon Dieu! Not Myrtle Street! I hope that you two didn't buy that tawdry little shack beside Bertrand Lebland. There was a good reason why it was on the market for so long, you know," Paulette said, leaning conspiratorially toward them and giving them an overwhelming whiff of his heavy cologne. Just what the 'good reason' was remained undisclosed, most likely because it didn't exist.

"That's exactly the tawdry little shack that we did buy," Simon cheerfully piped up. "Ghosts. Wasn't that the reason?" he said, smiling at Paulette's face that in closer view revealed quite a lot of makeup here and there, particularly around the eyes where wrinkles had been caulked in an attempt to shore up the bags and hide a few of the "laugh lines". One of Paulette's closest and dearest friends, upon hearing Paulette's crows' feet described as laugh lines, had quipped, "Deary, nothing could be *that* funny." It was that sort of a crowd.

Unabashed by his faux pas, two French words that *should* have been in his vocabulary, La Pompadour went on. "Well, the fact that a murder was committed there is one thing, but I couldn't get my realtor to tell me what else was wrong. But I suppose it's too late to warn you now, ha ha!" and perceiving that his news did nothing to impress them, he moved on to greet other, more malleable and impressionable possibilities among the arriving brunch crowd.

The only negative reason Hal and Simon could think of concerning their new house was its proximity to Bertrand Lebland's vocal gymnastics, but they said nothing about that, knowing that it would get back to their illustrious neighbor, who, at that very moment was coming onto the patio and greeting what he perceived to be members of his fan club. Even if Bertrand were only going out to his own mailbox, he dressed as if he were ready for a photo opportunity: today he wore a tan linen suit and a light blue shirt that reflected his magnificent gray eyes, and he positively dazzled his adoring public. He nodded hello to everyone in the style of a visiting movie star, and then swept past.

Not all of the men lining the patio walls were stand-ins for Quasimodo, far from it. The beach town sported quite a bevy of the young and beautiful, men who could have easily been seen on the sets of Hollywood films; in fact, a number of them had been. One such contingent arrived, led in by Chester Flint who had for many years been comptroller at one of the larger film studios in Hollywood. His retirement to Laguna meant bringing a steady flow of 'talent' through his house, and often parading them before the envious crowd foregathered on The Blue Cove's patio.

"Oh! Here's Chester! Chester, darling!" Paulette crooned, edging closer into position to meet Chester's entourage of beautiful men. "How are you? Oh, and how did the dog problem work out?"

"Hello Paulette. You're looking ravishing. Must be that new makeup artist I sent you too. Do stay out of the sun, though. And the dog barking has ceased, thank you."

Chester's neighbors had a large dog that barked as soon as they left every morning for work, and continued to bark until they returned home. Because Chester was retired and therefore at home much of his day, he was understandably annoyed. At first he requested that his neighbors do something about the dog. Nothing. They refused to believe that their precious dog made a nuisance of himself. Then Chester called up some friends in Hollywood. They arrived with movie-quality recording equipment and made a tape of the offending dog's daytime barking. That night, Chester aligned two large speakers toward the neighbor's house, and played the tape.

Lights went on next door, and soon the neighbors arrived to complain about Chester's dog. "But I don't have a dog," Chester replied as he closed the door. As soon as he was sure that the neighbors had gone back to bed, he played the tape again. This time the police arrived at Chester's house to insist that he silence his barking dog. "As I have said to the neighbors, I do not own a dog. You are welcome to see for yourselves." The police confirmed that no dog was found, and they left. Fifteen minutes later, the tape resumed. And the following morning, all was silent from the neighbors' house. No dog, no barking, nothing but peace.

Chester had hoped that his earlier request to his neighbors about their dog would be enough to remedy the situation, but he soon surmised that these two were not true Lagunatics, but were instead rich interlopers who had no sense of the ethos and mind set that formed a kind of corporate regard for and among the people who lived there. He had to take matters into his own hands, and he had won the battle. He wondered about the war that might ensue, but he only briefly thought about it. Now he reveled in the company of his beautiful companions, as he greeted old friends on the patio of The Cove.

A number of these had attended last night's show of *Oklahoma!* and variously saluted Bertrand according to how they had found his performance. There was a wide gamut of expression: some were moderately congratulatory, some effusive, and some looked downright embarrassed as they shook hands with the glowing Bertrand who was oblivious to anything except praise.

Apparently that performance had been something less of a success than the management of the dinner theater had counted on, only ten tables of thirty having been seated for the show. This news had already circulated through the very efficient grapevine that kept its attention focused on anything to do with 'the arts'. Nevertheless, our Bertrand was generally greeted with the fascination and awe granted to anyone who finds himself in spotlights on stages. He had sung like never before last night, giving his rendition of Curly everything he had, and consequently had spent his voice. He was now speaking in whispers to preserve what was left of it so that he could sing a few songs later when Vi Winters showed up to accompany him.

While Bertrand was enjoying what he regarded as accolades from his fans, George and Marty arrived, the latter known far and wide merely as Martha, the one who spoke all sentences as if they were questions. George and Hal had been to university together, both were teachers these days, and had kept up their friendship over the years. Martha worked for a large department store and, through mere longevity, had become one of its assistant managers despite what many regarded as his annoying manner of speaking.

"Well, look who it is? It's Hal and Simon?" Marty shrilled as if they had not arranged to meet at The Cove in the first place. "George and I haven't seen your new house?"

"We haven't had time to organize a party yet, but don't let that stop you from coming by," Simon said. "You just missed Tom and Mark who were here yesterday." Martha's complete and observable jealousy of Tom's good looks, and of Mike's when they were a couple at the Shadow Lane house, had never abated; for this reason, Simon delighted in giving him news about them.

"Oh really? And they haven't broken up yet? I'm surprised they're still a couple since I know what I know?" Martha intimated. When actual dirt was scarce, Martha had no qualms about implying some.

Hal and George had been talking to each other about school while Martha's attentions were turned to inventorying the crowd, but Hal noticed that George seemed to be watching the entourage that accompanied Bertrand who was busy looking over his adoring fans in an effort to cull out a few to join him at his table for brunch. "Been to see his show yet?" Hal asked, looking in the same direction and abandoning school topics.

"Uh . . . no, not yet. Marty doesn't like live theater. Remember when I dragged him off to watch my kids do *Hamlet?* That was years ago and he still bitches about sitting through it. Think that his show is worth seeing?" he asked, nodding toward Bertrand.

"Let's just say that we've already heard all, and I do mean all, of Curly's songs in it. The star lives right next door to us, you know."

"Really? Have you met him yet, I mean, is he a nice person? He's certainly handsome as hell," George said, watching as Stockley ushered Bertrand and his chosen guests inside for brunch.

"Goes a long way when you're on the stage," Hal said. "And yes, we have met him. Now, you two planned to have brunch with us, didn't you? Martha sounded surprised that we were here."

"Sure, we did. And he knew we did. What that was all about is anybody's guess. Might get us a table sooner if we double up." George said, and Hal went off to report to Stockley.

"I'll never understand what anyone sees in that aging actress Bertrand?" Martha remarked as he came back from scanning the patio. "Where does he buy his clothes?"

"Apparently not from your store," Simon noted. Hal returned and they were shortly ushered in to their table.

A large piano bar dominated the interior of The Blue Cove; the service bar was installed on one side of the room, with as many booths and tables as it was possible to set up along its other walls which were adorned by original paintings by local artists, usually of beach scenes of the town, and sold to anyone who had the purchase price. Stockley had lately given up joining the ranks of oil painters after a brief and unsuccessful career as an interpreter of landscapes. One of his paintings had gained a brief celebrity on the walls of the restaurant, and to his utter humiliation had been jeered at. It had been a derivative study, reminiscent of Andrew Wyeth's work, specifically *Christina's World*, except that Stockley had replaced the prostrate Christina with a rustic shack in the foreground. The same hills appeared as did the ominous storm clouds which prompted an upstart critic to name the piece *Lightning Strikes the Crapper*. Stockley's abrupt removal of his masterpiece from the wall that day signaled the end of his painting avocation, and propelled him to think about his real love, the stage. His earlier appearances as an actor had been as disappointing as his painting, but he thought that perhaps time had mellowed his 'persona', that the sibilance with which he spoke might have become less noticeable to allow him another chance at footlight stardom.

He was, of course, star-struck over Bertrand, and having given him and his guests the best table in the house, flew frequent trips over to it to ensure that every glass was filled with complimentary champagne, and that every wish the 'star' had was granted insofar as it was within Stockley's ability to grant them. Hal, Simon, George and Martha were seated at the adjoining table.

"Would you mind if we trade places?" George asked Hal. "I don't care if I have my back to the piano." Hal acquiesced, menus were brought, and brunch ordered. The new seating arrangement kept George in full view of Bertrand's table.

It didn't much matter if you were facing the piano or not since Vi Winters' loud banging on it would scarcely be less annoying regardless. They had almost an hour before she was scheduled to start her repertoire that was as predictable as it was dated. She would invariably start with something rousing from *Gypsy*, and in her best Ethel Merman imitation, let loose with "Things Are Swell", or maybe it was "Things Look Swell", she was never really sure. Didn't matter; she felt that it got the set off on the right foot. That showstopper would be followed by selections by Cole Porter, Gershwin, and Berlin. Not that there was anything wrong with these American greats; it was just that Vi's rendition of them tended to diminish their luster. By mid-set, she would be joined by Bertrand, again cajoled into singing perhaps one of the songs from his current show.

Anticipating this, Hal whispered to Simon, "Maybe we'll be out of here before that act gets on its feet. Eat fast and I'll take you out for drinks at the hotel, what do you say?"

"It's a deal. It'll be nice to see Roger down there." Their friend Roger had been the manager of the Hotel Laguna restaurant for a few years now, having finally told Denise off when he quit working for her. Hal's whisper had been louder than he thought.

"I was looking forward to hearing your neighbor, you know," George said. He seemed miffed. "You don't sound as if you want to." It had begun to occur to Hal that George had been looking over at Bertrand's table quite a lot, had seemed therefore preoccupied, and more than once had to have the table's conversation reviewed for him. Hal noticed; Martha apparently had not, but of course, Martha never noticed anything but Martha.

"Well, like I said earlier, it's just that we've heard him practicing next door, George, and we've heard all of the songs by now," Hal explained, looking carefully at his friend. "You don't need Simon and me to hang around, do you?" But George's attention had once again drifted toward Bertrand's table.

"Uh... what? No, of course not," he said distractedly. Their food arrived, and for a few minutes, even Martha wasn't talking while they ate. Hmm... Hal thought. I wonder what *this* is all about. By the time they were halfway through their meal, Bertrand's table was finished with brunch, and they were leaving with Bertrand saying goodbye to the admiring coterie who had dined with him.

Hal stopped him as he was passing their table. "Bertrand, please come have another mimosa with us. I want to introduce you to some friends. This is George, and this is Marty." Hal thought George looked faint as he took Bertrand's hand and as Bertrand gazed into his eyes. After a cursory handshake with Martha, a chair was found, placed on George's left, and Bertrand sat for the offered drink.

Predictably, the table conversation turned to the show, with Martha vainly trying to gain everyone's attention by interjecting interesting tidbits from the fascinating world of retail sales. These attempts were skillfully overridden by Bertrand whose talent for upstaging anyone in his way had no peer. George looked entirely rapt as Bertrand went on about the mishaps and laughs that came fast and furious in the high-speed pace of show production. "No matter how well rehearsed a show is, there is always the possibility for something unexpected. Did I tell you about the night that Hazel's corset fell right out of her dress..." Even Martha was cowed into a smoldering silence, at least until later when he would be able to deliver a scathing comment or two about how Bertrand had 'just taken over our table?'

Vi Winters arrived and was settling in at the piano for her afternoon gig, a clear signal to Hal and Simon that it was time to leave. "We have some things to do, but we leave you in good hands, Bertrand," Simon said as they rose to go. Martha looked as if he could chew nails, glaring at the departing Hal and Simon who left him alone with the loquacious Bertrand. And George.

"You've started something, you know that, don't you?" Simon said to Hal as they walked down Coast Highway toward the hotel.

"Do you think so?"

"Don't give me that innocent spiel. George is purely ga-ga over Bertrand."

"Just stage worship, Simon. George loves drama and anything about it. That's all it is. I was just indulging his fantasies."

"Yeah, well I think he has more than one fantasy right now, and it isn't just stage lust if you ask me. He looked as if he could have eaten Bertrand for dessert."

"I doubt it. He and Martha have been together for about a century or so and I don't think I did anything harmful. I know that you and I can take only so much of Martha, but he and George have solidity."

"I guess you're right; after all, you know them better than I do. It's just that I have the feeling . . ." They came to the hotel and went into the restaurant bar to find Roger.

Ken was there too, having a drink with his lover in the off moments when Roger wasn't taking care of restaurant business. It was a fairly slow afternoon at the hotel bar which looked out over some of the finest beach real estate in California. "What are you two up to? Slumming, huh?" Ken kidded Hal and Simon as they took a seat.

"We're just coming down from the giddy heights of gay society, my dear," Simon said in his best fake haughty voice. "You've missed another stunning Sunday brunch at The Cove 'where the elite meet to compete' while you were sitting down here in this tawdry straight bar, soaking up champagne."

"Well, what's the husband of a busy waitress to do? I have to be here to keep an eye on the old girl so she doesn't get tempted into some upstairs hotel room by the out-of-town clientele," Ken joked back.

"Who's a busy waitress? Me? Wait 'til I get you home, you bean counter," Roger said, arriving to greet Hal and Simon. The bar was mostly empty; he furtively looked around, saw no one noticing, and kissed Ken on the cheek.

"See the kind of service you get at this place?" he said, putting an arm around his lover. "And you thought this was a straight bar, huh?"

"Well it probably was before the four of us got here," Hal said, hugging both of them. "So now we get to spend the rest of the afternoon with the gay Bickersons. How about the two of you coming up for dinner tonight?" "Uh . . . ok, but how's the noise level these days?" Roger asked.

"We think that the practice room has been moved to the other side of his house, if that's what you mean," Simon said.

"Of course, that's what I mean. The other day when I was there, he started in and he might as well have been making that racket right in your living room."

"You scoff, but of course we have a very appreciative fan in our house. Edward sings right along with him."

"That Edward is a creature of refined sensitivities; has Bertrand heard Edward's sing-along?"

"Probably not," Simon said. "Bertrand drowns out nearly everything within range, including ambulance sirens. Anyway, things are better, so come up and have dinner."

"Sounds great," Roger said. "7:00 OK?" It was, and drinks arrived. They took them out to tables overlooking the beach just as Roger was called to the front desk.

"I really don't mind spending Sundays this way," Ken said. Hal tried to detect any insincerity here, but decided to take what he said at face value. He knew however that Ken would have preferred Roger to have a work schedule that matched his own, one that allowed for entire weekends together.

"We do pretty well finding time together," he went on, sitting down beside Simon. "It's just that I'd like us to go on some weekend trips now and then. At least he's not working for the dragon woman. Remember those days when she would just burst into our apartment with her own key, anytime she wanted to?"

"Days I will never forget," Hal said. "She came to see us right after she heard we'd moved, you know. She has eyes and ears everywhere, and one of her spies tipped her off as to our new whereabouts. She wanted us to rent the back cottage to Carl. She's got her claws out for him for some reason, probably jealousy, and wants him out of her house." Roger had returned and heard what Hal said.

"Yeah, I know. Eric dropped in the other day and said the same thing. He didn't say what they plan to do," Roger said. "Need refills here? They're on the way."

Their gaze moved toward the beach, gleaming white in the afternoon sun, and washed by gently breaking waves from the turquoise sea beyond. The spring had not yet warmed the water enough for any but the diehards who seemed to swim in any weather, but the not-so-brave crowded the beach with towels and umbrellas. The onshore sea breeze brought a mixed aroma of iodine and sun tan oil into the open bar where the friends now sat enjoying each other's company and the day.

Probably nothing can compare with spending such an afternoon, sipping drinks, gossiping with friends, and watching the ocean and the beach on such a bright spring day, and the friends relaxed into the lazy and delicious ambiance of simply being contented. Roger was able to sit down and enjoy much of that congenial time too, and the four of them chatted "rubbish" as the Brits call it, just small talk that is the cement of close friendships. Halcyon days like this one, a day which gives an impression of eternity, or if not eternity, at least the feeling that life holds out kind promises for many more times like this lazy Sunday afternoon.

Hal looked over at Simon who was staring out to sea. How beautiful he is, Hal thought. He's everything to me, everything. Oh God, how I don't want to make his life a hell, but it's coming, I know it's coming. I'm going to need his strength and he's going to have to put up with a lot of crap, stuff he doesn't deserve. How will we survive it all? Can we survive it?

The first of the salvos across the bows of Hal's sense of well-being had been fired last week from a fundamentalist church near his school, the Christ Almighty Church of God. Its pastor, G. D. Torrents, had stoked the fires of hatred against gay people from his pulpit, and his fiery talk had set his self-righteous congregation to rout out anyone who fit the stereotypes delineated by their fuehrer. He remonstrated against the hotbed of gay sin concentrated in Laguna Beach, a known harbor of perversion, and sought to cleanse every possible institution that might have been contaminated by what he claimed on biblical authority to be the greatest abomination. One of those institutions was Hal's high school; G. D. Torrents convinced his flock of mindless sheep that the public schools had been infiltrated by a multitude of the unheavenly host, homosexuals who were busy corrupting the youth of an otherwise godly and holy community.

*Lagunatics*

A tract containing G. D.'s talk had been disseminated at school, and Hal had read it, becoming both angry and frightened by its message. The frustrating thing was that he felt powerless; what could he possibly do about such a diatribe that wouldn't jeopardize his job, his standing among his colleagues, and the respect his students would relinquish once he come out on the side of reason and justice? Nothing, nothing but wait and worry.

But here on the pleasant patio of the Hotel Laguna as he overlooked the untroubled scene of sand and surf, as he sat beside his lover and with his friends, his mood slightly lifted. He pondered what alternatives he had. He could fight or run. He could quit his job, or he could defend it against the gigantic evil forces that were organizing against him and his kind. There were options to living with the abiding threats that perennially kept his mind on alert to impending danger. Whatever he did, he thought, he would protect Simon, and he would protect their life together.

"So what Eric will do is the question. What do you think Carl will do, Hal?" Roger asked, jerking Hal back into the afternoon's chat from his reverie. "Where were you just now anyway?"

"Oh, uh . . . sorry. Just thinking. Carl? Who knows? I imagine that he'll stick with Eric no matter what. But I don't see them staying in the Dark Tower up there for long. Denise will have her way. She always does," Hal replied. Simon looked at him and knew that Carl and Eric's situation had been the farthest thing from Hal's mind a moment ago. He had honed his ability to read Hal over the years, and he saw the worry and concern in his eyes. "Did someone say something about another drink?"

They settled once more into the lassitude that the afternoon gave them, Hal relaxing into the warmth of their friendship and managing to put aside for now the cares and worries that would rise up again tomorrow.

\* \* \* \*

*"See, that's where the fags hang out, that Blue Cove place. Loaded with 'em. Somebody ought to throw a bomb in there some day. There he goes with his faggot boyfriend down the street, big as life, just like a normal person. Hey, they're goin' into the hotel. Let me out here. Meet me inside when you park the car. I wanna see what they're up to now."*

# CHAPTER 8
# *All the News That's Fit to Print*

Monday afternoon, and Norman's anticipated review hit the streets. The most salient parts of it are quoted here:

### Oklahoma! You'd Sooner Go to Kansas

#### By Norman Stands

The idea of having dinner while seeing a show seems a particularly good one, especially during the current production of *Oklahoma!* which plays for at least another week at the Beach Playhouse; that is, if the place can find an audience that long.

The chef there is superb and the menu varied with prices well within anyone's budget for a night out. I especially recommend the *Supremes in tarragon cream sauce* which are perfectly cooked and not over sauced . . . . We had a splendid chocolate confection along with several fine wines, expertly served by the waiters there. Certainly worth going out for such fine dining, provided you are prepared for the amateurish performance of the musical which you will have to endure while you're eating.

I must say that given the small space in which *Oklahoma!* is staged down there, the blocking and movement of the actors worked quite well. It was everything else that became a series of one dreadful event after the last. The cast sings accompanied by tape (there is no room for an orchestra), and the tape was the only thing that stayed on pitch. The singers, with the exception of the man who played Judd, all sang as if they had never seen, much less rehearsed, the score before that very night.

No one expects to hear Gordon McRae when they go to a local revival of *Oklahoma!* but one does hope to hear the old familiar tunes by Rogers and Hammerstein sung with something like recognition. Last night's performance of "Oh, What a Beautiful Morning" gave the impression of its having been adapted for something much darker, perhaps starring Vincent Price in some horror epic. The song's originally intended exuberance and nascent meaning of optimism was lost on Mr. Lebland whose voice failed to negotiate the higher notes needed to celebrate a new day. Nor was Curly's wooing of his lady love convincing, perhaps overshadowed by the appearance of a winsome cowhand, and the songs were perfunctory and often sung flat.

The restaurant itself is open several days during the week when the show is dark. I'd go then.

*  *  *

The article was much longer and went into detail about the menu, but it was this part that had the phone ringing the moment Hal got home from school at 4:00. "Have you read it? Have you READ IT?" It was Bertrand from next door who really didn't need the phone. "That son of a bitch! What does he know about show business anyway? With all that clinking and clanking from his jewelry, I'm surprised he can hear anything else."

"Hold on, Bertrand. I just came in the door, and no, I haven't read it, but I take it that is wasn't entirely a favorable review, huh?"

"To say the least. A pan like that could close the show. It's not fair . . ." and the rant went on with Hal holding the phone a good foot away from his ear. "Wait a minute, somebody's at my back door."

Coming up Hal's walkway at that very moment was the author of the review, joined halfway by Simon who was getting off work. "Well, well, Norman! Come in and have some coffee. Hal's probably already home," he said as they got to the front door. "Oh he's home all right," he said, watching as Hal was trying to signal him and Norman to get inside quickly. Bertrand came back on the line.

"Look, Bertrand, I know you're upset, but I'm not sure why you're calling me unless you just need to ventilate," Hal said, trying to wind down the conversation. "Now try to calm down. It's probably not as bad as you think.

55

The show will go on, I'm sure," he said, rolling his eyes at Norman and Simon who were starting to giggle. After something more from Bertrand, Hal said goodbye.

"Wow, let's see what you wrote, you vicious old queen," Hal said grinning at Norman who had a copy of the paper with him. "Hmm . . . well, I see. That bad, huh?"

"The worst! I was actually a lot kinder than my dinner companions were," Norman said, taking a cup of coffee from Simon. "I suppose I could have glossed over it a bit, but I do have a duty to my readers, you know." "Uh huh, right. Bertrand's on high boil over there, but somebody came in as he was winding down and things got softer. Anyway, are you over here hiding out?"

"Not at all, my dears. I'm here to extend an invitation. We're all going to dinner at the new hotel in Dana Point this weekend," he said, petting Edward who had meowed his way in to see who was going to feed him. "You'll never guess who the guest chef is so I'll have to tell you. None other than the famous Jean-Jacques, down from Los Angeles for the week. Won't Madame Lebouche be surprised when she finds out?" Norman crowed.

"I'd be surprised if she doesn't already know. She knows everything else. She's been here already to see if we'd rent the cottage to Carl—something we are not about to do—who has apparently got himself on her bad side. And we'd love to go to dinner," Hal said, getting a nod from Simon.

"Saturday night. Dress nice. Must go now," and jingling his way to the door, he was off down the walk.

Simon went to the windows that faced Bertrand's house and opened them. "Strangely quiet over there, don't you think? Fifteen minutes ago he was hot enough to burn the house down."

"Yeah, well let's not look a gift horse in the mouth. I need a drink. It feels like it's already Friday and it's only Monday. Did we ever have this much fun up on the hill, I ask you?" It occurred to him that he hadn't given the Briggs menace so much as a thought for a whole afternoon, but just as suddenly the clouds returned to his mind to darken his day.

# CHAPTER 9
## *Around the Neighborhood*

Hal's high school classes usually provided him with what he called 'normalcy', a term borrowed from educationese that he used to describe his life away from the commotion of singing neighbors, review-writing friends, drama queens at The Blue Cove, and ghosts in the back yard. Not that he disliked his life in that milieu, far from it. It was just that getting some distance from the seemingly constant parade of issues brought to their house on Myrtle Street gave him better insight on how to view the events that kept his and Simon's life more than fascinating. Likewise, Simon's medical practice supplied the same reprieve from the drama that played before him and Hal. How they found themselves in the center of the vortex of everyone else's lives mystified them. But there they were. Mercifully, Monday had not brought Hal anything further from the war against fags campaign; he counted it a good day, had gone about teaching his classes and caring for his students, and had even hoped for a moment that the fundamentalist church might have taken some time off. Of course, he knew better, that the hiatus was temporary, and that the evil ones were gathering strength for a new assault.

Both of them had thought to have a quiet evening alone. The boys had gone back to San Diego, Bertrand had moved his studio to the farther side of his house, Edward and his dog friend Augustus were curled up on the back patio, God's in his heaven; all's right with the world. A quiet dinner for the two of them, dishes done, and both men went to the living room to read. Then the phone rang.

"It's George for you, Hal." Simon had gone to pick up the kitchen extension.

"Hey George, what's up?"

"Nothing much. Just going out of town next weekend to a conference," George said. "Didn't you hear about it?"

"Nope, couldn't go anyway. What conference?"

"Just somebody telling us all how to teach better. I'll let you know how it goes. It's up in Santa Barbara." Although George's love was the theater, and his master's degree included nearly as many courses in drama as it did in social studies and history, he nevertheless had got a job teaching history. "Maybe there will be a few new samples of decent history textbooks on display," he said. "I mean, what kind of an American history book has a chapter on the Revolutionary War called 'Beating Off the British' I ask you?"

"I'm sure that gets a laugh from your kids," Hal laughed. "I've always wondered who writes textbooks anyway. There is that famous sentence in one of the grammars in the indirect object section: 'Mary helped Jack off the horse.' Now if think *that* won't stop a lesson cold."

George laughed too. "Well, maybe we should write books of our own. But anyway, I'll be looking around up there."

"What's Martha doing while you're away?" Hal asked, hoping that he and Simon wouldn't be called on to entertain him while George was out of town. Martha wasn't a bad person, just an annoyingly boring person, best taken only in small doses and in the comfortably mitigating presence of George.

"He's staying at home, I guess. He hasn't said what he'll do. Probably go out to The Cove. I'm only gone over Saturday night. Be back home on Sunday."

"If you're back early, say around 10:00, come by for some brunch," Hal said.

"Thanks, we'll try to make it." And with that they hung up.

"George is away on Saturday and Martha is at large," Hal reported to Simon. "Glad we have that dinner to go to with Norman. It will be good to see Jean-Jacques and Michel, huh?" Simon looked up from his medical journal and nodded.

"By the way, how is George dealing with the hate campaign?"

"Same way I am, I think. We haven't talked much about it yet, but the time is coming when we'll have to. Right now we've all got out heads in the sand hoping it will all blow over. I wish I could find out how much support we might gather against this group that calls itself a Christian church," Hal said.

"Don't you think there are more gay teachers around than just you and George?"

"If there are, they are so far into the closet that they look like the rest of the clothes hanging in there. Nobody else in my school lives in Laguna, of that I'm sure. Hey, let's just enjoy the evening, OK? How about reading right over here beside me?"

Another phone call was taking place next door:

"Dana! When are you coming down?" Bertrand asked. Dana was a close friend who lived in LA, took trips to Laguna from time to time, stayed with Bertrand, and made forays into The Blue Cove in search of prey. Dana's job as an actor on various TV shows had moved him into a successful career, and his good looks got him cast as everyone's ideal boyfriend, clandestine lover, and more rarely, as the best looking dad anyone could imagine.

"This weekend if you've got room. Will that work?"

"It will, of course, but I wish I'd known sooner. I could have got you a table at the dinner theater. You haven't seen my *Oklahoma!*, you rat," Bertrand kidded his friend. Dana was keenly aware of Bertrand's singing aspirations and had managed to evade his performances if at all possible, thus also avoiding having to comment on them. He liked Bertrand very much, but he could not admire his voice. "But the show is entirely sold out for the weekend."

"Well, I know it's short notice, but I'll be fine. I could meet you after the show on Saturday night. How's that?"

"Fine. Get here early and we could at least have a drink and I can give you a key. I've moved the place around a bit—more on that later—but there's still a double bed in the studio just waiting for you."

They settled on a time for Dana's arrival and said goodbye. Bertrand went back to practicing the finer points of "The Surrey With the Fringe On Top" which he felt was in need of more attention.

Down Myrtle Street, behind a white picket fence and a yard divided into flower beds, sat the house of Dorothy Eakins. Dorothy had lived in

Laguna all her life, had married twice, produced three children, buried both husbands, and resided in the same house in which she had been born. Her parents once owned the house that Hal and Simon now lived in as well, and, having spent part of her childhood in it, she watched over it as if she still had more than a little vested interest in the place. Her circumstances had been greatly reduced at the death of her last husband who had managed to spend a great deal of the trust fund that Dorothy had inherited from her parents. These days she made extra money cleaning a select list of the better houses in town, one of which was Hal and Simon's.

"That used to be our house, you know," said Dorothy Eakins to Cynthia Daley as they sat in Dorothy's back yard garden on Tuesday afternoon, sipping martinis. "We moved there when I was a girl. But after the trouble, my father bought this house back and this is where Papa and Mama died, both of 'em." Cynthia had heard this history before; in fact, she'd heard it many times, but she had grown to expect hearing it again after the two women had been through the first pitcher of martinis. "Did I ever tell you about the trouble? That's what my mother always called it, the trouble."

"I think you've mentioned it once before, Dorothy," Cynthia said, draining her glass and reaching for the iced pitcher.

"It's not over, not by a long shot," Dorothy said, handing her glass toward Cynthia who filled it for her. "Those boys who just moved in there have a shock in store."

"Oh Dorothy, we need another pitcher of these if you're going to tell that ghost story. I'll just go freshen this up," she said, unsteadily rising and heading for the kitchen. She hoped that by the time she got back, Dorothy might have forgotten about telling the story yet again. No such luck.

"It was a murder, pure and simple," Dorothy began as she always did. "You don't find somebody with an axe buried in their skull and call it accidental death, now do you? Well, that's what that fool coroner did call it. Said poor Uncle Raymond tripped and fell in the back yard while he was chopping wood, and hit his head on the axe which went right into his brain."

"It doesn't sound that far fetched to me, Dorothy," Cynthia said. This was her expected line and she knew better than not to say it.

"That's because you didn't know Aunt Clara. Now there was a piece of work, let me tell you. I was afraid of her the moment I saw her. She had that kind of dead look about her, eyes sunken in, real bony face like a skeleton. She was scary. If you'd have seen her, you'd think she would have rattled, she was that skinny."

Next line. "If she was that skinny, she must have been pretty weak too," Cynthia said, eating a gin-soaked olive out of her glass.

"Strong as a bull, she was, Cynthia. That's why she could have done it."

"Tell me again why you think she wanted to kill your uncle Raymond."

"Why else? He was playing around! Oh she knew, all right. Everybody knew. What nobody really knew was who he was playing around with! That's what made her do it when she found out."

Cynthia knew very well the answer to her next question. "Well, who was it?"

"Let's just say it wasn't a woman. And no, it wasn't a girl, either. Uncle Raymond had him a boy to play with. When Aunt Clara found them together out in that shed—now it's been made into that guest house—that's all she could take. That's when she decided to do what she did."

"It sounds like Lizzie Borden, Dorothy. How come they never arrested your Aunt Clara?"

"Oh they did, they did. But looking so frail and all, they thought she could never pick up an axe much less chop it into Uncle Raymond. But we knew she could. Used to watch her pick up the sofa and sweep under it, single-handed too. So she got away with it, right there in our own house. That's when Papa decided to move out."

"And now there's a ghost? Whose ghost, Uncle Raymond's or Aunt Clara's?"

"The Schenleys said they saw both of 'em in the back yard one night," Dorothy said, helping herself to the martini pitcher. "Said they were just sitting out there together as if they had finally made peace. Then they disappeared when Alice Schenley went outside to get a better look. Oh they're there all right. Just wait until those boys see 'em."

"Have you met 'those boys' yet? They look like nice men from what I can see."

"Oh yes. I clean their house, you know. Their cat comes over to visit every day. I hardly ever see them to talk to, they're both so busy. And I'll tell you something else. There's trouble brewing for them. You know that Hal and Simon are 'that way', don't you?"

"I would have guessed so. What's wrong?"

"People down there where Hal works are stirring up a lot of hate against gay men. Especially teachers. I read this paper at their house the other day by some crazy preacher. Wants to get 'em all out of the schools," Dorothy said, eating the last of her olives. "What I can't get is why people like that don't tend to their own business."

"Well, I have seen the ads for this Briggs amendment or whatever it is. That doesn't look good either."

"He's another one. Just plain nuts. Politician without a grain of sense. Hand me that pitcher, will you?"

"How's Bertrand been? You're old friends by now, I'd guess," Cynthia asked.

"Bertrand's busy with his new musical and I hardly ever see him these days either," Dorothy said wistfully. "Such a lovely man. Too bad he's 'that way'."

"Hell, three-fourths of the men in this town are 'that way', Dorothy. I hope you haven't been shopping for another boyfriend."

"Ha! At my age? And besides, look what happened to Ethel Declamber with that awful musician she had in her house. Took her for a lot of money, not that she'd ever admit it. Nope, no boyfriend for me."

# CHAPTER 10
## *There's No Business Like Show Business*

Hal's blithe encouragement to Bertrand, that *Oklahoma!* would continue somehow in spite of Norman Stands' scathing review of it, turned out to be prophetic. Not only did the show go on, its next performance, as Bertrand had rightly told Dana, would be presented in front of a sold-out house, proving the old adage that any publicity is good publicity. Possibly the dining public wanted to see for themselves if what they had read was true, but for whatever the reason, not a single table was available Saturday night as the curtain rose on the opening scene.

Many of Laguna's gay aristocracy were in attendance, some to bask in the glory of their local star tenor, others to await their turn at formulating their own review of the show. Hal and Simon were not there since they had been invited to Jean-Jacques's dinner. But there was one table to the left of the stage, almost obscured in shadow, where George sat by himself, and clearly not attending a teacher conference at all. He wanted to be unobtrusive, to be unnoticed by everyone, and he nearly pulled that off had it not been for La Pompadour who never missed anyone anywhere. "Why George! All alone over here in the dark? Why don't you join us at our center table? And where's Marth . . . uh . . . Marty tonight?"

George tried not to appear guilty although he felt as if he had just been caught doing something naughty. He had, of course. He'd lied to everyone to mask his real intentions of coming to Bertrand's show alone. He disliked lying, and he thought about how much of it he had found himself participating in over the last years. Sometimes it was merely evasion when it came to telling Marty where he was going. It was just easier than starting a firestorm over his wanting to attend a play, for instance, when Marty wanted him to stay at home. It would have been one thing if they had had anything to do at home together, but all Marty did these days was watch TV. But he wanted George there anyway although George hated almost everything he saw on television. So he had begun to find reasons to be at school at night, to manufacture mythical events that he pretended he was obliged to attend. Lying to Marty was one thing, but now he had lied to Hal, and that saddened him.

But not for long. There rang in his mind the heady song of adventure. His encounter with Bertrand last Sunday had started that song playing. He had no real hopes besides watching Bertrand and therefore being in proximity to him, but the strength of the song increased as he awaited the beginning of the show. He felt as if he were on a holy mission, one that thrilled his soul, and made him tremble.

Now interrupting his reverie was the annoying Paulette's invitation to join his horrid crew of harpies. He mustered as much savoir faire as he could. "Hello Paulette. Thanks, but I'm fine over here. I'm uh . . . writing a sort of review for my students and I'd need to concentrate. Marty doesn't really like theater, you know. He's at home watching his usual dose of commercial TV stuff."

"Well, I hope that your report will be more gracious than that snotty one that Norman Stands wrote. Really, how rude! And our Bertrand just singing his heart out, night after night. Oh, look the curtain's going up. Sure you won't join us?"

"Thanks, but I'm fine here," George said as the invisible orchestra struck up the overture.

Bertrand's appearance on stage heightened George's ardor, but as the show moved along, George was grateful that he wasn't really having to write anything about it; he ignored the music and kept his eyes on Bertrand who returned the favor by smiling at George. At long last the show was over, the curtain calls completed, the last bows stolen, and the curtain rang down on yet another night of musical grandeur. George left through a side door of the theater, mainly to avoid being seen by La Pompadour and her entourage, but also to find Bertrand. He waited for half an hour outside the stage door before the star tenor emerged, freshly cleansed of stage make-up. "Hi," George said. "I hope you don't mind if I waited."

Bertrand didn't say anything but instead, strode up to George, moved him into the shadows, took him in his arms, and kissed him passionately and deeply. He moved his lips down to George's neck and whispered, "God, I hoped you hadn't left. Let's go. Follow me in your car."

George did exactly that, and in the rarified air of illicit romance and with the heady manner of a man who has just been made love to with the promise of much more to come, he found himself parking his car in the alley behind Bertrand's house. Bertrand was instantly at his window. "Come on, I'll show you the way," he whispered as they went into his house through the back door. George couldn't help noticing that the house next door, Hal and Simon's, was very dark except for a dim light, probably in their hallway. He felt assured that he hadn't been seen by his friends as he eagerly followed Bertrand into his bedroom and closed the door behind him.

They took up where the exciting kiss outside the theater had left off; clothes were quickly abandoned as the two men, locked in each other's arms, fell onto Bertrand's bed. George was not prepared for the intensity of lovemaking that Bertrand presently invited him into. When he could think at all, he chalked up the passion to Bertrand's highly strung artistic temperament, let loose and visited on the very willing George who wasted no time in reciprocating. It was a night of heightened ecstasy that he had not anticipated; in fact, he had only vaguely hoped that he might get to have a drink with Bertrand after the performance. He had been stage struck when he met Bertrand at The Cove, no more than that. He had to admit that he had wanted him, had fantasized about being with him, and now here he was. My god, he thought, who wouldn't have the hots for this man? He's totally beautiful all over.

They were resting in each other's arms. "How did you know?" George whispered. "I never thought . . . I never even hoped . . ."

"You weren't the only one sneaking looks last week at The Cove. I saw you watching me, and I knew at that moment what you wanted. It was what I wanted too, but there was your boyfriend sitting right there. I don't think I made a very good impression on him, by the way. When Hal asked me to join your table, Marty—that's his name, isn't it?—looked as if I'd just peed on his foot."

George said, "Yeah, you're right. But never mind about Marty. I'll tell you later about all of that." He heard a noise that he thought came from across the hall. "What was that?" he asked.

"Probably my friend Dana who's here for the rest of the weekend just getting in from the bar, and from what I can tell, he's not alone," Bertrand said, snuggling up with George and petting his hairy chest. "I should never have shaved mine," he said. "It's constant maintenance."

"It's beautiful, whatever you do to it. So you like hairy chests, huh?"

"Well, I like yours," he said, burying his nose into George's chest hair. "I like this too," he murmured, moving his hand down George's front.

Exploring another man's body was by no means a new activity for Bertrand, but something about George's firm muscles brought him to remember the early days of his own sexual awareness, exciting days and nights that were conveniently engraved into his memory. He had, over the years, called on that bank of memories when other sexual partners had failed to prompt his libido; all he had to do was remember one of them, transfer it to the current bed partner who was subsequently made to feel that he had been the inspiration for Bertrand's sudden crescendo of lust. Bertrand had carried on this charade with countless men with the result that he himself had managed to have a satisfying climax with each of them. The cold light of morning usually did not sustain the manufactured fantasy of the night before, with the result that the partner in question was not summoned again to Bertrand's bed.

George's presence did not require Bertrand to dip into his libidinous bank account to retrieve a memory of a better time than he was having right then. What was it, he wondered, what *is* it about this man? We've only just met so it's not that I know him that way. But my God I like touching him. He felt George moving on top of him, and he seemed to melt into George's arms as he opened his legs to allow George to lie between them. He submitted entirely to George, and for the first time in many years, knew the genuine pleasure of being made love to.

It was 7:00 AM when George awoke beside his handsome bedmate, the time when he normally got up every other day. He knew that the bathroom was down the hall, and he carefully moved out of bed to go there. No need for clothes, he thought. Probably nobody else is awake at this time of the morning. He headed for the bedroom door, opened it, and switched on the hall light.

Suddenly the bedroom door across the hall opened and there, emerging for a similar errand to the bathroom, and standing in front of George, was an equally naked Martha.

# CHAPTER 11

## 'How sharper than a serpent's tooth'

"What do you think will happen now that her plot blew up in her face?" Simon asked Hal over their first cup of Sunday morning coffee. They had slept in until 9:00AM. "I'm glad of one thing, that Carl told her off right there in front of everybody."

"Well, one thing's for sure, he'll have to move out of Denise's house. That sort of leaves Eric to decide what he'll do, huh? Denise thinks she has him on her side, but she thought that one other time, remember? My guess is that Eric will do what's good for Eric. And we're agreed about not renting out the cottage to anybody no matter what, aren't we?"

"Absolutely. Besides, my mom is coming out for a week sometime and we'll need it. But imagine Denise trying to get away with that stupid sabotage plot. By the way, I've never seen her dressed like that; I mean, she blended right in with the rest of the diners. Obviously on purpose. She was there to watch what she hoped would be large-scale gagging."

"Nothing she does surprises me. She's one of the best business women in town, smart when it comes to running Le Bleu, but at the same time, she can carry out some of the most idiotic stunts imaginable. Remember when she set the restaurant curtains on fire with that awful fake Grand Marnier junk? Well, this was just one more of her hare-brained schemes that backfired. Want some more coffee? Who do you think will turn up for brunch later? I told George to come by if he got back from Santa Barbara early enough. He'll have to go home and collect Martha, I suppose," Hal said, looking out toward the street.

"I could swear I saw Martha crossing Coast Highway as we drove back last night. Seemed to be heading for The Cove."

"I saw him too. Finally got tired of TV at home without George, I guess." Their desultory and lazy Sunday chat evolved into other topics, with Simon talking about a patient he'd treated last week. "Of course, you'll know who I mean even if I don't say his name. He came in to see what could be done about some curious lesions that have appeared on his back. I hadn't seen anything like them except in textbooks, but several of us identified them as a rare cancer. We'll do some more tests and figure out treatment."

"Did you by any chance hear a lot of noise in the alley this morning around 7:00AM or so? Doors slamming, some loud voices, more doors slamming—this time a car door—and after that, somebody roaring off. Maybe Bertrand had a party after the show last night. I was too uh . . . wrapped up with you to go look."

"Something was definitely going on," Simon agreed. "Hey, here comes Norman. Better get your scones in the oven." Hal left for the kitchen as Simon greeted the turquoise adorned Norman at the front door.

"Quite a scene with Madame last night, wasn't it? I never would have thought that Carl had it in him to let her have it.

\* \* \* \*

It had indeed been quite a scene. Leaving Le Bleu under the supervision of her head waiter, Denise had headed for the Harborside Hotel with Eric and Carl where Jean-Jacques would be the guest chef for the invited elite of the coast towns. How she had managed to get a table at all was not so miraculous as it was underhanded; she had bought off a guest who had a reservation by promising him free dinners at Le Bleu, and kept his name on the Harborside reservation list, much to the horror of the maitre d' who recognized her when she and her two minions showed up. Before he could do anything about it, she had swept past him and gone to her table in the far corner at the back of the room, a table that had easy access to the kitchen. In her large purse, she carried a box of table salt which Carl was to pour into the lobster bisque after sneaking into the kitchen.

Much of what animated Denise's life was a keen sense of revenge. When Jean-Jacques had dumped her for a young man some years ago, her wounded pride had sat on brood ever since. The fact that he left her the restaurant and the house without any strings whatever had done little to mollify the simmering anger that she kept just under the boiling point all this time. Now she would get even, or so she thought, and Carl would be blamed. As usual, her ill-conceived plot lacked anything like a reasonable hope of success, but such was her nearly blind rage and determined sabotage that the basic questions of what might be wrong with her plan failed to cross her mind. Why, for instance, would Carl want, of his own volition, to wreak destruction on Jean-Jacques' dinner, and why anybody would believe what would be her accusation of him did not occur to her. For another thing, why she thought that she could count on Carl's complicity without his revealing its source afterwards was another piece of incredulity that escaped her. No, she was instead convinced that the plan would go forward, and equally convinced that she would emerge blameless.

No one was more cognizant of her and what she was capable of than was Jean-Jacques, and he had been informed of her surreptitious arrival. During their marriage, he had dutifully tried to get her pregnant—even the thought of what bravery that must have taken revolted Hal—but to no avail. Her years were against her for one thing, and after a series of miscarriages which Jean-Jacques came to believe she induced, they had given up. He had imported Michel from Marseilles, realized his real sexual interests, and left with him to take up a life together. They had stayed for a time in Hal and Simon's house on Shadow Lane, a fact that Denise added to her long list of accounts payable against anyone who had in any way moved against her.

Speeches and drinks preceded the meal of course, and at the point when Jean-Jacques was brought out and introduced to the dinner guests, Carl was sent to the kitchen with the box of salt. In he went, and out he came without the box. Naturally, Denise figured that her plan was on schedule, and that very soon there would be retching and gagging all over the dining room. The lobster bisque was served, eaten, and praised. No reaction from the contented diners. Denise gave Carl a withering look; he merely looked straight ahead. Next came the entrée, a beautifully cooked veal dish accompanied by fresh peas and potatoes Anna. Still nothing but ooos and ahhhs from the crowd. The salad arrived, a perfect venue for too much salt. It was eaten and its plates whisked away as more wine was served and dessert came out.

Of course, Denise and her mob ate right along with everyone else, and it galled her all the more that Eric and Carl were enjoying dinner as much as they did. Finally, "What deed you do wees zee salt?" she angrily whispered to Carl.

"Put it on a shelf in their pantry," he said, forking up the last of his charlotte russe.

"What? WHAT? You deedn't do what Ay told you?" Denise hissed at him, her voice rising with every word. "Why you teenk Ay bring you here?"

"I know exactly why you brought me here, and I came so you would think I was going to be a part of your dirty trick. Nice dinner, wasn't it, Eric?"

It was not easy for Denise's funereal pallor to rise much beyond the color of light pink, but on this occasion, her complexion went to an unaccustomed red. Livid with rage at the failure of her plot and even more furious that Carl had sabotaged it instead of Jean-Jacques's soup, she let loose with a combination of Belgian French and her version of English that cannot possibly be recounted here with any degree of accuracy. But the gist of her diatribe was that Carl had until tomorrow to get out of her house once and for all, a piece of oratory that drew attention to her table, not that she cared any longer who knew she was there (Jean-Jacques had known all the while).

Eric sat impassively while she fulminated against his lover, and as Hal predicted, waited to see what would be the best route for him to take now that Carl was no longer in favor with the czarina. Over the months since his return to Denise's bosom, if one could call it that, he had not been idle. His penchant for working undercover found an outlet with the opportunity to invest in a certain piece of property, and his crafty investments gave him controlling interest in the very shopping center where Le Bleu was situated; in short, Denise had unknowingly been paying him rent for the past six months. He held her lease there, and he could, if he wanted, make her vacate the premises. Having learned his lessons about such things as rental agreements and leases very well a few years back, he vowed never to be in a position of subservience again. His goal had been to gain complete ownership, but his controlling interest would serve him well at present.

Once Denise had ventilated her opinion of Carl, it was his turn to let her have it. Their table had suddenly become the show for the diners, and all eyes were on it. "Know what she wanted me to do?" he asked his newfound audience. "A box of salt into the soup. She thought that would make you all sick and would make Jean-Jacques look bad. She's furious with me right now, but she's been mad at him a lot longer. This was going to be pay-back time, she thought, and she also thought I'd help her in this nasty little trick. I couldn't do it." Here he paused and received a round of applause, prompted by Hal whose table with Simon and Norman was not far away. "And she's kicking me out of her house where I've been living with Eric here for some time. Know what Denise? It didn't take much imagination to figure out that you've wanted me out of your house for some time. Truth is, I've already packed up and moved most of my things. I've got a place downtown where I won't have to put up with you and your hideous walls that are covered with some of the worst crap ever painted, your pathetic bad taste, your bad manners, your wicked moods, and your genuinely evil way of living, if you want to call it living." Another pause and more applause. "If I thought that pouring water on you would make you dissolve like the Wicked Witch of the West, I'd do it." And he stalked off leaving a stunned Denise sitting there wrapped in the general abhorrence coming her way from the rest of the diners.

"As a matter of fact," Eric said once the attention of the crowd had subsided, "we'll both be leaving your house, Denise. I'm moving in with Carl. I know that you don't like him, and have never really liked him, and you've made that plain to him before tonight. We like living together and that's what we're going to do."

Things had backfired all around the wretched Denise. Her plans to discredit Jean-Jacques and get rid of Carl so as to have her beloved Eric to herself once and for all having vanished, her high color returned to its usual pallor, and then rose toward red again once she had processed the news Eric had just delivered. "Zen you don't have zee job at Le Bleu no more. Zat ees final. You go wees heem, and zat ees zat. What you do for money to leev on ees op to you."

"You and I have been friends, or at least what you think of as friends, for a long time, Denise. I am sorry you feel that I cannot work there anymore, but it will be as you say. Now we will leave here, find Carl, and drive back." With as much dignity as she could muster, Denise hauled herself out of her chair and marched through the exit.

Outside, Eric found Carl and put him in the front seat of the car, consigning a very nettled Denise to the back. The twenty minute drive to her house could only be described as icy, but by the time they arrived, Denise had rethought things. If Eric left, she would be without a valuable manager, one who not only knew the business but who could get along with her. Although she was not the most introspective of people, she did know where her best interests lay, and losing Eric was by no means in her best interests. "Ay tink we ave been too, ow you say, hasty tonight. Ay want you to stay at Le Bleu. You make good money dere and you good manager, Eric." He waited to hear what she would say about Carl. Nothing.

"I couldn't stay without Carl being there too, Denise, and I doubt that he will stay, knowing how you two hate each other."

"Correction, my love. I don't hate her. That would mean I have some emotional interest in her. I don't. The fact is my feelings are entirely neutral." Carl said nothing further and looked out the car window.

Eric was playing this for all it was worth; he wanted to see if he could get Denise to apologize, something that would be a first in the history of the city. Silence. "Just as I thought," Eric went on. "Here we are at your front door, Denise. It has been an entertaining evening. I'll be around tomorrow to give you the keys. Goodnight." He went to her side of the car, opened her door, and waited until she got out. But she didn't get out; she sat there stolidly and put on her pained look, the one she wore on rare occasions when she wanted pity, all of her bluster and bludgeoning having failed.

"Ay geev you beeg raise, you see," she said as a last ploy. Still nothing with regard to Carl.

"That's very generous of you, Denise, but no thanks. If you wouldn't mind getting out of my car, we'll go on to Carl's place." Slowly and deliberately she got herself out of the car and walked toward her house.

Eric was no fool. When he had accepted Denise's invitation those years ago to live in her house with his lover, he did so with the full knowledge that she could never be trusted. Thus, when she made him choose between her and Carl, he knew that the time had come round again when Denise's interests would ride roughshod over what anyone else might want or need for a happy life.

On Monday, Eric thought to himself as he drove off, he would double her rent at Le Bleu.

# CHAPTER 12
## *Dalliance, Delicious Joy*

Breakfast on Myrtle Street resumed after the tale of Denise's plot had been told; Hal's Sunday morning scones arrived at table, hot, lightly browned, and delicious, Norman wasting no time digging in. "What I want to know is how the show went last night. My neighbor said that he couldn't get a table when he called," he said, buttering a scone and slathering orange marmalade over it.

"It's been as quiet as a tomb next door, at least since seven this morning that is," Simon said.

A knock at the kitchen door, and in came Bertrand and George. "I hope that we aren't intruding," Bertrand said. "George said you wouldn't mind if we came over."

"Not at all, not at all," Hal said, ushering them into the dining room. "Please, come have some coffee and scones. I'll make you some tea, Bertrand." Hal was wearing a smug smile as he nodded at Simon who knew immediately what it meant. He returned his "I told you so" look. The new arrivals both said hello to Norman, Bertrand's beaming smile in his direction coming as a surprise, given the vehemence over Norman's article that he'd vented on Hal just a day or two before.

A lot of superfluous and nervous chat from Bertrand and George, chat that skirted the topic that everyone else wanted to raise, chat that was starting to get on everyone's nerves. George was waiting for Norman to leave so he could talk openly to Hal and Simon, but Norman, with his usual nose for news, showed no signs of going anywhere. George became more and more uneasy; he wondered where Martha was at the moment, what he was doing after having found naked George coming out of Bertrand's bedroom. He had of course, exploded, called George everything he could think of while conveniently forgetting that he had just risen from a bed of lust and licentiousness, and had dashed back into the bedroom where he had left Dana and his clothes, put himself together, and had stormed out of the house, and while he was slamming things, slammed his car door before speeding off.

"Well, you might as well know. I didn't go to a teacher's conference," George began.

"You don't say," Hal said, still smiling and frankly enjoying this whole turn of events. "Here's your tea, Bertrand."

"Yes, I went to Bertrand's show instead."

"Quite a long performance, I'd guess. The show apparently had more acts then we thought," Norman piped up. Despite his having fumed about what Norman had written about the show, Bertrand was apparently in a mellower mood than when he first read the review that panned *Oklahoma!* In fact, he hardly did anything except look at George. "I hear that the place was full. I should be irritated that my review was ignored by the general public . . . but I'm glad your show is still on."

"Uh . . . that's not the performance that I want to hear about. And who was slamming doors early this morning?" Hal asked.

At this point the whole embarrassing confrontation between naked George and naked Martha in Bertrand's hallway got an airing.

"We both just stood there dumbfounded for a minute," George said. Hal was by this time in stitches.

"Well, I'd guess you're used to seeing Martha naked in the morning," he giggled, "but probably not in somebody else's hall. What was he doing there?"

"He had been in bed all night with my friend Dana from Los Angles who's still asleep," Bertrand volunteered.

"Why that scamp! Imagine going out cruising and tricking as soon as he thought you'd left town, George. Ah, where have modern morals gone? Just gone, gone, gone," said Hal, rolling his eyes in fake outrage. George seemed strangely unfazed by his banter, and instead returned Bertrand's gaze.

"My, this really *is* news," Norman said, rising to leave and gathering up some scones to take along. "And now that I've heard it, I'll be going. Oh don't worry, it won't find its way into my column. And we'll talk later," this last to Hal as he jingled his way toward the front door. "Ta ta, all."

Everyone else settled down to more breakfast. "You know that any minute the phone will ring and it will be Martha wanting to come over here to tell his side of the story," Simon said, clearing plates and pouring more coffee. "Then what will we do?"

No answer. George and Bertrand merely continued looking at each other and holding hands. "Oh well, I see that breakfast has only been something of a fuel stop. Think you two have enough energy to pick up where you left off earlier?" Apparently they did, and shortly exited through the back door, back to Bertrand's.

Hal and Simon sat for a moment in silent amazement at the retreating figure of a different Bertrand. "Have you ever seen anybody so changed? What happened to that pompous arrogance that he brought with him the last time, that bragadocious attitude born of his imagined stardom? Not a word about the show or the stage or his usual boring reminiscences of show biz this morning. No attempt to impress anybody with his incessant name dropping," Hal said.

"He's in love, can't you see that? He never took his eyes off George the whole time," Simon said.

"He was even nice to Norman whom he wouldn't have peed on last week if he'd been on fire in the doorway," Hal remarked as he poured them each another cup of coffee.

"How vivid," Simon said. "What do you think will happen?"

"George and Martha are going to split up. I've been expecting it for some time."

"Bull! You just told me last week how solid they were to each other after all these years. You couldn't have predicted this and you know it. You might have been hoping for something to happen for George, but that's not quite the same thing."

"You're right, my love, on both counts. As tired as I am of Martha, however, I'm not so sure I'd have picked Bertrand for a substitute. But did you see how they looked at each other? I haven't seen such mooning since, since . . ."

"Since you and I met, you jerk. Remember? We were everybody's annoyingly in-love couple for a while; or at least we were until we started snoring at each other," Simon grinned at him. "It took a while before we got to be acceptable in polite company again. Some people still think we're a bit gooey." He moved behind Hal and kissed him on the top of his head.

"Gooey? Us? Well, maybe in some circumstances we get gooey," Hal smirked. "Anyway, it's going to be fun around here very soon. What do you say we get out of here before Martha turns up?"

"Best idea I've heard since scones for breakfast."

* * *

"Willy! Get away from the window! They're going out the front. Duck down. Where's that cat? Yeah, I had to hit it. Wouldn't stay away from here. Guess it knows better now. No pictures worth taking today. Know who else was in there? George, that's who. Another fag, I'll bet. We gotta get to the other side of the house. That's their bedroom where they do it with each other. That's what we gotta get pictures of. Hey, out the back, get going! Somebody's coming!"

# CHAPTER 13
## *A Bloodless Revolution*

It wasn't *Oklahoma!* that at the moment occupied Bertrand's Sunday afternoon. "I don't know what to say, George," he whispered as the two of them recovered from another delicious bout in bed. "I haven't felt like this for a very long time, maybe never before." And then something George didn't particularly want to hear, "I feel like singing!"

"I feel the same way, you know. This is all such a surprise, a wonderful happening. I can't think right now about anything except staying right here and holding you." Anything to keep him from striking up a solo. Oh God, how was he going to handle that, he wondered?

The ecstasy began to wane as cold reality crept back into both of their minds. Where would they go from here? Was this just a one-night stand? George looked into Bertrand's handsome face and certainly didn't want their night together to have been a mere sample. Bertrand smiled back at him. "What are you thinking? You look worried. Think I'm kicking you out?"

"I don't know what to think. I really can't think of anything except being with you, seeing you again, seeing you a lot."

"God, I'm glad you said that. If you only knew how long it's been since anything like last night has happened to me." Bertrand said.

"Man, you could have anybody in town that you want, probably anytime you want them. I just feel so lucky right now. It's OK if this is all there is; I mean, I'd be disappointed of course, but I can hope that there's more for us, can't I?"

"The curse of good looks, that's all. Sometimes I buy into my own looks too. When I get lonely and want somebody, that's when. But that's not what happened last night, George. Would it scare you off to tell you that I want somebody like you in my life, somebody who's solid and real, and not just a 'groupie'? And not just 'somebody', I want to see what we can have together. You, I want to be with you. That's how I feel right now."

"Not scared at all. If you did kick me out, I'd think I was the happiest man in town just for having made love with you for a whole night. Maybe I am a groupie, huh? But I don't think I really am."

"Still thinking we could see each other again, a lot, I think you said?"

"Yeah, that's what I said," George whispered as he snuggled Bertrand into his arms.

"What do you think we should do? I mean, you're not . . . you're . . ."

"Not free? No, I guess I'm not in some ways. But the truth is that it's been over between Marty and me for a long time. I suppose we like each other, but I'm not sure that we're really friends anymore. We're just used to living together after all this time. It's been seven years, no, eight, by now. We've grown farther and farther apart. We don't even like to do the same things, like going to live theater. Habit keeps us together; at least, that's what Hal says, and I think he's right. I only needed you to turn on the lights," he said, pulling Bertrand back into snuggling with him. "I don't know what he'll do. That's the only problem," he went on a bit wistfully. "He puts up a big front, he pretends to be independent, but he has a deep fear of living alone."

"There's probably going to be one hell of a scene when you get home. Are you ready for that?"

"I guess I'll have to be. Frankly I don't see how he can get too uppity about what happened. After all, he was across the hall right here, probably getting his brains fucked out by your friend. And speaking of him, when do I meet him? I've seen him on TV for years; always been a fan."

"Let's get him up. He has to drive back to LA this afternoon anyway. Oh, and don't say 'for years' when you meet him, OK?" Bertrand said, grinning at George and unwrapping himself. He headed for the bathroom.

Soon all three of them were gathered in Bertrand's living room. "I loved your portrayal of Atticus Finch in the re-make of *Mockingbird*," George enthused. "I thought that nobody could do that role like Gregory Peck, but you gave it a whole new look. Really fine acting, I'd call it."

Dana was flattered by this sincere compliment, and as used as he was to adulation from fans and critics, he deeply appreciated George's review which went on for some time, analyzing scene after scene of the play. "What are you working on now?" George asked.

"Some Shakespeare for the summer, and a couple of TV sitcoms for the fall. Nothing with me in the major star role; I'm getting to the age when those roles go to the young hot guys. Listen, I know we're not talking about last night, but now that I know that Marty is your partner, we ought to. He seemed more than a little upset when he slammed out of here this morning. This is pretty awkward, and I don't know whether to apologize or what."

"We did what we did," George said, shrugging. "Things will be a little rough for a while between us, and we have some decisions to make, but it wasn't your fault. Things were heading this way for a while. Neither of us wanted to own up to not having a real relationship anymore, but it's true."

"Well, what's awkward is that I'd rather like to see Marty again, I mean, if you think it would be all right. I feel like I owe him some explanations. I talked him into leaving the bar last night," Dana said, looking a bit ashamed of himself.

"Hey, if he hadn't wanted to go, he wouldn't have. Please, don't beat yourself up over what happened," George said. A bright prospect came into his mind. It may well have been Dana's idea to take Marty home, but knowing Marty as he did, he knew how absolutely dazzled he is with anything that smacks of Hollywood. And here was a known TV star asking him to go home with him. This could work out really well, George thought. I might have less to worry about than I figured. Hmm . . . Marty and Dana . . . "No reason why you shouldn't see him again. I'm sure he'd be very happy about that."

"That's very generous of you, George. He left without giving me his phone number though. Think I could call him before I leave for LA?"

"Certainly," George replied, writing down the phone number. Bertrand watched this exchange with great interest. He walked over to George, and caressed his cheek.

\* \* \* \*

There are a few examples in human history of peaceful changes of governments, of treaties actually preventing out-and-out wars, of the tranquil movements of one political force replacing another. In fact, these rare occurrences take a back seat to more dramatic events that erupt from the damaged pride of one nation another, of the zeal of armed revolutionaries that topple kings, and of full-on warfare that spawns endless stories of bravery and cowardice, heroism and perfidy. On such events is literature often founded, providing great novels with an automatic backdrop of human suffering and hardship.

Now we come to one of those rarities in the affairs of men, a transition from one partnership to another that took place with such ease and without anything like real acrimony, and so devoid of interesting and gossipy details, that a long description would bore anyone whose IQ registered above 50. There was, of course, the initial skirmish that looked as if it might develop into something warlike:

"So you had that planned all along? And you lied about going to that teacher conference? And all the time you were thinking of that awful Bertrand?" This posturing was necessary for the armistice to be agreed to.

"Partly true. I did lie about the conference but I didn't think things would get as far as they did with Bertrand. And he's not awful, by the way. It's just that he didn't pay constant attention to you the only time you two met. For some reason he wasn't too interested in the hot gossip from Nordstrom's." A singeing broadside in retaliation, also necessary to level the battleground.

"He was rude to me the whole time? He cut me out of every conversation? And now I know why?"

"Look Marty, this is going nowhere. We have to decide what to do. And we have to own up to something, each of us, something that we have ignored for a long time," George said, taking Martha's hand. "We just don't love each other anymore, and that's the truth, isn't it?" And it was the truth. It didn't take Martha long to get over whatever was jabbing his pride once George said, "And what about this Dana? He called you, didn't he, I mean today? He said he wanted to. I think he's more than slightly interested in my chic ex-lover who is the fashion expert at Nordstrom's."

Martha hadn't wanted to add this into the general negotiations, thinking that he had the upper hand if he left out Dana's phone call and what they had talked about. But now, he admitted to himself that things between him and Dana looked promising, that they had spent most of the night (when they weren't otherwise engaged) talking about all the things that fascinated Martha about Hollywood and TV. He had been invited up for a weekend to meet some of Dana's friends, a prospect that glowed in Martha's mind like a child's long-distance view of Christmas, and a piece of news that he omitted from the peace talks now going forward. He had said yes, even before the hallway encounter the following morning with George, and certainly before he had figured out how he might manage it.

They would live out the month's lease in their old apartment, but neither of them slept there again. Martha began keeping the road hot to Hollywood and Dana's house; George was warming the other side of Bertrand's bed. What astonished everyone was how quickly the changes and moves were made. Things that had looked so permanent only a month prior now displayed the quiet bleakness of an abandoned apartment that the two men had shared for some years. Nothing but bare walls and floors, cleaned out kitchen cupboards, and emptied closets. "However did Martha get all of her clothes out of here so fast?" Hal asked as he surveyed the empty nest with George. They were there to pick up the last of George's books.

"It was more of a miracle to see how they were stored here in the first place. I hope that Dana has lots of closets," George said, hauling a box toward the door. He looked around the apartment for the last time, nodded Hal out the door, and closed a chapter of his life with only a slight twinge of regret. He assigned his momentary sadness merely to the fact of change itself. He had been less than happy here with Martha for a long time, and although he liked the place and would miss some of its charm, he felt elated to be moving away, into a new life, and more than that, a new life with Bertrand.

"It was amazingly calm," George reported on the way to Myrtle Street. "It was as if we both knew that it was over and that we both needed a new start. I know you thought Marty was a pain in the ass among a lot of other things, but he was dependable, and I guess that went quite a ways to keep things stable. But the fire had gone out years ago. Can't remember the last time we had sex. Some things just die a natural death, I guess."

"Welcome to the neighborhood. Now it won't be so far to come to breakfast, that is if you ever get out of bed on the weekends," Hal grinned.

# CHAPTER 14

## *'The cares that infest the day'*

Hal saw Marty's departure to Los Angeles as perfectly satisfactory, as an adjustment to a condition that he had long thought in need of correction. "How they managed it for so long is beyond me," he said to Simon over dinner that night. "I never asked George what it was that got them together in the first place, but they had almost nothing in common. Nowadays Marty is in his element, rubbing elbows with the Hollywood famous, and advising everyone on the latest in Nordstrom fashions."

"George looks like a man reborn, don't you think?" Simon replied. "But talking about what gets people together, you don't imagine that it was Bertrand's singing that had George so smitten, do you? How do you think George will deal with Bertrand's singing career?"

"As long as it stays on the other side of their house, I don't care," Hal said, reaching for the wine. "We'll find out, I'm sure. I'm just glad that he's happy, that he has found somebody who has more to talk about than the price of men's pants."

"People probably say the same thing about us. How boring can it be to hear a doctor go on about diseases."

"But you don't. And what you do tell me is interesting, leading me to believe that you carefully edit everything. By the way, how's that cancer patient doing, you know, the one with the rare skin problem?"

"Not so well. You know who it is, don't you? Wilbur Initson."

"What? Marsha's husband? The people who bought our house on the hill? No, I didn't know. Not doing so well, huh? Any idea why not?"

"We've tried a number of standard skin cancer treatments only to have the lesions come up somewhere else. It's more systemic than we thought.

It's called Kaposi's Syndrome and is less rare in Africa and among older men along the Mediterranean, but almost never seen in this country."

"By the way, I remember where I saw him. Years before you moved here there was a small gay bath house in Dana Point. Everybody from here went there from time to time, and one night I saw Wilbur skulking out of the steam room. He looked entirely spooked and no wonder given what his wife probably knew about his little trip into the world of instant gay sex. Nobody was in there solely for the therapeutic benefits of steam and sauna, I can tell you. Besides, his towel was tented straight out in front."

"What does Wilbur do for work? I don't think I ever knew," Simon asked.

"Imports, mainly from Central American and the Caribbean. I think Marsha told me that he goes to Haiti fairly often."

"Interesting," Simon said. "And don't worry; we're treating his condition with the utmost caution. I want to hear more about that bathhouse in Dana Point."

"Ha! You do, do you? I'm only glad it's gone out of business. You know, I can't exactly remember what its real name was. It had lots of nicknames. The Crab Cooker was the most popular one. If you didn't get a dose of crabs in there, you just hadn't been playing hard enough. They put in a pizza place where it used to be. Still can't bring myself to buy pizza there."

"Why not? Can't be any diseases hanging around there by this time," Simon said.

"It's just the idea. There was the big syphilis scare a year or so before it closed. Almost an epidemic. Always clap, of course."

"Ugh, I see. And how did you manage to get out unscathed, or did you?"

"I didn't. Got the worst and most tenacious crabs you can imagine. Once I got rid of them, that marked the end of my illustrious career at the baths. You weren't hoping for snappy stories too, were you?"

"Of course! You didn't just sit in the place alone, watching the passing crowd as if you were at a bus stop, did you?"

"Ah my love, you are becoming a voyeur. Tell you what. If we run into any of the boys who frequented the place when I did, I'll let you know and tell all, fair enough?"

"Fair enough. You didn't have anything to do with Initson, did you?"

"No, and a good thing too now that you tell me what's wrong with him. Do you suppose it's contagious? He's apparently found some other place to meet men behind Marsha's back. There are plenty of bath houses in LA, and one in Long Beach, so he's probably sneaking up there. Well, maybe you'll cure him and she'll never be the wiser."

"No, it's not contagious in and of itself, but we can't figure out exactly why it's so resistant to treatment. My God! Hear that?" Simon started up from the sofa. Edward was also on the alert and started vocalizing too. "I thought he moved his studio to the other side of his house. Talking about things infecting the world. How do you think George is going to deal with it?"

"Let's go visiting," Hal suggested. They headed next door with a neighborly bottle of wine.

"We'll go broke if we have to short circuit every practice session with a bottle," Simon said as they knocked on Bertrand's front door. The 'music' stopped and the door opened to present a George they hadn't seen before, wearing a facial expression they hadn't seen before either, a mixture of quiet despair that gave way to grateful relief.

"Oh come on in! Bertrand! Hal and Simon are here!" he said with great joy.

Beyond the fence and through the windows, they could hear Edward continuing his own concert, all by himself.

# CHAPTER 15

## *The Oasis*

Probably everyone has visited a town or a city or a locale that instantly tugged at the heart, that beckoned a welcome, that made a visitor feel as if he or she had always lived there or wanted to. Many such places like Cannery Row in Monterey, California, celebrated by John Steinbeck, are like that. Similarly, San Francisco has people leaving their hearts there. The smells and sounds of New Orleans often lure visitors away from their humdrum life in say, Possom Butt, Kansas, and into the milieu of romantic existence among the history and charm they find behind its levees along the Mississippi. Places like these appeal to most of the senses, all at once and overwhelmingly, and as they do, they become more than a mere destination, or simply a charming town. They seem to aggregate their attributes into a soul of their own, one that speaks to the soul of the smitten visitor as the two of them carry on a dialogue that may have no conscious beginning, but that subtly and surely embraces and enfolds until the visitor is no longer a stranger; he lives there now, breathing in the beauty that every day greets him, and he continues the conversation as if with an old friend. He belongs, and his belonging emboldens him to defend his new love against anything that he perceives may endanger it.

Laguna Beach was such a place, engaging not most, but all of one's senses. Its sweeping cove in the center of town that hugged its main beach was best seen from the cliffs slightly to the north of it, displaying the gem of ocean azure that lay mounted by embracing shores. A barefoot walk along that beach brought the smell of the sea, the sound of the surf as it swept gently along the sand, and the caress of the on-shore breeze. The cool damp sand completed the rapture in which all of one's senses were vibrantly awakened.

What had been recognized and prized by artists early in the century as a special place, Laguna Beach had by the 1970s gained popularity among an ever burgeoning influx of people wanting to share its seaside beauty. The town had become nationally famous as a gay mecca, and its attractions for many young gay men have already been alluded to. It also had prime real estate, the prices of houses more than doubling in less than three years from 1975 to 1978. Regardless, Laguna had became the best place to live in Orange County. The town was sanctuary and safety and harbor for any who came and fell in love with her.

The gay 'community', if you will, met in its various bars. The Blue Cove has already been introduced; it shared patronage with two other establishments, The Boom Boom Room in the Coast Inn hotel, and the Main Street across the street, the latter owned by a ferocious lesbian named Marian whose experience as a bar owner in Puerto Rico had fortified her with a vitriolic temper; she hated men, and she had a passive and lovely partner named June. Gay life revolved around these places, and many of Laguna's gay men could be counted on to turn up at one or more of them from time to time.

That is not to say that there weren't other gay venues. There arose in those days a tradition of Sunday brunches in private houses, often using the 'potluck' format, expecting participants to contribute something to the common meal. Gay men, being the creatures they are, soon began vying with each other for more and more elaborate menu items that made their appearance at various homes around town. Strangely enough, the lowly tuna and noodle casserole retained its popularity, and variations on its basic recipe taxed the ingenuity of the most inventive of gay cooks. Tuna and noodle casserole showed up so often at gay brunches that it became known, somewhat derisively, as fairy pudding.

Regardless of the social charms that had grown up there, it was certainly the beauty of the town itself that was its chief allure to those who visited and then decided to make it their home. Beach-front cities like Miami had allowed row after row of high-rise hotels to spoil the landscape; Laguna Beach disallowed the kind of exploitation that hindered views and ruined the natural aspects that its famous cove provided. The only major 'improvement' that did not meet with wholesale gay approval was the reconstruction of Main Beach and the imposition of a long boardwalk there, a project that meant the destruction of old buildings that many considered charming and a part of old Laguna's beach heritage. Nevertheless, the beach was cleared of those venerable buildings including the one that had housed Breakers, another gay bar.

Laguna was a happy place, inviting and cordial, and no self-respecting Lagunatic wanted to see the tone of the town changed. A sense of pride, not only of ownership, but of belonging pervaded the thinking of the townspeople, and while they were content to be invaded every summer as the Pageant of the Masters brought thousands into town, they were equally happy to have the town restored to them after the stage sets of that illustrious production came down. It was that sense of community that produced among the citizenry a wariness against other, more inclement invasions, particularly from the right-wing political and religious forces that besieged the town's generally liberal fortress now and again.

The townsfolk were, of course, losing the battle. As more conservative elements came to buy houses, the politics at Laguna's city hall inexorably began to mirror their views. An erosion of liberty had begun, and although it would take time, the old ways would finally be swept away, victims of an unstoppable onslaught of wealth. Some saw the trend, and like Cato in ancient Rome, railed against what they saw as the encroachment of a puritanical agenda on the social milieu that had mightily evaded them.

But for the moment, there seemed to be hope for a continuance of life as usual, of life free of prejudice and ill-will. Gay men felt safe no matter where they were or when they went out at night, and the general ebullience in the hope that the Briggs Initiative would be defeated bolstered the faith among many that their town, their beautiful Laguna Beach, would be theirs for years to come.

Hal did not harbor such a hope or such a faith. His brush with gay hatred represented by the Briggs Initiative, now on the ballot as Proposition 6, had not planted any such seeds in his heart, quite the opposite. A studied caution replaced any optimism he might have ever had, and he proceeded with vigilance. He carefully weighed to what extent he might get involved politically, always keeping his and Simon's safety as a mitigating factor. He managed for the most part to keep his concerns secret, and to display a kind of joy which he borrowed from simply living in his beautiful house in his beautiful town and with his beautiful lover. It was a guarded joy, and he knew that he was not fooling Simon in the least. Simon knew his moods better than he did himself, and part of how they loved each other revolved around their mutual sensitivities.

It had been five years since they met, five years of relative peace and quiet, but five years during which a higher visibility of gay life had steadily risen on the public's consciousness. Gay Pride Parades proliferated in many large cities across the nation, principally in New York and San Francisco when the anniversary of the Stonewall rebellion against police tyranny was celebrated. These were of course televised, raising the anger level of biblethumping preachers against the newly publicized gay 'abomination'. The struggle for equal rights had begun and nothing would take that liberated segment of the population back into obscurity. Hal wondered to what extent the in-your-face tactics of gay liberation were a good thing, but he reasoned that any objections he might have arose from his own sense of threatened security. His and Simon's.

They would take walks together, mostly along the beach at sunset, renewing their determination to carve out a life together regardless of what might come their way. Here Hal's waning optimism received a respite. Sometimes there were long periods of silence as they sat on the sand holding hands, silence that they each knew was in and of itself a deep communication between them. The ocean calmed them and restored to them their original impressions of this special place. They breathed in the intoxicating sea air as if it were a tonic, and while watching the sea's horizon, they felt the surf-cleansed sand beneath them. Like the mythological Anteaus, their strength and endurance returned from the very ground. An almost meditative frame of mind obtained as they walked together, affirmed in their mutual regard for each other and for the wonder of the oasis that was Laguna Beach, this place that gave them peace, however temporary that peace might prove to be.

# CHAPTER 16

## *Paying the Piper*

Curiosity having fueled a slight resurgence among the theater-going population, *Oklahoma!* at the dinner house managed to break even, but after that sold-out weekend, tickets and seats went begging. An ad campaign was mounted which offered two-for-one prices, but even that attractive offer, coupled by tempting descriptions of items on the menu, failed to fill the room. The show closed after only two more disappointing weekends.

"Don't worry, Bertrand," George soothed. "There will be other shows. I hear they are putting on *The Little Foxes* at the Laguna Playhouse next season. You'd be perfect as Horace Giddons in that play."

"But it's not a musical, dear. I'm born to sing," he said somewhat hoarsely, following a cough.

"Well, it would be just a stop-gap until another musical comes along," George said. "And when are you going to have your throat looked at? You've been sounding strange ever since the last night of *Oklahoma!*"

"It's nothing. Just natural hoarseness."

But it wasn't just nothing. On the following Monday, Bertrand had his throat examined. "Mr. Lebland, you have some serious polyps on your vocal cords. Your larynx is badly enflamed. The polyps will have to be removed, of course. Let's see when we could schedule surgery."

"Surgery! Are you sure that's necessary? Won't they just go away on their own if I take it easy. The show's over and I won't be singing for a while," Bertrand croaked out, his voice raspier than ever.

"No, they won't go away; in fact, they will only get worse unless we take them out. There is the possibility of their becoming malignant. It's a fairly simple operation if we do it right away. Local anesthesia, done in fifteen or twenty minutes. After a period of healing, you'll have your voice back without that rasping you've been experiencing. But I don't think I'd strain my voice again if I were you. That singing you've been doing has obviously been the trouble. Straining the larynx is always dangerous," the doctor said. "The polyps, and possibly worse, could very possibly return if you abuse your vocal cords in the future."

"Not sing? Why, singing is my life! I must sing, People expect it of me," Bertrand rasped.

"Well, if they do, they won't expect it for long because you won't have a voice to thrill them with. You can get a second opinion if you'd like, but I think it will be the same opinion. That said, when can we do the surgery? The sooner, the better."

A defeated Bertrand acquiesced, arrived at a date for the procedure, and sullenly left the doctor's office for home. George was still at school and the house was quiet. He sat down at his piano, played his usual arpeggio that he used every day as he vocalized, and lowered the piano lid and the keyboard cover, locked up the instrument, and wept.

Every relationship has parts and sections that each member must keep to himself, and George's secret was that he hoped for the end of Bertrand's singing career. How could he say to his lover that people laughed at him behind his back, that his singing produced ridicule and giggles rather than the adulation he thought he was receiving? George, in short, was embarrassed for Bertrand, yet at the same time, proud to be with him. What he couldn't stand were the covert smiles, the rolled eyes, the widely held scorn heaped on his lover. He was not, however, prepared for the brutal way that he would get his wish. He arrived home from school to find Bertrand in the back yard and on his third double martini. "Uh oh," he said, going over to kiss his lover. "I guess it wasn't good news, huh?"

"The worst. They want to cut out my voice," Bertrand croaked, slurring his words as well.

"Oh come on. Cut out your voice? You're not on stage now, my love. Just give me the doctor's report with as little drama as possible,"

"So, I'm dramatic, you think? How'd you like it if some doctor told you that you might have cancer," Bertrand ranted, making the most of this.

"Cancer! No, it can't be! What exactly did he say, for God's sake?"

Bertrand finally came out with the truth. "I'll never be able to sing again, that's what he said. They can take away the polyps, but I can't put my voice through the strain of singing again. Ever, ever . . ." he sobbed.

George sat down beside him and held him while he cried. "It's not the end of the world, my love. Lots of people can't sing after a while, and they go on to do other things, like just acting. You're a natural actor, and you're always the best looking person on any stage. This could be a new start for you. You won't have to worry about your voice, and you'll still be on the stage. Now come on, your number one fan needs a hug back."

Bertrand leaned up and hugged George, planting his wet face on his neck. "God, I'm glad you're here. I've felt like hell all afternoon, but I'm OK now. I'll be better tomorrow," he said, rising to the higher drama of his new vision of bravely going on despite his bad news. A vision of Bette Davis in *Dark Victory* appeared in his mind.

"Yes, you will," George consoled, kissing Bertrand's hair, and thinking that once Bertrand got over the distress of his lost singing career, the future without it could look pretty rosy. He would encourage Bertrand to take acting roles. "When will you have the surgery?"

"Next week. The doctor says it's an easy procedure. Just some healing afterwards, sort of like having tonsils out," Bertrand said, recovering from his bout of self-pity. "I'll have to take a couple of days off from the bank."

"You've got a hairy-chested nurse right here to make pudding for you," George smiled. "It'll be fine, Bertrand. Thank God it wasn't cancer. How about my sharing that last martini?"

Naturally, the news of Bertrand's condition and upcoming operation spread next door to Hal and Simon's, the clearing house for gay chat. They were waiting for the doctor's report too. "Well, that's that," Hal said, checking on the cookies he was baking. "Can't say I'm all that brokenhearted."

"Callous, that's what you are," Simon said. "All that jealousy over Bertrand's singing successes that you've been harboring can be laid to rest," he joked.

"And you, my love, are a cynic. Want a cookie, little boy? Hey! Here's Norman. You're just in time. I'll put on some coffee."

"Hello you two," Norman said, jingling his way into the kitchen and plopping down at the table. "I come bearing news."

"If it's about Bertrand Lebland, we already know. But maybe you don't know," Simon said, putting out cups and plates. He described Bertrand's condition and the procedure that would ensue in his best medical terminology.

"A gift to the collective human ear," Norman said at the end of Simon's recitation. "I feel just fine being a bitch about it since what he has isn't fatal or even all that serious. And no more vocalizing from next door. Edward will have to find a new partner to sing with." Edward had entered when Norman did, fascinated as he always was by Norman's dangling jewelry.

"So what's the news, Norman?" Hal asked.

"The news is that I'm going on a month's trip to Europe, entirely paid for by the newspaper," he said, centering the particularly large turquoise pendant on his necklace. "They want me to co-author a book on dining there."

"But that's great! A restaurant tour, huh? Where all will you be going?" Hal asked.

"It's an exhaustive list, dears, but know that Nancy Navajo here will wow them in the major capitals of the free world. Here comes the other part. I need somebody to write my column for that time. How would you like to do it, Hal? The pay's not bad, it's only about a page of text, you'd get to take Simon out to dinner, and you're a good writer. What do you say?"

Hal didn't say anything for a few minutes. "It's a tempting offer, Norman, but I'm not sure I can drum up good things to say about some of those godawful places the newspaper makes you go to. What was that one place called, Bottom of the Rusty Barrel, or something like that? That place that featured meatloaf."

"Oh, you'll get used to that. You always know when I don't like a place, don't you? Even if the restaurant itself thinks it's reading a good review? It's a just word craft, and you could easily learn it. It would help me a great deal if you'd say yes."

"What do you think, Simon? Are you willing to eat fancy meatloaf and god knows what else with me?"

"I think it would be fun, Teach. And Norman's right. You're perfect for the job. When does your trip start, Norman?"

"We leave in two weeks. You don't have to make up your mind this minute, my dear. Think it over, talk more about it, and have a look at these." He produced from a briefcase a large stack of reviews and notes. "You'll soon see how this is done. Well, I'm off, as much as I hate to leave these newly quieted precincts. Call me and let me know." He removed Edward from his lap, grabbed up several cookies, and jingled off toward the door.

It really didn't take much to convince Hal that he would accept Norman's offer. "But only if you're my constant dinner companion," he said to Simon. He dialed Norman and it was a done deal.

# CHAPTER 17
## *Desert Adventures*

"What? You haven't been to Palm Springs? Oh my dears, it's becoming the new gay watering hole. We've just bought a place out there," Leonard enthused over drinks at The Blue Cove one evening. Hal and Simon had met this couple a few weeks before while waiting for a brunch table on The Cove's patio. Leonard and his partner Sid lived up Bluebird Canyon in Laguna, and had been together for over thirty years. "We got to spending so much time out in the desert in the winter that we went ahead and found the cutest place."

"What's so cute about a triple-wide trailer," Sid piped up, getting a searing look from Leonard. "Oh come on, Len. It's a trailer, for God's sake. He likes to let people think it's a real house."

"Well, it *is* a real house. And never mind Miss Wetblanket here. I've been putting up with his raining on parades for at least a century. Anyway, you guys just have to come out for a weekend. We have lots of room—and . . ."

"Yep that trailer has about six bedrooms," Sid interrupted, "and you'd be welcome to any but one of 'em."

Hal looked at Simon who was smiling at the two trailer enthusiasts. "How about next Saturday?" Simon asked. "I'm off all weekend, and we could drive over in the morning if that works for you." He and Hal had been talking about taking a short trip somewhere, a little getaway that they both felt they needed. This invitation might be just the thing.

"Perfect. Come for lunch. That gives me some time to get the place in shape."

"In shape?" Sid exclaimed. "He's been over the whole goddam trailer with a toothbrush already. In shape? Hell, Simon, you could do surgery on the kitchen table, it's that clean."

"I meant buy a few things for our best guest room," Len said, getting a groan from Sid. "And it's a mobile home estate, not a trailer park, if you please." They all finished drinks and went off to dinner.

Hal and Simon dutifully set out for Palm Springs on Saturday morning through light traffic, the heat of the desert increasing as they drove on. It was April, but the desert town was unseasonably warm. "We should get there by noon. Isn't that when they said to arrive?" Hal asked. "I hope they have air conditioning. It's really getting hot out."

"They said noon-ish, in time for lunch. And I'm sure that everyone has air conditioning out here. This is fun, don't you think? We haven't been out of town for a while. Sort of a mini-vacation. Free, too. We should take them out to dinner, though. They made reservations at a new restaurant." Simon was full of excitement. "I've never been to the desert, not really. I had to drive across it when I came to California, but that really doesn't count."

"No, my love, that doesn't count. This will be a relaxed and civilized weekend with nice people. Did you bring the sunscreen?"

"Yep, can't wait to slather it all over you by their pool." Their anticipation of the good time ahead almost made them miss a turn. But soon they were on Highway 111 that led into Palm Springs itself.

"Their trailer court is on the other side of town according to the map they gave us," Hal said.

"And don't call it a trailer court. It's a mobile home estate," Simon ribbed as they drove through downtown Palm Springs, passing the famous Follies Theater where retired stars, mostly women, still put on great shows. They rounded the curve out of town, driving another mile or so. "Slow down, I think we're almost there." They drove into what was certainly a trailer court but had the new name on its sign of Rising Gorge Mobile Home Estate. They wound their way around through the grounds and finally found Len and Sid's triple-wide. A deep and shaded front porch full of patio furniture and rather forlorn-looking planters full of dying flowers greeted them.

"The Wayfarer. Isn't that just precious? This thing isn't wayfaring anywhere. It's cemented to the ground," Hal said as Simon pushed the doorbell button.

Len greeted them with a drink in his hand. "Well, here they are at last. We began to think you'd got lost. Drinks have been flowing here for an hour or more. Come on in and meet some of our friends." He led them into an enormous living room that had been made of two of the triple-wide trailers. To its right was the kitchen, obscured by a large bar on which sat pitchers of Bloody Marys. "You gotta try one of these Marys. It's Russell over there's recipe. Here, just drop your stuff and grab a drink and I'll introduce you around."

Since Palm Springs is something of an elephant burial ground where the old go to spend their last days, there is a thriving business in resold furniture, most of it having been fairly expensive, and available at a number of estate sale stores. Leonard had made forays into these places, and his and Sid's living room in the triple-wide reflected his successes. Arranged around the room and seated in an eclectic selection of easy chairs, sofas, and recliners was the morning drinking crowd in various states of consciousness. Drinks in hand, Hal and Simon were paraded around the room and given everyone's name. "Now there's a test on this later, so pay attention," Len hooted, amusing himself with this tired old joke. Hal wondered if it might help to alphabetize: Al, Ben, Danny, Henry, Kenny, but then he gave up; they began to all look alike. Seats were found for Hal and Simon, and they fell into a rump-sprung sofa, vintage 1935.

Pitchers of Russell's Bloody Marys went around the room again, with no sign of anything like lunch, and not even so much as a potato chip in sight. Russell himself looked as if he'd tried every batch of his famous libation, and he was currently swaying over a seated guest, his drink dripping onto him. Hal and Simon tried to make small talk with the mannequin seated next to them. The mannequin, a man of a certain age, sported hair dyed an unsuccessful yellow, and he had dyed his eyebrows to match, just for verisimilitude. He was darkly tanned, his skin having achieved the color of brown shoe leather. The three of them were stuck into the fearsome grip of the sofa, but unfazed, the mannequin maintained a frozen smile through which he managed a few syllables, mostly having to do with the desire for a refill of his glass.

Conversation, what there was of it, among the six or eight attendees consisted mainly of local gossip. "Oh Sal, that mad old queen! He bought that hot Chilean, you know, paid for him to come up here to be his houseboy. Ricardo, I think's his name. All he gets done is make food for his lord and master."

"I'm sure that's not all he gets done. If that Sal gets any fatter, though . . ."

"Violet told me that her husband's been missing for five days."

"Again? Well, you know where he is, don't you? He's over at the Desert Palms, shacked up with some man. And you know that Violet knows too. She's not stupid, just dumb."

And so the talk went as glasses emptied out. After the initial introductions, no one seemed at all interested in the newcomers from Laguna Beach. That worked both ways; Hal took instant stock of the Madame Tussaud Wax Museum collection arranged around the room and decided that his and Simon's weekend was not exactly going the way they thought it would. "I think you said you had a pool here," he said to Leonard who was passing by with his ubiquitous pitcher.

"Oh yes, but they are redoing it. It's closed for a while. Fill you up here?" Hal declined. The closed pool was one more nail in the closing coffin lid of their weekend getaway.

More drinks were made, the pitchers refilled as were glasses around the room, the clock ticked another hour off, and still nothing like lunch. "They did say to come for lunch, didn't they," Hal whispered.

"I'm sure they'll be getting lunch ready very soon."

"This collection of mummies is by no means eager for anything, particularly food. I'm starving, aren't you?" One of the guests across the room leaned into another one and went soundly to sleep.

"They did say lunch, and if something besides the celery in these drinks doesn't show up pretty soon, let's take off for some food somewhere," Simon whispered back. "We can say we forgot something in the car."

"It had better be soon or we'll both be too sloshed to drive."

"What's all this whispering over here, you two?" Leonard asked, hoving into view, pitcher in hand. "Let me just top those up for you."

"Thanks, but we've had enough for now. I don't want to be rude, but did you say to come for lunch? I mean, it's nearly 2:30 and we haven't eaten since early this morning."

"Oh, that's changed and I forgot to tell you, ha ha! We're all going over to Elmer and Jake's for lunch later. They always eat late, never before around 3:00 so we thought we might as well just have a drink or two before we go." Sid, Hal noticed, was nowhere in sight. "They just live on the other side of our little neighborhood here. You'll absolutely love Jake. Hot, hot, hot!"

Sid sidled in through a side door with a bag that looked suspiciously like it had come from MacDonald's. He made a dash for one of the back rooms, and closed the door behind him. "That was the undeniable smell of French fries," Hal said. "My God, I'd kill for a bag of French fries right now. In fact, murder is coming up in my mind quite a lot at the moment. This is just plain rude, Simon. Let's go get some food of our own. And speaking of rude, if Sid can sneak back in here with a stash of hamburgers and fries, so can we." They got up to go and were immediately intercepted by Len.

"Sorry Leonard, we have to eat. Health reasons, you understand. We'll come back after we get some lunch," Simon said on their way out.

"Well, if you just can't wait . . . We are going over to Elmer and Jake's, and he's hot, hot . . ."

"Yes, so you said," Hal interrupted. "Say hello for us." They left a bit unsteadily and headed for their car.

Returning an hour later, they found the living room in the triple-wide populated pretty much as it had been when they left with only two casualties having bit the dust, and replaced by two others of similar alcoholic tolerances. "Oh here they are," Leonard sang out as Hal and Simon came into the room. "You were right to go out. Elmer called to cancel and we're trying to decide what we'll do for lunch." It was nearly 4:30.

"What time are those dinner reservations you told us about?" Hal asked.

"Oh, let's see. 7:30, I think. Where's Sid? Sid! What time are we going to The Velvet Liner?" Sid poked his head out of the bedroom and said, "7:30" and disappeared again.

Hal and Simon found the pool deck, and as Len had said, there was no water in the pool. They decided to get some sun there anyway, waiting out some of the time before heading off to The Velvet Liner for dinner. "We will definitely drive," Simon announced. "The gallons of vodka we've seen washed down in there today could have filled the pool here. Is this what they do in Palm Springs, just drink?"

"No, they also rub suntan lotion into their lovers' skin, like this."

"Don't get frisky, honey. This isn't a gay club, you know. Hal! Keep your hand out of my trunks," Simon laughed. "What a dirty old man you are."

"Yeah, well I have wonderful inspiration," he said, stealing one last grab of Simon's butt.

In an hour or so they were back at the triple-wide where all was silent. The wax works had vacated and nobody seemed to be around. Their bags had been removed from the living room where they had dropped them, and they searched for what might be their bedroom. One closed door, the one that Sid kept popping in and out of. There were a couple of open ones in the farthest reaches of the place. In one of them they found their bags and quite a lot else.

Leonard had been busy decorating, aided and guided by his daily intake of vodka. The headboard on the king-sized bed consisted of what might have been carved wood, painted a bilious green with gilt edging, sculpted in high rococo with deep curls and swirls that ended up in the middle in the shape of a huge heart. This enormous piece dominated the entire wall and its motif was reflected in a matching chest of drawers, bedside tables, a quilt stand, and a wash stand, all illuminated by a similarly painted chandelier. Denise would have loved this, Hal thought.

Hal and Simon simply gaped at the room, and then at each other. "Close the door before you say anything or do anything," Simon said, fighting back a guffaw.

"Where in the hell does anyone find furniture like this? I mean, you don't just go to Macy's and see this sitting around, now do you?" Hal said, convulsing with laughter.

"The chandelier's on a dimmer. Look!" Simon said as he turned on all fifty of the chandelier's 'candles'. It was bright enough in the room to shoot movies.

"God! Turn it down! No, turn it off," Hal said, still laughing. "What are we going to say when we're asked about how we liked the décor, oh great master of tact and diplomacy?"

"We'll rave about how comfortable the mattress is. Come here, you, and see for yourself. And while you're here, how about putting a hand or two down my trunks?"

The expedition to The Velvet Liner got under way late; in fact, it left at 7:30, the time of the reservation. What amazed Simon was how put together Leonard and Sid were after a solid day of swilling down alcohol. Much haggling over who would drive had finally yielded Simon as the driver of the night after an appeal to "it's the least we can do for putting us up in that indescribable guest room." Leonard and Sid were installed in the back seat, directions given, and they were off.

They needn't have worried about being crowded out of their reservation. No one else was in The Velvet Liner. No one at all, not even a waiter at first. In the foyer stood a table with mints in a bowl and a stack of business cards that read Décor By Shel, printed in highly florid script. When no one greeted them, the four men chose a table and sat down.

Dark purple velvet entirely enshrouded the walls, thus the name. The ceiling had been painted black, and only dim lights here and there ensconced around the draped walls emitted what light there was. Great care had been taken to install enormous gilded framed pictures over the drapery, pictures of dark woodland scenes, night vistas of lightless harbors, and one of the dreary hallway of a large house. Denise would have loved this place too, Hal thought.

As far as Hal was concerned, it was exactly what he imagined it might be like to eat inside a large coffin. Suddenly, the waiter appeared. In the dim light he seemed appropriately cadaverous, wearing a dark suit, and carrying large menus. "Good evening," he said, distributing menus, and silently disappearing back into wherever he had come from. The general theme of The Velvet Liner, as conceived by Shel, its owner and decorator, was one of formality and decorum, set in a room that he thought would inspire a sense of one's having arrived at a very elegant place. The waiter had been instructed to work in the style of an English butler; aloof but at the ready, formal but with enough humanness to enhance the right tone of the restaurant.

Hal's ears perked up. No, he thought, it couldn't be. He hadn't seen the waiter's face, but he knew the voice.

The waiter reappeared with a pitcher of water, filling each glass. When he got to Hal's, his studied reserve broke down and his hand shook.

The waiter was none other than Hal's ex-partner, Bill Redding.

"Bill! Imagine seeing you out here," Hal exclaimed. "I thought you were living in Newport with, uh . . . what is his name?"

"Hi Hal. Yeah, well, things didn't work out there too well. I met Shel one day and he offered me a job and here I am."

"Meet Simon, my partner," Hal said triumphantly. "And this is Sid and Leonard. We're staying with them this weekend. It's good to see you looking so well, Bill."

Bill didn't look all that well as a matter of fact. His stint with a sugar daddy named Cliff in Newport Beach had propelled him into a life of drinking and drugs. His face was sallow and sunken, and he had lost weight. He had left Hal years ago owing him months of rent and utilities, defecting once he figured that Hal was not able to provide him with a life of luxury. As Hal looked at him now, he wondered how he had ever been so in love with him back then.

"We've just opened this place," Bill said. "Not much business yet, but Shel says that it will catch on. Have you decided on dinner?"

Hal looked over his menu at Simon who was smiling like the famous Cheshire cat. "We'll both have the filet, rare," Simon said, knowing exactly without asking what Hal would want. Bill got the rest of the table's order and disappeared behind one of the purple curtains.

"Well, well, well, so that's Bill," Simon said. "I always wanted to see who my predecessor was."

"Let's just say that I've come up in the world since those days," Hal said as he smiled back at him.

"Yes, let's just say that."

# CHAPTER 18

## *Land Ho!*

Carl's apartment on Gleneyre now also accommodated Eric who had removed himself from the dark precincts of Chez Labouche after that fateful evening when everyone got everything off his and her chest. Eric had been through these tiffs with Denise before, but this time relations between them looked permanently glacial. He had to admit that theirs had been more of a truce than a friendship; certainly, he knew that he could never count on her as a friend to come to his aid should he need help. She had proved that her interests lay with her own concerns when things had gone bad for him. When the two of them had reconciled, it was as if two lions had agreed to hide their teeth and share the same territory, waiting until some tempting prey would shatter their fragile détente.

But he and Carl were not immediately concerned with Denise or Le Bleu or anything else except the delicious Miguel who was sandwiched between them in their large bed. He is one of the people every inch of whom is beautiful, no matter from what angle or view, Eric thought as he watched Miguel and Carl in a deep kiss. Miguel wasn't much of a gardener, as Denise found out, but he had other talents that she would never know about. The three of them had found that they liked three-ways, and Miguel had all but moved into the apartment as well.

Although Eric's first attempt at acquiring property, or more exactly ownership of a business, had been a disaster, he had learned from his mistakes. His painstaking salting away money had paid off. These were the days of a land boom in Laguna Beach, and Eric was not about to miss out. Within the past six months he had bought and sold two houses, made an enormous profit on each, and once more had put the proceeds in the bank. He also owned, as has been noted, controlling interest in the property company where Le Bleu paid its rent, and unbeknownst to Denise, he was her landlord. The apartment that Carl had found was in a building that was also for sale. Eric bought it, the rents from the other five units more than paying his mortgage.

What he had wanted to do more than anything else was to personally present Denise with her newly increased rent bill, but he thought better of it. Better to stay in the shadows, letting her believe that the consortium that owned the property had made the decision and not he alone. I'd have given a lot to have been there and heard the French when she got *that* bill, he thought, lazily petting Miguel's back and butt. All he knew was that she paid it.

He had other plans for both Carl and Miguel besides lolling around in bed. He would need managers and overseers for his increasing real estate holdings. He was able to keep track of everything himself, but just barely. That was one reason that his leaving Le Bleu did not hurt in the least in terms of income; in fact, he had planned to leave anyway to take care of his own affairs. Denise simply made it all happen sooner with her inane scheme to sabotage Jean-Jacques' dinner and Carl's refusal to be a part of it. He would train Carl and Miguel to help out, pay them well, and that would allow him to move further into the world of investment real estate. These exquisite thoughts were interrupted by Carl's moving in his direction and bringing him more fully into the highly charged events taking place on the bed. Yes, life was good, very good.

\* \* \* \*

Eric was right. There had been a great deal of very blue French in the air at Le Bleu on the day when Denise opened the letter announcing that her rent had been doubled. She was on the phone in a fury: "Ooo ees zeez? Ay want to spik to zee managair of my property ere." The madder she got, the thicker her accent. Finally her call was given to a prim voice at the management company.

"May I help you Mrs. Lebouche?"

"Ay want to know why my rent she ees twice zee amount of last month," Denise said fairly frothing at the mouth.

"One moment, Mrs. Lebouche," said the maddeningly calm voice. "Do you have your account number, please?"

"No, Ay don't. And you don't need eet. Ay ave been paying zee rent ere for years."

"One moment, please," and Denise found herself on hold. What seemed like ten minutes later, "Oh yes, your increase. I'm looking at your rental agreement here, and it seems that you did not choose to opt for a lease which would have frozen your rental amount for a specified length of time, depending on the terms of the lease. Since you did not make that option, the owners have the right to raise your rent, and that is what has happened."

"Ay don't op for anyting except for zat rent zat Ay always pay. And you want me to pay twice! Ay won't pay eet! Ay won't pay eet!"

"Of course," the cool voice went on, "that is your choice, Mrs. Lebouche, but if you do not pay your rent, the owners can move to evict you within sixty days. I hope you will reconsider. Good day, Mrs. Lebouche." The voice hung up.

Denise stood holding the phone for another two minutes or so, then slamming it down, alarming her kitchen staff, all of whom were relatively new. "Is there something wrong, Madame?" her new daytime cook asked, coming into the dining room.

"Get back to work! Ay don't pay you to listen in on my conversations," Denise shouted back to the quickly receding figure. But there was plenty wrong. She sank into a chair and began trying to figure out when it had all started going wrong. The facts that her entire restaurant staff had totally changed over the past six months, that her husband had run off with a man, that her only friend Eric had similarly left her for a life of his own, only peripherally figured into her calculations of what had gone wrong. Nothing like her own actions were added in; these she considered above reproach. Others had caused her current state of unease with how she found life these days. While she might not have liked Hal, she could always trust him to do his job when he worked for her. Roger, dependable Roger, who never did anything against her or the restaurant, had been the best manager she ever had, but he was gone too.

But this crew she had these days! She distrusted every one of them. The day cook had to be told everything to do every day. Steve the night chef was getting stoned more and more often, sometimes getting entire orders wrong. The waiters were sloppy and did cart service badly. She couldn't seem to keep decent busboys, and she was sure that the bartender was stealing. Profits were down and expenses were up, and here came this big raise in her rent! For one of the rare times in her life, she felt like crying, but of course, she didn't. No, she would find a way out of this mess. She always had and she always had done so on her own.

After another lecture to the day cook about how to make crêpes (how many times must she tell him, she wondered), she drove home to Chez Lebouche, whose outer aspects matched her bad mood. The plantings in the front yard had long ago died and their withered stems and stalks bore evidence of the neglect by design that characterized her property. Her idea was to make the place look formidable, thus scaring off would-be burglars. That, like so many of Denise's ill-conceived schemes, had not worked, and as she got to her front door, she found it ajar. She pushed the door open admitting late afternoon sunlight into her otherwise gloomy hall, and she cautiously walked in. Complete silence. She switched on lights as she proceeded toward the back of the house, and as she did, she saw that her precious art collection was still there, all of her French paintings of unknown 18th century aristocrats still hanging in their dismal frames.

Every drawer along the way had been opened and rifled, their contents spilled out. Still nothing seemed to be missing. Suddenly panic filled her and she raced for her bedroom. Again she found her things scattered around, but it was one set of locked drawers that she was interested in. The lock had been jimmied open as well, but her sacred bank books were still there. They had been opened and obviously read, lying as they were creased and flattened. But they were still there. One more drawer to check, her jewelry drawer. The thieves had found it, and all of her jewels, including her large diamond ring, were gone.

It was too much, even for the iron-clad Denise. She sat down on her bed and wept out of frustration and misfortune. She had, of course, brought on dismay all by herself. She had neglected to take out insurance on her jewels, always regarding insurance salesmen as thieves who dressed well. She wept out of aggravation for a day's worth of events that had been the culmination of some of her life's harder knocks.

She did not weep for long. She phoned the police who soon came to inspect the burgled house. They left after a thorough investigation turned up no finger prints, but they had a complete list of the missing jewels. They asked her who had keys to the house. Her mind turned to who might have done this, who knew that the house was empty since Eric and Carl had left, who could have watched her leave that morning? Miguel, of course. He was the perfect suspect. He had no money and no job, and he knew the house and how to get into it. And she knew where the police could probably find him.

All it ever took for Denise to recover from whatever calamity she brought on herself was to find a scapegoat, and the hapless Miguel found himself in the city police department being grilled as to his whereabouts on the afternoon when Chez Lebouche was robbed. He knew exactly where he was and exactly what he was doing, and of course, with whom he was doing it. He told the police the first bit of information, but withheld the second. A phone call to Eric.

"We're holding a man named Miguel down here and he says he was in your apartment all day today, but we picked him up on the beach half an hour ago. We'd like to corroborate his story," Detective Fenster said into the phone. "Aha, he was, huh? And he didn't leave that entire time? Does this Miguel work for you, by any chance? No, huh?"

"He's a friend of ours and we're teaching him English. What's he charged with anyway?" Eric asked.

"I don't mind telling you that there's been a burglary. Mrs. Lebouche is missing a lot of expensive jewelry. If this guy was a US citizen, I couldn't divulge this information but since he isn't, it doesn't matter. And what was he doing in your apartment all this time?" Silence on the other end. "Sir? If he wasn't working for you there, what was he doing? Ah, just socializing. He says that his clothes are at your place, Mr. Greason. Is that right? Do you know, sir, that this Miguel is an illegal alien, that he has no papers to stay in this country? Do you know also what the penalties are for harboring an illegal alien? We'll be in touch." Eric headed for home to tell Carl.

Poor Miguel whose English wasn't all that strong did manage to realize that he was in trouble, that he was about to be deported back to Mexico. But at least he was off the hook for burglary. "Do you have any keys to Mrs. Lebouche's house, Miguel?" Detective Fenster asked. "Keys, to the doors," he repeated. Miguel shook his head. The police had already turned out his pockets, producing nothing.

He had indicated that what he owned was in a suitcase at Eric and Carl's apartment. "We're driving you over there to get your things. Then you're off to Santa Ana, my friend." Within a few minutes the police car arrived at the apartment. "We'd like to look around your place, Mr. Greason. If Miguel here managed to slip out while you weren't looking and do a little robbery, he might have left some things. Do you mind?"

"Not at all, officer," Eric said, remembering very well his own brush with the law a few years ago. "But I can tell you again, that he was here all day. He came over this morning and only left an hour or so ago." Miguel was made to wait in the squad car while the police looked around. Eric saw his dejected face through the window, and knew what his fate would be. He also knew that the resourceful Miguel would be back within a week or two. He walked outside toward the police car and smiled at Miguel, a reassuring smile that said that he knew things would be OK. Miguel smiled back and then dropped his head once more.

"Well, nothing here. Thank you, Mr. Greason," the cop said, getting back into the car and driving off with Miguel.

Denise again, Eric thought. That evil bitch, trying to pin this onto Miguel when she knew how vulnerable he is.

He went back inside and got his own car keys. He would make a visit to the police station too.

# CHAPTER 19
## *More Sunday Comics*

April signaled spring break, the herald of summer, and the town was beginning to fill with its annual crop of male beauties. Beaches, particularly West Street Beach, had already seen the beginnings of what the Sunday brunchers at The Blue Cove predicted would be one of the best seasons ever in terms of the hunters and the hunted. Young men flocked to Laguna to pursue a wide variety of interests. Some came to surf and be summer beach denizens; some came to find summer jobs in restaurants and hotels; some came to seek fame and fortune and to capitalize on their youth and beauty; still others simply came to see about relocating more permanently, preferably with a wealthy and generous gentleman whose loneliness they would assuage during the long summer days and warm summer nights.

The culling of the herds was as serious an activity as it is on the African plains, a contest between hunter and prey. The only difference was that here in the famous "fishy little sleeping village", it was not always clear which was which. Determining the state of things provided no end of discussion for the sharp tongues gathered on the patio of The Cove. Conversations tended to be aimless at best, but they set the tone for the lazy summer just ahead. Gossip reigned supreme among the oldies gathered there, with no reputation left in tact if possible.

"Well, *that* one's still here, survived an entire year up in Wilbur Yates' house. Getting fat, too. I do wonder how long it will be before skinny Wilbur starts to look around for a replacement. Plenty to choose from who make that Ben look like a sack of potatoes." The object of their notice was walking onto the patio, and it has to be said that their assessment of him wasn't far off. He had been a ravishing blond only a year ago, his presence on the beach commanding universal attention, particularly from the older and well-to-do gay men whose competitive hunting for prey gave the term "lying in wait" a whole new meaning. Ben's perfect body, adorned with just the right amount of blond hair, gleamed like a beacon, and before long, he was on the auction block to the highest bidder. Wilbur had won. That was a year ago, and a year of easy living in Wilbur's large house, replete with innumerable dinner parties that featured rich food, had given the lovely Ben a plumpness that this year would not have got him much addulation on the beach; in fact, the keen and discerning eyes of the hunters would easily pass him by for more comely and leaner physiques.

"Oh deary, it won't be long. I saw Wilbur on the beach last week taking a look at the new herd of sleek gazelles that have arrived. That Ben's days are numbered," Paulette said, smiling while sipping his martini. "He's been something of a snot anyway, putting on airs and acting like the lady of the manor." It was well understood that Paulette's attempts at seducing Ben had been rebuffed, and Paulette never forgot an insult.

"Look there! Talk about one of the beach beauties that has kept it all together for years," Bruce said. As Paulette's chief conspirator and confidant, Bruce subtly pointed his drink toward Chad and Hank, a couple roughly in their early thirties who had similarly found each other on the beach some five years ago, had escaped the usual gauntlet of voracious hunters, and had instead begun life together. "Hello, beautiful men," Bruce said as they came by. The two men nodded smiles in his direction and headed for the bar.

"Well! You'd think that I'd rate more than a nod after all I did for *that* one," Bruce sniffed.

"Still nursing that old wound, are we? And remember, doll, I'm the one who knows what you presumably did *to*, not *for*, that one. You are lucky to get so much as a nod, if you ask me," Paulette said, rolling his eyes.

"Crabs isn't a fatal disease, you old cow. How did I know I'd give them to Hank during that one lovely night at my house? I didn't know myself that I had them until later. You'd think I'd given him syphilis the way he's acted toward me ever since. Anyway, it's ancient history. Oh look, here's Ken and Roger. Hey! Over here, you two!"

"Hi Bruce, Paulette. Have you seen Hal and Simon? We thought they might be here by now," Roger said looking around the crowded patio.

"Palm Springs is what I heard," Paulette said, finishing off his drink. They were invited to Leonard and Sid's place for the weekend. I hope they were ready to drink. A LOT. That's all those old girls do over there, but what else is there to do? Rounds of cocktails from house to house, staggering off to the bars later. I feel like a tee-totaller by contrast."

"And no one would ever accuse you of *that*, my dear," Bruce said.

"They cut their stay short out there," Roger said. "Called this morning to say they'd be back in town by brunch and that we should meet them here."

As if on cue, Hal and Simon walked onto the patio, and seeing Roger and Ken, came right over to them. "If ever we deserved a drink—not that we haven't had plenty since yesterday—it's now. Did you guys get a table yet?"

"We escaped. It wasn't so hard to do since nobody in that trailer—and that's what it is, a trailer—gets up much before noon, and then only to make a trip to the fridge for pre-mixed Bloody Marys, just to get the day rolling again," Hal said, once they had been seated for brunch. He and Simon took turns recounting the events with a description of the stultified guests at Leonard and Sid's place, leading up to dinner at The Velvet Liner restaurant. "Nobody wanted to stay once we finally got there. We were the only party in the place for one thing, the menu looked expensive for another, and out of nowhere, there was my ex as our waiter."

"Frankly, I was having a hell of a good time," Simon piped up. "I'd been wanting to meet Hal's ex, and there he was, living with Sheldon who owns The Velvet Liner, and working as his chief, and I might add, only waiter in the newly decorated coffin." A detailed description of the place had everyone rolling. "You won't believe it. It's worth going over just to see it. That alone may keep it in business," Simon laughed. "Anyway, we left just as things were getting interesting."

"Yeah, interesting, he says. I just wanted out of the place like everybody sensible"—this got him an elbow in the ribs from Simon—"and we were out on the road in search of another restaurant. We had ordered steaks which were on the menu but not in the kitchen. They hadn't stocked the place at all; the only thing they had was some sort of fish that Bill admitted had been frozen. So we left. It was the weekend of the Dinah Shore Open, don't you know, and every lesbian in the world had come to Palm Springs to participate. I don't think they were all playing golf, for that matter, but that meant that all restaurants within miles were filled with them. We finally gave up once we saw their parking lots crammed with campers."

"We ended up at the Gene Autry Hotel restaurant, the straightest, most conservative, gay-hating place on the highway," Simon added. "As soon as the frosty maitre d' got a look at us, he sent us off to some remote corner of the place where we were waited on by a lovely man named Tommy who was gayer than a pink parasol and very happy to see four fags get seated at his station. Hal and I were starving by then—did Leonard and Sid ever eat anything?—and ordered steaks. Big tip for Tommy, and we were headed back to the Rising Gorge Mobile Home Estate where we went directly to bed.

"Guess what Leonard had planned for us for today if we'd stayed. He wanted Hal to cook dinner for twelve or fourteen of their closest friends over there. Lobsters, no less. We were to go shopping for them, work all day getting dinner ready while the other guests guzzled down more booze, and then serve dinner at some undisclosed time. We just went along with this scheme last night and sneaked out this morning," Simon said.

"Know what? You could serve Alpo with ketchup on it to that bunch of drunks and they would never know the difference," Hal said. "I wasn't about to spend the day cooking for a crew like that. I guess we're probably in hot water, but we at least spared the lobsters from joining us in the boiling pot."

"It wasn't quite the weekend from hell, but close enough," Simon sighed, forking into his eggs Benedict. "I don't think I ever want to see another Bloody Mary."

Another stir from The Cove's patio as George and his famous partner Bertrand arrived. Bertrand's polyps had been removed from his vocal cords on Friday, rendering him unable to speak except in a whisper. "He not even supposed to do that," George told the fans who had gathered to offer condolences over Bertrand's ill-fated singing career. Their sympathies were not altogether genuine; in fact, there were more than a few among the wellwishers who saw Bertrand's 'retirement' from the musical stage as a milestone in the history of the genre, one that would put them on the road to more sincere congratulations when he resumed a non-singing career.

"What are you two doing here?" George asked when he saw Hal and Simon.

"We'll tell you later. How are you feeling, Bertrand. Oh, don't speak, don't speak, I didn't mean . . ." Hal said.

"It's OK," George replied. "He can only whisper for a few days, but his voice will come back." He put his arm around his ailing partner. "Got room at this table for us? Or do we have to ask Stockley?"

"Sit, sit. You know Roger and Ken?"

They did, hugs all around, and menus arrived from the unctuous Stockley. "Special drinks today, gentlemen," he proudly announced. "Halfprice on Bloody Marys."

# CHAPTER 20
## *All In a Day's Work*

The neighborhood quieted down on Monday morning after nearly everyone on the street had left for work. Edward took up his usual patrol of the back yard, greeting his friend Augustus the dog from next door who came through a hole in the fence to give Edward a big sloppy dog kiss. Then, as suddenly has he had arrived, he stopped dead in his tracks. The fur on his back went up and began to growl. Edward joined in, his tail bushing out as he hissed in the direction of the cottage at the back of the yard. Both animals slunk away, highly agitated. Something in there, something they sensed more than saw, something fearful to be avoided.

The window blinds inside the cottage shot up, and that noise was the last straw for Edward and Augustus, and they repaired to safer parts of the yard. Movement behind the windows, and through the curtains, the outline of a dark face that cautiously looked out over the lawn. Then it disappeared, the blinds were lowered, and all was silence.

* * * *

"You idiot! You want the whole neighborhood to know we're in here? Now you got that dog nervous out there. Sometimes I wonder why I bring you with me, Willy."

"You know damned well why, Dick."

"Yeah, well let's get out of here. Nothing to see or take pictures of anyway. Get through that hole in the fence. I'm right behind you."

"I know you are, Dickie, I know you are. Hey, how'd you get the day off anyway?"

* * * *

Two weekends of relative fun and ease, but now that they were over, and Hal arrived at school the next day with the foreboding he had been carrying with him every time he came to campus. He tried to fight it off, tried to remember how sunny and bright his days at school used to be, days free of the anxiety that steadily grew over the issue of gay teachers. He couldn't dispel the clouds and the awful feeling that there were worse times ahead. The uncertainty and apprehension fought against his desire to teach his classes as he always had, and it was with a great deal of mental exertion that he pushed his fears to the back of his mind.

Hal's second period English class was leaving the room, students on their way to their next class. The last to leave was Barry; he was always the last to leave, the kid who always wanted more help with his work. Barry was cute in a feminine sort of way; a delicate face topped by dark brown hair, clear light brown eyes, good complexion, slim body, and excellently shaped legs that protruded from his shorts. He was eager to please, always ready with a smile that showed the salutary effects of many visits to a good dentist. He was particularly ready with that smile for Hal. Barry had a crush on his English teacher.

"Mr. Schroeder, could you take a look at this paragraph? I can't seem to make it work with the thesis somehow," he said to Hal who was straightening up his desk.

"Didn't we go over this last week, Barry? I thought you re-wrote it."
"Well, I did, but I'm not so sure."

"But don't you have a class right now? We don't have time, do we?"

"Yeah, we do, I dropped algebra. Flunking it anyway. So I'm free this period. What do you think of this?" Barry asked, putting his essay down on Hal's desk. Hal didn't have a class coming in either, but he longed to get to the teacher's lounge for a coffee before his next one. Nevertheless, he started in on Barry's second paragraph.

"There's nothing wrong with what you've said here, Barry—change that 'it's' to 'its' though—and you might want to put in a transition word right there," he said, pointing at one of the sentences. "You're doing fine. It's going to be a very good essay. Just go write it," he said, trying to give closure to this conference. Barry didn't budge; in fact, he moved closer to Hal, brushing his leg against him.

"There's something else," Barry said, looking into Hal's face, "and it doesn't have anything to do with my essay. My parents are punishing me for . . . being . . ." his voice trailed off and something like a sob caught in his throat. Then he broke down, tears streaming down his face, and sobbing, he turned toward Hal and lay his head on his shoulder. Hal moved toward his distraught student and put an arm around him while he cried. He cringed and cried out in pain.

"For being what, Barry?" Hal asked, smelling the fresh scent of Barry's thick curls.

"Gay! I'm gay! There, I said it! I'm gay and according to my mom, I'm going straight to hell, and if I don't quit being gay, they will kick me out of the house and send me to a camp where they fix kids like me. There, now you know. And I suppose you hate me too, don't you?" Barry cried, quickly moving away from Hal.

Was this a trap? Hal's newfound wariness thanks to the atmosphere surrounding the Briggs horror had heightened his suspicions that he might be the prey for a particularly evil hate campaign sponsored by the local fundamentalist church. He sat for a moment, looking at the distraught Barry. If Barry was part of a trap, sent in to tempt Hal out in the open, he was certainly a good actor. "Who all have you told about this, Barry? What other teachers, I mean? And why are you telling me in particular?"

"No, you're the only one. Who else could I talk to? Not those snotty counselors in the front office who can't keep anything to themselves, that's for sure," Barry said as he wiped his eyes.

"What made you blurt all this out to your parents?"

"I didn't want them to know, but my mom found a magazine in my room, a gay one, and that got my step-dad mad as hell. Started yelling at me, and . . . well, you know . . ."

"Wait a minute. When will you be eighteen?" Hal asked.

"June 14th, why?"

"Because they can't send you to some camp unless you want to go after you're eighteen, and that's only two months away. You're officially an adult then and can do what you want. Hate you? Of course I don't hate you," Hal said, standing up. "Let's sit down and you try to be calm, Barry. Come on, sit down," Hal said, coaxing Barry to relax. But Barry didn't sit down. Instead, he moved close to Hal and put his arms around him.

"Do you think you could just hold me for a minute? I just need somebody to hold me, somebody who doesn't hate me. Please, I'm sorry, I'm really sorry," he said, starting to cry again as Hal wrapped his arms around him. My God, Hal thought, what this kid has been through and he isn't even eighteen yet. Hal's own fears receded farther back in his mind as he tried to comfort his student. He felt Barry relax as he held him, standing there trying to ease the kid's pain. As they stood there, Hal was aware of something else happening. Barry was getting an erection that jutted into Hal's groin. Alarmed by this, Hal tried to maneuver Barry into a chair.

"Barry, we need to talk about some things. Think you're ready to talk for a while?"

"Yeah, sure," Barry said, seeming to be more collected.

"First, how do you know that you're gay? Have you ever had sex with another boy?"

"I just know that's all. Well, yeah but that was a year or two ago at camp. All the guys were beating off together, so I don't think that counts. I think about it all the time, and I dream about being with a man. I don't want to be with a boy. I dream about men. I dream . . . about . . ."

"You don't have to tell me, Barry; in fact, I wish you wouldn't tell me," Hal said, suspecting the truth.

"But I want to tell you, Mr. Schroeder. I want to tell you that I dream about you. About you and Simon and how I'd like to be in bed with both of you. I dream about you, man, you . . ."

"How do you know about Simon? How?" Hal nearly yelled at Barry, alarmed that he had brought up his private life in such certain terms.

"How do you think? I know where you live. I know about your house on Myrtle Street. I even know your cat Edward," Barry said, looking rather pleased with himself.

My God, another lurker, Hal thought. Years ago someone else had watched his house from a car across the street. That episode turned out to be fairly benign, but now this! He was instantly on guard again. "How long have you been watching my house, Barry? How long?"

"I'm not going to rat you out, Mr. Schroeder, promise. I'm sorry if that makes you nervous, that I watched you, I mean."

"Nervous? It makes me very nervous, Barry. Please promise me you won't do it again, OK?"

"This got turned around today, huh? I stayed here for help, for some understanding, and you're worried about what I know. Don't know what you're worried about. More people know than you think. Just add it up. You teach down here but you live in Laguna. No talk about a Mrs. Schroeder. You never hang around after school for anything unless you have to. I'm not the only kid here who's curious about you, you know. Ever heard Mr. Palmer go on about queers? He's a member of that church my family goes to, and they hate queers. Talks about it all the time in math class. That's one reason I don't go much. There are more queers here than me and you, Mr. Schroeder."

Hal felt a bit sick. He had, he thought, carefully guarded his life, kept it away from school, and while there were a couple of trusted colleagues who knew him and Simon, they weren't about to broadcast the fact that the Advanced Placement English teacher was gay. And here was Barry, needy and horny, who knew more about Hal's life than he wanted any student to know, particularly a student whose parents were confirmed fundamentalists. He tried to think what he could do to defuse this whole situation, but he came up with nothing.

"Barry, you're sure that you haven't told any of the counselors about your situation at home?" Hal asked.

"Are you kidding? Nobody in that whole rat pack down there wants to hear about a queer kid's home life."

"Good. Let's keep it to ourselves. Tell me something else, though. Are they physically abusing you? I mean, do they hit you or harm you in any way?"

"Yeah, once in a while the old man wallops me with his belt, just to take out his frustration on having a fag in the house, but not often. I stay out of his way."

"Is that why you cried out a minute ago? When was the last time he hit you?" Hal asked.

"Yesterday. That's when I told them I was gay, as if they didn't know already. He really let me have it across the back."

"Can you raise up your shirt and let me see?" Barry did, and there across his lower back were the welts. "How far down do these go?" Barry undid his belt and fly, and let his pants drop down. Then he took down the back of his jockeys to expose more welts across his buttocks. "Barry, how would you like to get out of your parents' house right away? You can, you know. All we have to do is show these marks to the principal. The police will be called and they will get you someplace else to stay. What do you think?"

"Stay where? Some foster home? No way. I'll take my chances with the old man. He probably won't hit me again for a while, especially since I promised to not be gay any more. Course that was a lie. I'm pretty used to lying, good at it too."

"Maybe you can dodge your step-dad for a time, Barry, but sooner or later he's going to come at you again. Will you let me do some checking for you, maybe find you a good place to live that isn't what you imagine? I don't want you hurt anymore; I want to help, but it has to be on my terms. You understand what I'm risking here, don't you?"

"Yeah, I do, but you're forgetting something. I love you, Mr. Schroeder, and I'd never hurt you or put you in danger." Hal bristled, knowing full well that things could easily be taken out of their hands, that Barry's avowal of love and confidence would mean nothing if the wrong people knew any of what had just been said.

"Promise me you'll be OK for a day or two. Promise me to stay out of your step-dad's way until we can figure something out, will you do that?" Hal asked.

"Sure, Mr. Schroeder. I can do that. You know, I feel a lot better, thanks. I'm not crying like a baby anymore, am I? It's just between us, I promise," Barry said, touching Hal's hand and looking into his face. "I'd better go and let you get some work done." He moved toward Hal as if to kiss him, but Hal moved away to prevent that possibility.

"We can't, Barry, we can't. It doesn't mean I don't like you. It's just that we can't. Please know that I want to help you if you want me to, and I want you to be happy. You're going to be OK?"

"Sure, I'll be OK. See you tomorrow," he waved as he left Hal's room.

Oh God, now what? Hal thought. He remembered his first crush in high school on his homeroom teacher, a coach who wouldn't have given him the time of day otherwise, and he remembered how many afternoons he spent masturbating over seeing just one hairy arm or part of a hairy leg if Mr. Douglas exposed one. He knew what Barry was feeling; he also knew that while he wouldn't for the world have told Mr. Douglas about his ardor for him, that Barry lived in a more open time, a time that on the one hand allowed him the audacity to intrude on Hal's life and tell him about it, and on the other, a time that would land Hal in jail for even the slightest hint of any relations with a student. Could he trust Barry? That was the question. Who should he see about Barry's being abused? He was legally bound to report such incidents, and he would have to do so before the evidence went away.

He headed for the principal's office where found out more than he thought he would.

# CHAPTER 21
## Sotto Voce No More

Bertrand's days of whispering while his throat healed came to an end, and with them, so did his patience. Home alone on the afternoon after the doctor had tested his voice and found it returning very well, Bertrand turned on his tape recorder, sat down at the piano, and tried a few illicit arpeggios. The top notes hurt like hell, and he closed the piano lid with a bang. The doctor's warnings rang in his head: "Take it easy for a few more days. You can talk normally, but don't strain your voice. I wouldn't try to sing. Keep your voice low in its natural range and you'll heal up just fine." He turned off the tape recorder and left the piano bench.

No singing! Bertrand was convinced that once the wound caused by the surgery had healed that he could ignore everything that the doctors had told him before and he could restart his career on the musical stage. No singing, ha! But he immediately came to the conclusion that they were right, that making his voice move into the upper registers not only hurt, but could also bring back the polyps problem. Damn it, he thought. I'm a cripple. It's like finding out that you're going blind or something. Or losing a limb.

He crumpled onto a chair and indulged himself in a good wallow in self pity, almost bringing himself to tears. He wasn't a man accustomed to such setbacks. His had been a life of relative ease and pleasure, and although his banking career might not have been his first choice, it was an easy job that gave him security and time to pursue his other love, singing. He had given life the benefit of the doubt; he acknowledged that he wasn't twenty-one any longer, and he vaguely believed that his body would change somehow now that he wasn't young. But the reality of those changes and of any other aspect of life's moving on inexorably and without his permission had not set in, had not become a part of his thinking. He had always had his own way, had always healed from the few minor diseases he'd ever had, had always triumphed over everything that had threatened him. His overweening belief in a kind of undefined immortality for himself, accompanied by the utter denial of anything like death, had him living in a kind of fantasy world. Fate and his own determination had fortified that world, and that's where he wanted to live. Always.

He truly believed that he could. Here was George in his life, wonderful George who adored him and whom he was loving more every day on an equal basis. Almost like having a Prince Charming arrive and plant the awakening kiss to live happily ever after. Until now, until this throat thing brought down the walls of his paper castle and left him exposed to the world and all of its harms. Damn, he thought. If only he could turn back the clock to when his voice . . . oh, what the hell, it was useless to think that way.

He sat in the late afternoon dimness of his studio looking at the silent piano which loomed there as a symbol of what he had once had, of what he could no longer have, a monument to his defeat. The great black bulk of it seemed to mock him, and he turned his chair away from it and toward the French doors that led to the patio. There he sat brooding.

Just then George arrived home from school. "Hey! Are you home?" he called into the house.

"In here," Bertrand shouted back. Shouted! His voice volume was returning, but raising his voice hurt.

George found him in the dim studio and walked over to kiss him. "Hi, my love. You shouted! Your voice is back, huh? Why are you sitting here in the dark? What did the doctor say?"

Reluctant to play the whole afternoon again for George at first, Bertrand finally gave him a summary. "No singing. OK, OK, I tried it once I got home. Hurt like hell when I tried to hit anything above an F below middle C."

"Hey, you know what? I think your voice sounds different, even better," George enthused. "Maybe you can't tell the difference, but I can. Read something into the recorder and see what I mean."

Bertrand turned on his tape recorder and read into it, replaying his reading to hear his own voice. Not bad, he thought, not bad at all. In fact, he detected a new resonance that he had not heard in his speech before, a deepening of tone and a richness that produced what he realized was a pleasing reading voice. He tried it again with equally satisfying results. George was right; his voice had changed somehow.

"What do you think?"

"It's great, honey. Your voice sounds great," George said, beaming at his lover.

"Yeah, but I still can't sing. You should have heard how that sounded," Bertrand said a bit sadly.

"So what? You can do lots of other things. Here, look at this," George said, producing a flyer which advertised auditions for parts in a Tennessee Williams revival to be staged at the Laguna Playhouse in June. "What do you think about trying out for a part?"

Bertrand eyed the flyer as if it were announcing that he'd won the lottery. "It's so like you to bring me this, George. This is great, and I'm going to do it. I'll try out for anything they want," he said excitedly, reaching up for George and pulling him down into a kiss. "You always think of me, don't you?" he whispered into his ear.

"Nah, not always," George chuckled back. "It's just that I want to see my handsome lover up on stage, wowing the women and exciting the men. Hey, auditions start next week. Is your voice up for it do you think?"

"I'm fine. No sign of the polyps or anything else in there. This is going to be fun. But you're not off the hook here, you know. I don't know beans about Williams and you'll have to help me."

"No problem, my love. Williams' plays were part of graduate school and I know them well. Could we go back to that nuzzling in the ear part we were doing a minute ago?" All George could think of at the moment as he unbuttoned Bertrand's shirt was not Williams, but a Shakespeare title: *All's Well That Ends Well*.

In the next yard another low voice was making itself known. Edward had taken to adopting the growl that cats have when they are being threatened. He did it every time he ventured near the cottage, and Hal noticed it. Edward's generally haughty manner was also gone, and in its place was a noticeable fear, a kind of apprehension that bristled the fur on his back and tail. Hal noticed something else too. The drapes in the cottage were closed, and he was sure that he had opened them yesterday when he went in to look around. Had he locked the cottage when he left? He was sure he had. Well, maybe Simon had gone in after him and closed the drapes. But no, Simon hadn't; he was sure of that. He went in to look around, and that's when he saw it for the first time. A wide board in the back wall was lying on its side on the floor. Through the hole that it left, he noticed that a piece of the fence separating the property from the alley was askew. Somebody was getting in and out of the cottage this way, but who? Hal hadn't noticed anything else odd inside the cottage, certainly no evidence of anyone having been there.

Hammer and nails fixed the problem with both boards, and Hal felt that he had secured the cottage from the alley side. Strange, he thought. We hardly ever lock the place anyway. Whoever wants in could come in across the back yard and through its front door. He took a more scrutinizing look around to see if he could find anything left by the mysterious person who had gained access to the place. He found nothing, but decided to lock the cottage door behind him before walking toward the main house's kitchen.

He had other problems to think about now, more pressing ones than the cottage mystery. What would he do about Barry? What could he do? He had been vague with the principal while he tested the waters to see what legalities were involved with a suspected abuse case. John McHenry, the principal, had pressed him for details, but Hal had pretended that his wanting information was merely academic and that no real case had come to his attention. One thing was clear: Barry would be better off away from his horrid parents, particularly the one that beat him with a belt. But where could he go? Where would he consent to go?

Hal worried about his own situation in the midst of this. The Briggs Initiative had just gained enough signatures to become Proposition 6; it would be on the November ballot. If passed by the voters, it could prohibit all gay people from teaching in the public school system. The angry rhetoric that promoted the ban of gay people from schools had been loud and vehement, and the ballot measure's success seemed assured if the rightwing papers could be believed. But resistance to it was also mounting. Like many other gay teachers however, Hal was keeping a low profile until things could be better assessed.

Suddenly here was this trouble plunked down into his life. He wondered who would need more help in the coming months, himself or Barry.

"What's up with Edward?" Simon asked, coming through the back door. "He looks like he's seen a ghost."

"Maybe he has. Something's going on in the cottage that's spooked him. He won't go near it, and when he does he growls and his hair goes up," Hal said, reaching over to hug his partner. "Oh Simon, there's another mess going on," and he nearly broke down as he related the problems with Barry, the Briggs Initiative, and his job.

"One thing at a time," Simon said as he held Hal. "What do you think can be done for Barry? It sounds like he needs another place to live, but where? He certainly can't live here. That would hang you good and high once anyone found that out. Otherwise we could have given him the cottage until things cool down."

"There's one thing in his favor right now. He turns eighteen in early June, and he graduates right after that. He'll no longer be a minor and nobody can be prosecuted for helping him. Problem is, can he hold out at his parents' place until then? I don't know; his step-dad beats him, but Barry says he can stay out of his way. Maybe we can get him out of there right after his birthday. No, no, not here. There are other complications with that." Hal told Simon about the boards in the back of the cottage. "He says he's in love with me . . . well, us, actually. He's been watching the house. Says he fantasizes about sleeping between us, for God's sake."

"But that's it! Frank Binder, rescuer of lost souls! Frank has never replaced Mike and Tom from the days when they lived up there with him. We could ask him, anyway."

"There's more, Simon. Barry isn't like Mike or Tom. It's as if he's been a foster child in his own home, mostly neglected in some ways, but dominated and abused by irrational so-called Christians in others. I've observed this at school, who his friends are, what he does, and how he acts. His essays relate a troubled life, one in which he has had to fend for himself. I think that he's basically a happy person regardless of his home life. Sometimes he writes so beautifully that he makes me cry. On the other hand, he's learned to be a bit irresponsible and self-indulgent, not surprising given the home life he's probably had. We'd have to be entirely up front about all of that with Frank."

"OK, but for now, have you talked to anybody in the teacher's union about what your rights are and how you need to protect yourself? That's probably a good next step, don't you think?"

"Yeah, you're right. I can talk to Youngman—he's our union rep—tomorrow afternoon about it. I haven't done anything as yet except talk to McHenry who was as benign and noncommittal as he usually is, and I didn't tell him anything specific about Barry," Hal said, starting to rise from his doldrums. "Hey, why don't we go out to dinner tonight? I'd like to take my best boyfriend out on a date."

"Your best boyfriend needs a nap and a shower and after that, he would be very happy to accept your kind offer," Simon smiled at him as he moved toward the bedroom. "But I do wonder what is wrong with Edward. Now he's outside just glaring at the cottage again. I'm going out there."

Simon took the key and unlocked the cottage door. He hurried inside and found nothing and no one. They had never bothered locking the cottage before, but now he closed and locked the windows, locking the door behind him as he came back to the house. Somebody was using the place. Was it indeed Dorothy Eakins' ghosts? he laughingly thought. Simon was far too scientific to believe in that possibility, but somebody was getting in and staying when they could. He retraced his steps to the cottage door and unlocked it before he returned to the main house for his nap and shower.

# CHAPTER 22
## *Lofty Neighbors*

Ken and Roger lived in a smart and newly renovated condominium in an older building that they took pride in furnishing and decorating according to their desire to make their home both comfortable and in step with modern styles. While they were not slaves to the latest trends, they generally admired what their contemporaries in the world of home décor were presenting, but they had a good eye of their own, one that kept their home from being merely a showplace, and instead one that looked inviting from a first glance through their front door. They were, as Hal liked to kid them, the neatest and tidiest people he had never known. "Has anyone ever seen a speck of dust in their entire place at any time? Does anyone else that you know fold the top sheet of toilet paper into a triangle in the guest bathroom, anyone who isn't a hotel maid, that is? And that kitchen! We all know that Roger can cook as well as anyone, but who could tell? Every pan looks like it's never been used."

Roger and Ken rather liked this joking from their good friend, and they were getting a full dose of it at Hal and Simon's one night with another couple in attendance, Hank and Chad. "As if this place were a pig pen by comparison," Roger said. "Who's cleaning for you these days anyway?"

"Dorothy Eakins, who else? This used to be her house, you know. She does a pretty good job although she's not able to reach up very high these days," Simon said.

"Right. Anything tits high and below gets a good going over. Anything higher doesn't," Hal said, pouring more wine. "But it gets her into the place to look after her ghosts in the back yard. She creeps through our gate at night to watch for them. She thinks we don't know, but we've seen her sitting out there in the dark from time to time." "You've got ghosts?" Chad asked.

"Yep, according to Dorothy we do. She'd be glad to tell you the grisly history of murder and mayhem that happened right here, anytime you'd like to ask her. It's one reason we don't hang around while she's cleaning the lower three feet of the house. Plus we hide the gin," Hal said.

"Well, we've got new neighbors, did I tell you?" Roger said. "An older couple of men in their 70s who just arrived from the Midwest to spend the rest of their days here in sunny California. Ken doesn't like them."

"Well, I didn't say that . . . exactly," Ken replied, thinking back to when the couple in question had made themselves known one evening. "They rang our bell and waltzed right in . . ."

\* \* \* \*

"Hello, we're your new neighbors. I'm Gerald and this is Hans. We've just bought the penthouse, but you probably know that already. I hope we aren't intruding, but we did so want to meet you." Ken had been mixing drinks and setting the table for dinner. Yes, they were intruding.

"No, not at all," Roger said, inviting them in. "We were just having a drink. May we offer you a martini?"

"Oh thank you, no. I haven't touched a drop in forty years. Used to be a hopeless alcoholic, you know, but I dried out, and Hans doesn't drink either." They walked on in, looking the condo up and down. It was clear that they were taking notes.

"We were wondering what the other units looked like. We just had to have the top floor. Hans can't stand anyone living over us, never could. Now isn't this interesting? Hans, look at this *lovely* painting. It looks like an exact copy of somebody from, what would you say, the classic period?" Gerald said with the removed voice of an art appraiser.

"Actually, it's an original from a local artist who sells a lot of his work in New York these days. He's a friend of ours and we were very glad to get this particular one," Ken volunteered.

"Yes, yes, so many amateur painters around, aren't there? What *lovely* furnishings (apparently Gerald's favorite word for something he didn't particularly like was '*lovely*'). Isn't this an interesting chair, Hans? So midcentury, almost an antique. You know, I've been a decorator nearly all my life. Studied at a school near Chicago years ago. Oh, if I could even remember all of the clients I've had along Lake Michigan . . ."

"You want to listen to Gerald when he gives you advice about decorating," Hans suddenly said as if he had just heard his cue.

"I'll be glad to help you out when you want to change things in here," Gerald said, reaffirming his decorating superiority.

"The truth is that we have just finished redoing this place," Ken said. "It's pretty much the way we want it."

Gerald ignored this. "You might want to warm up this part of the room. It could use some hot color over here. A bright painting would be just the thing." All of this free advice was starting to work Ken's nerves.

"You know what? I guess we're pretty lucky to have you close by in case we want some decorating tips. But for the present, we'll just put up with what we have if that's all right with you," he said rather sharply.

"Oh I didn't mean to butt in, of course. Everyone to his own taste said the old lady . . . but you've heard that before, ha, ha ha! No, your place is really quite something given what you've done to it." Meanwhile Hans seemed to be taking inventory of the condo, and Ken had the feeling that he was adding up what he considered to be decorating mistakes.

"Gerald is a great cook," Hans said distractedly, perhaps picking up on the fading tone of the decorating advice. "You must come up for dinner sometime."

"Oh yes, please do. How about next Saturday night?"

"Roger works on Saturday nights, all of them," Ken said.

"Oh well, any other night would be fine."

A low-voiced conference between Ken and Roger while they looked at their calendar. "Nothing could induce me to get any closer to these two than we are, we on our floor, they on theirs," Ken whispered. "Who the hell do they think they are?"

"Calm down," Roger whispered back. "I think they mean well. Let's at least go up to their place once for dinner and see how that goes. Monday looks OK."

"Under duress," Ken said. They agreed on dinner and the two oldsters left.

\* \* \* \*

"And you two went to their place for dinner?" Hal asked. "How did that go?"

"Just as I expected it would," Ken said. "Roger has to agree that they were a bit sniffy when then came over to our place. And you should see theirs! My God, what stuff they have. They collect some kind of glassware that they think is rare, all of it entombed in glass cabinets all over their condo, on display under lights."

"Sniffy? As in snooty and dismissive?" Hal asked.

"Yeah, sort of. Gerald mentioned at least five times that he had been an interior decorator in some former life, I'd guess around the 1950s given the looks of their décor. He didn't exactly criticize our place, but there was a look on his face that said everything he was thinking. Hans gave us the exact number of pieces of that glass junk they have. He counts things. It's in his blood to count things."

"Ken's right," Roger said. "Their place doesn't really look bad or anything, just out of date. They like furniture that's nondescript, that's all. Gerald told us about all the clients he's had over the years, some wealthy people back where they came from."

"I wouldn't say the junk on their walls is nondescript. All very abstract, lots of hot colors in a too obvious effort to offset their bland white carpets and sofas. Gerald took a look at some realist paintings we bought and turned up his nose as if a painting that resembles anything you'd recognize was too ridiculous for words," Ken said. "Did you notice that huge red blotchy thing over their dining room table? And we had to eat under it. I've figured out that people who insist on what they think is abstract art are the same people that wouldn't know a good piece of realist art if it bit them in the ass. And the food! Some sort of gawd-awful stew that they both praised and wanted to give us the recipe for. I wouldn't spread that stuff on the lawn —well, maybe I *would* spread it on the lawn."

"They probably think the same thing about our place, honey," Roger said, "and the food wasn't that bad. It will be interesting when they come to our house for dinner and I give them some real cuisine."

"What! You didn't invite them, did you? Oh God, Roger. Why are you so damn nice to everybody? We'll have to hear all over again about their good work for several charities in Chicago. You get the feeling that they don't really like people that much, but they like charities. Keeps their hands clean, and they don't have to deal with anybody in particular." Ken was on a roll.

"Hans has lots of opinions about everything, all of them heavily laced with suspicion and cynicism. If somebody else gives money to one their charities, Hans sits around figuring out what benefit the donor might get from the gift. It never once occurred to him that his own motives for charity work might be in question. Oh, they're a pair, all right. And we have them all to ourselves, right upstairs."

"Not to change the subject, but what are we going to do about this horrid Briggs Initiative?" Roger asked. "Maybe we should get Gerald and Hans in on that cause."

"Lots. There are fundraising rallies going on all over the state, particularly in San Francisco and Los Angeles. In Laguna we're starting up one of our own. $50 per plate dinners, right here on Myrtle Street," Simon said. "We're very concerned for Hal's job, you know."

"They know you're gay down there, Hal?" Ken asked.

"Who can tell? I don't exactly wear a dress and high heels, but it has recently been pointed out to me that our lives here are more transparent than we thought," he said. He didn't go into details about Barry's stalking techniques and what he might or might not have said to anyone at school.

"Count us in," Hank said, getting a nod from Chad. "In fact, let us contribute right now if you can get the money to the right people."

"Why not wait until next week for the first of the fundraising dinners? Same time, same place, same Bat-channel," Hal said as he served up slices of a freshly baked apple cake.

# CHAPTER 23
## *More Rain on the Dark Tower*

"And how long did Miguel Gonzalez work here for you, Mrs. Lebouche?"

"He deedn't work ere, he only stay ere." Denise hedged.

"That's not exactly the report we received. We have it that you hired him under the table to be your gardener and pool man. Are you telling us that he merely stayed here as your guest?"

"Zat's right, my guest," Denise said emphatically.

"Did you know that he is an illegal alien and that it is against the law to harbor someone who does not have proper papers here in the US?"

"Ay deedn't ask about hees papers," Denise shrieked. "How do Ay know hees got no papers?"

"Did you get to know him very well, ma'am?"

"Yes, very well. He stay ere over a month."

"And in all that time, you didn't know he was here illegally? What did he do all day while you were at your place of business?"

"How do Ay know zees? Ay don't keep track of heem every minute!"

"And this is the man you accused of robbing you? This is the same man?"

"Yes, zat ees heem. Ay trust heem, and den he steal my diamonds."

"We were unable to find them on him before we sent him back to Mexico, ma'am. Do you have any other idea who else might have stolen your jewelry?"

"No, only heem. He needs zee money. Ay feed him, Ay geev heem zee place to stay, and he do zees to me!" Denise's voice rose in indignation.

"Well, thank you, ma'am. That will be all for now, but you can expect a visit from the immigration service. Goodbye."

Denise closed the door after the officers left and walked back through the gloom of her front hall to the kitchen and poured herself a glass of wine. She began to add up a number of things that had gone wrong lately, but the ills that beset her were too many to easily enumerate, and she was feeling as if she were under constant siege. The restaurant wasn't doing well with the staff she had hired. Her house that had once been her bulwark and her place of refuge had been violated. Eric had once more disappeared from her life, her precious jewels were missing, and on top of everything else, this threat from the immigration department. Her usual reserves of self-preservation and drive seemed inadequate to the problems that faced her, and for one of the few times in her life, she wished that she had a close friend to confide in, to tell her troubles to, someone who would be sympathetic and consoling.

But no such person existed in her life any longer. The closest possibility was her cousin Bertolde who owned a restaurant a few miles away, but Denise had managed to alienate her as well, and although they were on speaking terms, Bertolde could certainly not be counted on to take up the duties of a close girlfriend. Disconsolate and worried, she poured herself a second glass of wine. She could think of no one that she might tell her troubles to at first. Then she thought of Roger.

Roger had been her restaurant manager during the years when everything ran smoothly, when the staff knew what to do under his direction, and most importantly, when money was pouring in from the filled tables, night after night. Oh, those were the days! They came up in her mind like a mythical golden age, a time when the world seemed to be at her feet, and when she was in total control of her destiny. Roger only left because of some silly disagreement that she was certain hadn't been instigated by her. What was he angry about, she wondered? Like all of her unpleasant encounters with people, she had conveniently forgotten the details that led to Roger's leaving the restaurant, and try as she might, she could not bring those details into focus. But maybe enough time had gone by. Maybe Roger would reconsider, or at least, maybe he would listen to her problems and help her out of them.

Cheered by these reflections, she got herself ready for an excursion to see Roger. Out of her copious closets came what she considered to be her most fetching outfit. She called the Hotel Laguna to ask after him and found out that he was at work. She would drop in, just by accident, perch herself in the hotel bar, and let him discover her there. Surely he would make some time for her, after all the years he had been her good and faithful manager. Surely by now he would have forgotten their little spat.

If Roger had forgotten "their little spat", he had not forgotten much else. He rounded the corner of the bar when one of the bartenders came to find him, and there she was, splayed out in a booth, looking like something out of several fashion magazines from which she had selected an amazing accumulation of dress and accessories. As accustomed has he was to Denise's sense of style—or lack of it—her appearance today topped the charts. This was, he supposed, her version of the 'lost and helpless little girl' look, which started with a red velvet cape complete with hood, worn at what she considered a becoming angle, that covered her blond head. The yards and yards of this garment opened in the front to reveal a kind of dirndl top, but Belgian instead of German he guessed, crisscrossed over her front with laces made of pink ribbons. The dirndle descended to a full skirt under which she wore white stockings and probably the largest Mary Jane shoes ever made. Not content with the relative simplicity of this ensemble, she had put on everything that hadn't been stolen from her jewel box including a collection of 'native' beads which competed with the pink ribbons down to her middle. Bracelets of various kinds and colors completed this picture, and Roger wondered why guests passing through the bar weren't crowding around to take photos.

"Hello Denise. They told me you were here to see me. I must say, you look incredible," Roger said, sitting down across from her.

"Ay come to talk wees you after all zees time," she pouted. "Ay am not mad at you anymore."

"That's very nice of you, but do you wonder if I am still mad at you?"

"Why should you be? You were zee one who leaves me in the lurches, jest lak zat!"

"I don't imagine that you remember the reason, do you? No, of course you don't. It was because I had had enough of your cruelty and selfcentered hatred for anyone who gets in your way. Eric had been your friend, probably your only friend, and you were ready to send him to the guillotine for trying to steal that framed junk that you refer to as a valuable art collection, remember?"

"Ay don't remember all zat. Eet was a long time ago."

"Not so long ago, maybe four years or so. So what brings you here today in this remarkable get-up?" Roger asked, knowing pretty well why she had come.

"Why you tink Ay must have a reason to visit an old friend? Ay tink eet ees time zat we be frens again, zat's all."

"You and Eric have split up again, that's my guess. He and Carl have left your house, I know that. That means you have no friends left and you think that I'll come back into your circle somehow and for some reason."

"That Eric! I don't know what comes over him. It is that Carl who is the problem. Ever since he move in with us, he has make a difficulty between Eric and me," she said.

"Thank you for dropping the accent, Denise. Everybody knows you can turn it on and off like a tap, so you don't have to pretend with me. I know that you use it to 'charm' people who like accents, but to me, it's as phony as your Little Red Riding Hood outfit and your reasons for showing up here." Roger looked pointedly at her. "So you're out of friends, huh? Well, that's not new. What else is going on?"

"I always thought you were a kind person, Roger," she said, almost tearing up. "But you sound like zat Hal, and accuse me when I am in need of somebody to listen to me. Zee uh . . . the restaurant is not doing so good. They doubled my rent last month. I have these idiots who can't cook or do anything right. Somebody robbed my house and took my diamonds last week. The police came to see about the robbery, but I am in trouble because I hired zat uh . . . that Miguel who ees illegal. Everyting comes down on my head all at once. You always had a kind heart, Roger. I tot you might . . ." And the mighty Denise, Denise the Merciless, Denise the Iron Woman broke down into tears.

She was right, of course. Roger was always the last person to cast stones, even at an arch sinner like Denise. His compassion for her was, however, guarded. He'd been fooled by her ploys before, and his distrust of this sobbing mess of a woman sitting there in her ridiculous clothes only partly melted his heart.

"Try to compose yourself, Denise. This is a public bar, after all, and we have customers who don't need to see this. I'll listen to you; I have listened to you. And frankly, I have no idea what you can do to get out of this fix. What you could do is pay your staff a decent wage, after you get rid of the incompetents, that is. I can help you find better people, but I don't know what you can do about the immigration department. Face the music, I guess."

"Oh, if I only had a decent manager, Roger, somebody like you who could run the restaurant and get work out of the waiters and busboys. I'd pay more, I really would."

"OK, I know somebody who's looking, but honest to God, Denise, if you screw this up, I'll never help you again. Here's what you need to pay him." He disclosed an amount that made the already pale Denise even whiter.

"But zat ees more zan I ever pay anybody before," she exclaimed, falling back into her Belgian French accent.

"Yeah, well that's why you've got the one you have now. Either you pay Paul—that's the man's name—the salary I suggest, and put it in writing, or you can figure out your own problems. You decide. I've got to get back to work. You can let me know later today." He left the wilted Denise in the bar and strode away.

She sat there calculating. Double rent, and now quadruple salary for a manager. Gulping down what was left of her drink, she gathered up her cape, slung it around her, and left the bar.

# CHAPTER 24
## *Mirrors and Ghosts*

The auditions were called for *A Streetcar Named Desire*, hereafter given the chummy nickname of *Streetcar* by the cast and crew who gave the impression to their friends and those outside the theatrical elect that they might have been chatting recently with Tennessee Williams as his intimate friends. Before this circle of smugness was entirely formed up, a great many hopefuls had been eliminated, a procedure that was conducted with a ruthlessness and sometimes downright cruelty that would have been the envy of a Grand Inquisitioner. The sheep having been separated from the goats, and the goats shown the gate, the sheep got together to bleat out their mutual congratulations on having been collected inside the fold of theatrical superiority. They were, they felt, the crème de la crème, the best that the city had with which to produce on stage the playwright's intentions.

Among these, but not quite in the center, was Bertrand who was only slightly smarting from the sting of not having been selected to play Stanley Kowalski. He was instead given the role of Mitch Mitchell, Blanche Dubois's would-be beau, a role that he felt would not show off his acting abilities quite as well. Stanley Kowalski would be played by one Brett Harrison who not only had the muscles for it, but also the youthful looks needed for the part. It was the remark about youthful looks that stung Bertrand. He had to admit that alongside the lovely young actress who would play Stella, Brett Harrison was a perfect choice.

"Do you think I look old?" Bertrand asked George that evening over dinner.

Uh oh, George thought as he bit into his chicken. He had become accustomed to countering Bertrand's increasing fears of aging and looking like one of "those old aunties," as he put it, who lined the walls of The Blue Cove every Sunday afternoon. So far, George had succeeded; at least, he thought he had. "What makes you ask that? Aha, something happened at rehearsals, I'll bet."

"We haven't really started rehearsals, but I didn't get the part of Stanley. It went to that muscle-bound ape who looks like a million bucks. It remains to be seen if he can act," Bertrand said.

"I imagine that the director has Brando in his head and he's trying to find a similar actor, that's all. You're not a muscle-bound ape, and apparently that's what he wants."

"You didn't answer my question."

"Come on, Bertrand, you know that you're the handsomest man in town, and you know how proud I am of being with you. What's 'old' mean to you? That you aren't twenty-five any longer? OK, so you're not twentyfive. In fact you're not thirty-five. But who cares? There isn't a man in this city, gay or straight, who wouldn't sell his mother for your looks. You know that. You still turn heads wherever you go, and I get to be envied wherever we go together," George said, moving around the table toward his lover. Bertrand looked up at him and took his hand.

George consoled where Bertrand's mirror failed. His traitorous mirror exposed the tiny, and not so tiny wrinkles starting here and there when he examined himself closely, but at this moment, he saw himself reflected in George's eyes, and he felt loved. George kissed him and returned to his side of the table.

Bertrand followed him with his eyes and he wondered if he had ever really been loved before he met George. He had spent his life trying to gain genuine admiration and approval of everyone; his alcoholic parents first—they had generally ignored him—and every man he'd met. Oh yes, he had been admired. Lots of people envied his looks and even his stage career, such as it was, but none of that had ever satisfied him. He had never trusted anyone's adulation for long, and with good reason. Without a constant stream of positive feedback, he soon lapsed into doubts, then into bad moods followed by plans to be rid of the man of the moment whom he had imported into his life to feed his ego. He had wondered at first how long George might last; as he looked at him and watched George return his gaze, he feared that George might one day leave him instead.

"You won't, will you?" he asked as if George could read his thoughts.

"Won't what?"

"Leave me. When I get older and older and more wrinkled, and less and less attractive, you'll find somebody younger and better looking. You'll leave me," Bertrand said, moving his gaze toward the ceiling.

"Bertrand, you can quit acting. This is George, your George. Haven't you figured out by this time that I'm here for the long haul? That you're more to me than your looks? I guess I should be worried that you'll throw me out when I get past a certain age, huh? Know what? I'm not worried about that possibility. Should I be?"

"No, of course not," Bertrand said once again looking into George's eyes. "No, never." And it was his turn to come around the table to put his arms around his lover. "What I can't figure out is what it is about you . . ."

George rose and turned into Bertrand's arms. "Why don't we go see if you can find out," he said as he led him out of the kitchen.

The six-foot board fence between the two houses hid their respective windows from view, but did little to muffle any sounds coming from them. In the bedroom facing the fence, Hal and Simon were engaged in similar bonding activities. "Listen! They're at it again. Who knew that Bertrand was a moaner? Got to say, it's better than hearing him vocalize in other ways," Hal said as he stroked Simon's chest.

"A lot better. They probably hear us too. You make more snorts than a bull elephant getting it off with a herd."

"Yeah, well that's not what people would hear from our bedroom from the uh . . . bottom of the deck, now would they?" Hal said moving his hand to Simon's ribcage.

"Don't! No tickling, remember? Now stop that, and let's give the neighbors a competitive run for the money," Simon said as he straddled Hal and felt his very big cock positioned at his rear. "Oh yeah, exactly like that," he sighed. "Exactly like that . . ."

In all that ensued, they were unaware of some slight clicks outside their window, the clicks that a camera makes. Quite a few clicks.

139

What they did hear once the festivities had subsided, was a window closing in the cottage. "What the hell was that?" Hal bolted upright. "Somebody's in the cottage again. How come we can never catch whoever it is?"

"I know who it is, don't you? It's somebody who needs an emergency place to sleep for now. I've been leaving food in the fridge out there. It's always gone by the next day."

"Well, who is it?" Hal asked. "I don't think they are getting in through the fence anymore."

"Our ghosts, that's who. Ask Dorothy who it is and she'll tell you it's her long-dead relatives, but it isn't," Simon said, nuzzling down beside Hal. "Haven't you noticed that Edward isn't spooked back there anymore? He knows who it is too." Edward, now that things had settled down on the bed, had curled up in his favorite sleeping spot, between two sets of legs.

"Right. What ghost needs you to supply food, I wonder?" Hal replied, wrapped around Simon. "But who the hell cares right now. If you don't, I don't," as he began to drift off to sleep.

But Hal did care, and he couldn't get to sleep. He had an idea who might be making their cottage into a temporary (he hoped) home. He'd talked to Eric and knew that Miguel had managed to return to Laguna after having been deported, and he suspected that Miguel was the 'ghost', presently in residence in the cottage. If that were true, Miguel certainly kept things tidy. Any visit to the cottage during the day revealed that nothing had been disturbed, no signs whatever of anyone living there.

At 2:00 AM, Hal woke up and quietly slipped out of bed. Putting on a bathrobe, he headed for the kitchen where he picked up a flashlight. He opened the back door and silently made his way toward the cottage. He listened at the door for a few minutes. Sure enough, he heard breathing. He slowly turned the doorknob and slid inside. He stumbled slightly over somebody's shoes, two pair actually. The breathing was louder now, and pointing the flashlight toward the bed, he turned it on.

What he saw scared the hell out of him. Yes, there was Miguel, all right, his muscular brown arm encircling another body, a body whose head Hal could just barely see. It was this second body's identity that shook Hal. Lying there, sound asleep in Miguel's arms was Barry.

As soon as he could compose himself, Hal doused the flashlight which fortunately had failed to arouse the two sleepers, slowly backed toward the cottage door, slid through it, and retraced his steps into the kitchen. He sat down at the table there and poured himself a drink. Scotch, and a double.

Oh my God, he thought. What next? Once anyone found out that underage Barry is living on my property, I'm off to jail. Scandal first then jail. Just what the Briggs people need to fuel their anti-gay teacher campaign. We have to get him out and we have to do it so he won't blab. How? How?

He didn't want to awaken Simon who had to work early in the morning, but this was no frivolous event. Simon would want to know. He finished his scotch and returned to their bedroom.

"Simon, wake up. I'm sorry to do this, but you've got to know something right now." Hal's voice was high with panic as he told Simon what he had just found. "His birthday is more than a month away. He's a minor, Simon, a minor and a student in my school," Hal was nearly frantic. "They could fry me for this, especially now that McHenry the principal knows I've been nosing around, asking about child abuse cases."

"But you, we, didn't do anything. We didn't ask him here. He just showed up and found the cottage. It's another thing that he found Miguel in it too, but this is explainable, Hal."

"It's how it looks, Simon. It's just the sort of thing the gay bashers love to get a hold of. We've got to get him out of here. I wonder how he's been getting to school. And if this is the first time he's stayed here. I'll talk to him at school tomorrow and see what I can find out. Damn it! The little bastard has really screwed things up. How can I possibly go to the authorities with a child abuse report? Where do you think his parents believe he's been?"

These and other questions plagued Hal the rest of the night and of course, he got no sleep. He made Simon go back to bed and held him until he was assured that he was sleeping. Hal crept back out to the kitchen to wait for tomorrow.

Unlike Scarlet O'Hara, Hal didn't share the optimism in her famous line,

"After all, tomorrow is another day."

\* \* \*

"We got him now, that queer bastard. All we got to do is get these developed and turn 'em into the police. We'll nail that queer, get him fired for being a faggot. He's keeping somebody in that cottage of his too. Could you see who it was in there? Hard to tell since he boarded it up again and we can't get in from the alley. Probably another bunch of queers. Let's go. And don't make any noise this time, you hear?"

# CHAPTER 25
# Hard Days at Tara

"Hal, you haven't slept all night. Call in sick. Don't go in today. Get a sub and just stay home," Simon pleaded, looking clinically into Hal's eyes and feeling his pulse.

"Did you check the cottage? Are they gone?"

"Yes and yes. It amazes me how completely Miguel cleans up after himself and now after . . ."

"Barry. No, I've got to get to school, Simon. I'd feel worse all day here not being around if anything is going to happen. I know you mean well and I love you for that, but I can't just hide out here. And from what, exactly? I'm just having the jitters, maybe over nothing." It was Hal's turn to try to smooth all of this out so Simon wouldn't fret. "Look, I'll call you at lunchtime. Now go to work, my lovely man, and don't worry. You're the one who told me that everything will be all right, remember?"

Simon glumly put on his jacket and picked up his briefcase. "OK, let's just put in a normal day and see what happens," he said as he kissed Hal and walked toward the kitchen door. "And it will be all right."

As Hal heard Simon drive off, he was less than convinced that 'it would be all right'. He suddenly felt himself in danger, the career that he had worked hard to establish in jeopardy. Not a year ago a male teacher had been accused of having sex with a boy student in Santa Ana and was nearly convicted of the charge. The boy who made the accusation finally confessed that he was getting even for the teacher's having given him a richly deserved "F" in his course. But that confession came too late. The wronged teacher had been dragged through hell, through the courts, and through endless suspicion and ridicule in the press. Once he had been exonerated, his credibility had been destroyed, and although his job had been restored to him, he knew that he had no alternative but to decline it and move to some other town where there might be a chance that no one would know what had happened.

Hal had followed the events of that case carefully, and it was his compassion for the maligned teacher that he now brought home to himself. What would happen if Barry turned on him and made similar accusations? His story would be laced with what would seem to be undeniable evidence that he had stayed over at Hal's place, even if not inside the house. Who would believe Hal in these dangerous times for teachers, these times of prejudice and hatred against gay people which had occasioned the Briggs Initiative, Prop 6, to be put onto the ballot? What would he do if he had to quit? What would happen to him and Simon, to his entire life that only six months ago had looked so full of promise?

These thoughts swirled around in his head as he drove toward school that morning, and he was at sea about what he could do to fight against the invisible forces that he felt were on full attack. Oh come on, he thought. Nothing has happened yet and maybe nothing will. Just because Barry found Miguel . . . Oh God, what a mess! Did he do this just to get even with me because I didn't respond to him? No, maybe he really likes Miguel. Who wouldn't, after all?

He arrived at the parking lot with the feeling that he was being watched, that his life had become transparent, and that he was indeed in some sort of danger from forces as yet unidentified, from a hidden but very real enemy. Paranoia? Yeah, maybe, he thought. There was Dick Palmer the math teacher, also just arriving. "Hey Hal, how's it going?" he asked. Was that a smirk on his face? Hal thought no, probably not. Just me being paranoid.

"Things are OK, Dick. How about yourself?" Hal asked. They walked into the center of campus together, exchanging the usual meaningless amenities. But there was that look, that smirk that was unmistakably plastered over Palmer's face. What does he know, Hal wondered, or thinks he knows.

He managed to get through his first two classes, but only barely. He kept the door to his classroom ajar, and since it gave onto a sidewalk rather than a hallway, any noise his classes made would not disturb anyone. He wanted to avoid the feeling of being closed in, of being confined. He thought about taking his fourth period English class out to the lawn, just for a change, but no, that would be too public a display. He equivocated between lying low and challenging the dark forces that he could not dispel from his mind.

Barry was absent from class. Damn, Hal thought. Now what's he up to? Hal went to the attendance clerk to find out if Barry had been at school that morning. He had not. Hal headed for the principal's office. "McHenry in, Betty?" he asked the secretary.

"Just a minute, Hal. He had someone in there with him earlier, but I think he's free now," she said, picking up the intercom phone. Hal went in, not entirely knowing what he would say, but he managed to tell what he knew of Barry's situation without mentioning that the boy had spent the night in Laguna. "I've seen the marks, John. I know he's being abused," Hal said. "We've got to get him out of that house. He's gay, or didn't you know that? His nutcase religious zealots of parents are determined to beat it out of him."

"And he's confided this to you, Hal? I mean, did he tell you he's gay? Do you think it could just be a story that he's made up to gall his parents?"

"No, I don't think it's made up, John. He's going to be eighteen in about a month and when that happens, he can do what he wants. It's the meantime I'm worried about him. What do you think we can do? He says he won't go to a foster home."

"First thing is to get the authorities in on this, Hal. You will have to file a formal report, you know. You're obliged to under the law. Hal, I need to know how involved you are with this kid. I know he's in your English class. Is there anything else that I need to know?"

Can I trust him? Hal wondered. How much does he know already? Nowadays in the anti-gay teacher atmosphere of hatred stirred up by the Briggs Initiative, what side would John McHenry be on? Hal quickly weighed the alternative of saying nothing more. It wasn't much of an alternative; he needed this man's support and he'd have to take the chance that he would get it. So, having gone this far into Barry's story and hoping that what he had told John McHenry would be enough, he slumped backwards into his chair. "Yeah, there is something else. Barry says that he's in love with me. But I'm here to tell you, John, that nothing has happened between us, nothing. I know that you know I'm gay although we've never talked about it. Why would we? But what you need to know is that he's fixated on me and on my partner Simon. And here comes the real kicker. I found him last night sleeping in our cottage with another man we know, a guy named Miguel who is probably an illegal alien. This is such a mess, John, and I need your help here. I'm nearly crazy with what might happen." Hal's eyes filled with tears and he began to tremble.

"Hal, Hal, it's OK. Try to be calm. You're right, it's a mess, but it's not the worst mess I've ever seen. We have to handle this carefully, that's all. It has the smell of dynamite and the last thing any of us wants is the sort of thing that happened in Santa Ana. If you've told me the entire truth, you've got me on your side. You're one hell of a good teacher with a great career ahead of you, and I want to help you preserve it. Just stay below the radar for now. You'll have to file that report, but as you know, those reports are anonymous. The parents won't know who is moving against them. But we have that boy's well being to think about. I'll get the papers ready for you."

Hal brightened and was able to compose himself. Somehow he felt much better. Maybe it was the unburdening of the story that had done it. Maybe it was John McHenry's surprising reassurance that he was Hal's ally here, but whatever it was, Hal left the principal's office with a much lighter step. It was lunchtime, and he walked toward the office to phone Simon.

* * * *

"No, it's not an arrest warrant; I'm not a cop," the detective was saying to John McHenry that afternoon. "At present we are merely conducting an investigation of possible molestation charges." He had shown his credentials and a paper with Hal Schroeder's name at the top, along with Barry's, with a list of Hal's whereabouts for the past week printed on it.

"I've just had an interview with Mr. Schroeder who has told me everything that has gone on between him and this student, and I am here to assure you that there has been no molestation or any other impropriety."

"You know that he's a homosexual and lives with another man in Laguna Beach, don't you?" the detective asked. "Take a look at these." He handed over some photos. "These were taken by a professional photographer just two nights ago." The photos showed Hal and Simon in bed, naked and having sex.

"Excuse me, but isn't it illegal to photograph private citizens in their own home without their permission?" John McHenry said, feeling himself getting angry. "I'm quite sure that your spy didn't have their permission, isn't that right?"

"In these days and times, many people want to protect public morality and their children against homosexuals. We're just gathering information, that's all. But where there's smoke, there's fire, ha, ha. We want to interview some other students of his, that's all."

"That's all? That's ALL? You may be too young to remember the last witch hunt we had in this country during what's called the McCarthy Era when thousands of innocent citizens were hounded out of their jobs and livelihoods because they were suspected of being communists. This is just another witch hunt, sir, and you'll get no help from me to support it. You are on this campus solely with my permission and only as far as this front office. You will not go any further, and you certainly will not be interviewing our students here."

"I'm sorry you feel that way, Mr. McHenry," the man said, pulling out another sheet of paper from his briefcase. "Please take a look at this." The paper was a copy of an official complaint filed by Barry's parents against one Hal Schroeder, claiming that he had taken advantage of his position as Barry's teacher to alienate the boy's affections from his loving parents, and of seducing him into the 'homosexual lifestyle'.

John McHenry's face did not betray his feelings as he read over the complaint. He foresaw some trouble ahead for Hal, but he wasn't about to indicate any of those thoughts to this smug jerk who was obviously a bigot whose sympathies lay squarely in the Briggs camp. "This is only a complaint. Nothing more. You would have to accumulate real evidence before such charges can be made official, sir. Now if you have nothing further . . ." and John McHenry ushered the detective out of his office.

He got on the phone immediately. "Chief Sanders, please. This is John McHenry calling." He wanted to detail the two interviews in his office to his old friend Mike Sanders. They had been to university together, roommates for three of their years there, had been best man at each other's weddings, and their families often shared vacations. "Mike, hi. Yeah she's fine. Look something's come up concerning one of my teachers. Oh, you know already, huh? Well, tell me where you think this is going." Mike filled him in on the official front. "That's it so far, huh? Good. Well, I've got a bombshell for you, too. We're filing child abuse charges against the parents. The student came to school last week beaten with a belt. Had welts all over him, and probably still has some. Yes, the same teacher saw them. Yes, we'll have papers on your desk this afternoon. Mike, this teacher is somebody I trust. He's not a liar and he's not a child molester. Good. OK, yeah, let's get together this weekend." And he hung up. "Betty," he said into his intercom. "Get Hal Schroeder down here, will you?"

# CHAPTER 26
## The Unexamined Life

Bertrand had buttressed himself with the dictum, often attributed to Bette Davis, that there are no small parts, only small actors, and he dived into the relatively minor role of Mitch in *Streetcar* with his usual diligence. Rehearsals found him mooning over the decaying Blanche Dubois with more fervor that was absolutely necessary, while trying to maintain the moral code that would eventually deny her availability as a suitable wife. Oh how the anguish of that internal debate showed on Bertrand's brow at every opportunity, giving the director, Tim Calloway, a full-time task of keeping him from absolute scene stealing. No mean feat. While Bertrand acquiesced to the director's plans of staging and positioning, he was less eager to listen to suggestions concerning his interpretation of the role.

Rehearsals did not require makeup for anyone, but Bertrand, overly conscious of his age, appeared in full paint in an effort to make the amorous Mitch even more appealing to the aging Blanche as well as to a prospective audience. His preparations in front of a dressing room mirror took an hour, minimum. But when he appeared on stage, he looked, or at least thought he looked, fabulous.

He did not, to his mind, appear on stage enough, and offered ideas about how his character might enrich the production by being in more scenes. "Bertrand, I didn't write the play. Tennessee Williams did and he's dead. We can't ask him to write in more lines for Mitch. You're doing it just fine, very convincingly," Tim told him. "Call me a purist, but let's just do the play in the way Williams wrote it, OK?"

It wasn't OK. When he wasn't in a scene, Bertrand roamed around making suggestions for what he thought would be better lighting, a better place for tables and chairs, shouldn't we use microphones for the scenes between Mitch and Blanche? Wouldn't it be better if Stanley didn't take his shirt off? And on and on until Tim had had it. After one particularly testy rehearsal during which lines were dropped, actors were not on cue, timing went to hell, and everything that could go wrong, did, Tim lost it: "Look Bertrand, and I'm telling you for the last time. You are getting very close to being thrown out of this play, do you hear me?" Everybody could hear him, no problem. "Either we do it *my* way without any further proposals from you, or you can get out. Period." And he stomped off the set to cool down.

Bertrand retreated, pouting his way off the set in the other direction, and sitting by himself, began to reassess his position among the cast. He had, of course, assumed that he was the star performer, the veteran actor whose invaluable experience the cast and crew craved, and whose advice would be translated into the way he thought things should proceed. As he recalled the rehearsals and readings up to this point, he realized that none of his ideas had become reality, and that realization brought him to the horrifying idea that he was being merely tolerated, coddled, put into the production out of pity or some misguided sense of his longevity in the theater. It was a jarring conclusion, and he wondered how many other great stars had suffered the same indignities. Joan Crawford's last roles were hardly starring ones, but there she was anyway. Same with Bette Davis. Same with Bertrand Lebland.

Having lumped himself into such august company, he took heart that he would uphold the finest traditions of the theater anyway, would act out his role as if it were a great one, and would by doing so, end his days . . . Oh my God! Not end his days! He stopped acting inside his own head and emended that last sentence: and would by doing so, end this production . . . Whew! That was better. End this production with the acclaim that would doubtless come his way for having been the show's best supporting role. Yes, that's what he would do. That would be noble and fine, he thought as he rose from his earlier despair with the high resolve to perform the role as Tim wanted him to.

And George would be proud of him. Now there was a thought that was new, or at least one that he hadn't trotted out since he was a boy trying to win the approval of his indifferent parents. He unexpectedly became aware that he wanted George to be proud of him, to see him as a real actor. He hadn't been convinced that George really did see him as such; he had hardly ever commented on his role as Curly in *Oklahoma!* after all. Any time he had tried to get George's opinion, George had become evasive, had moved the conversation into how fine he had looked on stage and then into lovemaking. Yes, this time he would do this role so that he wouldn't have to hint around for praise. George would be proud of him.

Two more weeks of rehearsals and then opening night. As Bertrand collected his stage makeup and left the theater. He headed for The Blue Cove. George was teaching a night class; no need to rush home. Vi Winters would be playing tonight, and what he needed to do was sing. It had been some time since the final curtain of *Oklahoma!* and weeks since his brush with permanent vocal damage that he had dodged after the musical had closed. The pain in his throat had gone away, and with it the memory of how he got polyps in the first place. So what? he thought. I'll just take it easy, sing a few easy songs, get the old pipes back into some sort of shape.

Many of the old gang had gathered onto their usual barstools and tables as Vi was holding forth with her usual repertoire. It must have been 8:30; that's when she geared up for "Hello, Dolly" and a few other songs from that musical. She did it at every appearance and at the same time, as dependably as a clock. That made things very handy for the regulars who could pick and choose what they wanted to hear, showing up in time for their favorites, or avoiding the songs they particularly disliked. It was like having a live juke box.

"*Dolly'll never go away! Dolly'll never go away AGAAIINNN!*" Vi hit the final chord in time for the usual applause from the usual people. In came Bertrand who had been waiting for the finale of the song before making his entrance.

"Bertrand! How good to see you!" trilled Paulette from across the bar. "Such a pity about your voice. Of course we heard all about it. Now don't ask me how or who. And we don't expect you to sing. Now come have a drinkie right here on your barstool." Bertrand acceded to Paulette's invitation, accepting greetings and good wishes along the way. Once settled with a drink in front of him, Paulette asked, "Tell us how the new play is going? What a shame you didn't get the Kowalski part! But look who did! My, my what a piece of beefcake! But can he act? That's what we want to know. Oh, he'll have to go some to outdo Brando. Now my dear, I'm sure that you could have done it just fine, but age comes to us all, more or less, doesn't it? And

Stanley is supposed to be twenty-something, isn't he. And my dear, despite your very fine looks," Paulette said conspiratorially, "I for one know that you aren't twenty-anything. Of course I'm not talking about any measurements, ha, ha, ha!" He put a hand halfway up Bertrand's thigh and began to move it upwards. Before it reached its destination, Bertrand stopped it and gently moved the encroaching hand off his leg.

His high spirits when he entered The Cove began to come down a few notches as he tried to rise above the source of this bitchery from this drunken and aging queen who had too much money and nothing to do but sit in the bar from opening to closing every day. He looked around at the rest of the clientele. Depressing, very depressing. There was old Danny, once a great beauty but these days as wizened and wrinkled as a forgotten apple. Beside him sat Henry, just barely conscious and nodding into his scotch. And the roll call of the old and tired and jaded went on as Bertrand surveyed the sorry crowd that had for many years made up his audience.

He tried to remember the glowing nights when he came here often, singing to these same men, basking in their praise for his renditions, and waiting for them to beg him to sing more. Those memories failed to brighten his darkening mood, and he began to see the whole scene as more than a little tawdry. Where were those nights when he felt so elated while singing show tunes with Vi Winters, he wondered? She was on break at the moment, and he tried to think about what he would want to sing when she returned.

Paulette, undaunted by having his advances rebuffed, said, "Now how are things there on Myrtle Street with that nice George? Nobody would have ever suspected the two of you would get together. I mean, you're so different, aren't you? He's a bookworm and you, my dear, are an artist on the stage, a great actor and singer. Well, at least you *were* a singer. What do you find to talk about? He never comes in here, never did, even when he was with that Martha person. Always acted too good for the likes of us, don't you know. And here you are without him! Isn't that interesting?" Paulette rattled on.

George would not want him to sing and injure his larynx again, but he also knew that he would never actually forbid him or say anything judgmental. Nevertheless he felt as if were betraying a trust, an unspoken agreement between him and his lover, merely by being here at the piano bar and thinking about choosing a song to sing. Oh come on, he thought.

It's not dangerous to sing something soft and vocally undemanding, surely. No, probably not. But that wasn't exactly what gave him pause. It was an accumulation of things: the same drunken, sunken faces, the gossipy Paulette, the cigarette smoke—all of these assailed him as he sat there hearing but not listening to the prating Paulette.

Before Vi's break was over, Bertrand slid off his barstool and headed for the door leaving Paulette in mid-sentence. "Well, you could at least say goodbye!" he screamed at Bertrand's back. And, "Piss-elegant old queen!" once Bertrand was out of earshot. "Talk about a has-been, honey," he said to someone on his left. "That one is a never-was. Always had a big idea of being a star. Ha! Couldn't sing then, and can't sing now. Could I get another drink over here?"

Bertrand walked down the steps to the beach, dangerous steps along dangerous places where men often found each other in the darkened under house overhangs and behind obscure rocks. The police knew about this place and patrolled it frequently, netting a few men having sex. But he was not interested in what might be going on around him at the moment. Before he reached the beach itself, he had had more than one implied invitation for an encounter. These he ignored, his thoughts entirely elsewhere.

What had made him leave so suddenly? Paulette? When he thought about The Blue Cove, a slight feeling of distaste displaced the old lure of the bar and the piano and the mike. What had been almost his second home for so many years suddenly emerged as a cheap, empty, sordid place, filled with men for whom he seemed to have nothing but contempt. These same people whose applause he had craved only weeks ago materialized in his mind like a crowd of ghouls awaiting in front of a gallows for the entertainment of a hanging. He wondered how he could have ever found them anything but repellent.

No, he thought. That can't be. Those are my old friends up there. I've known them for years. OK, so Paulette is a pain and a bitch. What about . . . ? Or there's . . . Nothing golden or fine came to him as he replayed everything that made up his life at the bar. All of the flimsy trophies, all of the empty accolades, all of the shallow praise for his life among the harpies of The Blue Cove paraded before him as they really were, utterly worthless.

He walked along the margin of the beach and stumbled slightly over a rock that protruded through the sand, falling forward enough so that he almost lost his balance. He took off his shoes, and sitting down on the margin of the surf, looked out over the starlit sea to the horizon where it disappeared into the dark sky. He wondered how long it had been since he had simply taken the time to ponder the endlessly moving waves, feel the surf wash his feet, and smell the onshore breeze. Exhilarated as he gazed out to sea, he breathed deeply of the salt air when the distant sounds of the bar reached him. Looking up toward the cliffs, he could see the lights from The Blue Cove. A short while ago they had called to him, inviting him into another night of what he used to think was fun, times of careless laughter and singing. Now those same lights confirmed his present feelings, and they glowed as if from the entrance to hell, serving only to illuminate his memories of years of wasted time. How many nights, weekends, years of them had he spent there? Owning that realization of time absolutely and irretrievably lost, saddened him as he sat watching the waves.

Turning once more toward the ocean, an ever increasing sense of loss rose within him as if it came from the depths of the sea itself, dark and cold, chilling him at first, and then propelling his spirit upward toward an inner light. The mists and fogs of the life he had so valued, lifted and dropped away, and sitting there on the darkened beach, he saw his own reality more clearly than he ever had before. My God, what has just happened to me, he wondered as he lay back on the damp sand.

George's face reappeared in his mind as if to answer his question. He smiled at the very thought of him and wished that he were there beside him. He reviewed their fairly brief history in his mind, one that really began that day when he had breakfast with Simon and Hal and their 'kids'. How he had envied their life, their sharing a home and a family, their loving each other. How empty he had felt when he had returned to his own house where he lived alone. The hollowness of his life before George, a life that he now saw had been as superficial as it was meaningless horrified him. Forty-five years old and what had he done to be proud of, to point to as accomplishment? He could not bring up a single event or person or anything else that had made his life anything other than a day-to-day existence in which he mindlessly searched for the idle and fleeting praise of people who didn't matter.

George had dropped into his life and excited him that first night just as many other men had over the years, and it was not exactly that he was in love with him right off. He had long before got out of the habit of falling in love with anyone, but something attracted him in some way that he put off trying to define. Maybe it had been that George was so transparent, had nothing plastic or artificial about him, and who from the start demonstrated a devotion to Bertrand that seemed entirely guileless. He had been up front and candid about his relationship with Marty, a history that other, less honest men would have kept hidden. True, many other men had seemed devoted to him in the past, but they often had ulterior motives, were only along for the coattail ride of his local celebrity, or had even more sinister designs for being kept as his houseboy.

At first Bertrand had harbored some suspicion of a man who had no pretenses, no drama, was not high maintenance, did no posturing. Instead of the disingenuous fakes he'd encountered throughout his life, he became aware that he only received genuine regard, respect, consideration, passion, and love from George. Now sitting by the ocean he watched the relentless surf that rolled up to his feet, bringing him a recurring and instantly clarified vision of where he stood in relation to what was sweeping into his being as real love. As he thought about his life with his lover, his communion with nature produced an even stronger light, and a greater warmth spread through him and made him happy.

Something else was disappearing as well. Like many men who had never found Mr. Right, Bertrand cherished a vision of who his ideal lover and partner would be, what he would look like, how he would act. It was a vision that he had recalled to mind nearly every day, but he was having trouble bringing that old apparition into focus; instead, he could see only one face in his mind's eye, the smiling good looks of his lover. How odd that the old and comfortable but now fading picture of the supposedly ideal lover, so often brought into consciousness and longed for, presently vanished like the foam of the receding surf.

He stood up just as a wave from the rising tide extended its flush toward him. He almost allowed it to flood over him, thinking that such a wetting would provide a kind of baptism. A baptism? He hadn't thought about anything religious for years. Maybe going too far, but on second thought, maybe not. As he stood there listening to the surf, a deepening sense of genuine happiness grew stronger within him, flooding through him as relentlessly as the waves at his feet cleansed the sand. An unaccustomed emotion of being an extension of nature gave him the urge to strip down and jump into the surf and emerge somehow transfigured, but he knew that stripping down would likely get him arrested. So he plunged in, clothes and all. He dived into an incoming wave, coming up on its other side, and swam for a while just outside the breakers, returning to the beach by body surfing his way in. He found his shoes and dripped his way toward his car. The late spring breeze should have chilled him, but if it did, he didn't notice.

His new sense of well-being erased all traces of the self pity he had wallowed in after the operation on his vocal cords, and although he felt like singing as he strode across the sand, the euphoria he was experiencing transcended mere song. He couldn't think of what he would sing even if he could. He didn't care that he couldn't; he only knew that there was a new song of joy inside him, inexpressible and whose melody he could not entirely make out but one that vibrated throughout his being, and that his life now had more than a possibility of meaning and truth.

He climbed back up the beach stairs and past the subtle sounds of men having sex among the rocks and under cantilevered buildings. One unengaged man watched him reach the first landing, gave him a lascivious grin and nod, an invitation into a similar tryst. Bertrand benignly smiled back and walked on.

He was treading the way of the newly converted, the high road of enlightened possibility for his future. He had for a brief time sung with the Episcopal Church choir and a line from a hymn came to him: "Ransomed, healed, restored, forgiven . . ." He wasn't entirely convinced that he had just had anything like a religious conversion, but whatever it was that just happened filled him with joy.

Old habits die hard in spite of profound, life-changing experiences and realizations like the one that Bertrand just had. As he passed The Blue Cove, he looked through its open door and heard its familiar music mixed with loud conversations. For an instant, he thought about going back in to test whether or not his new sense of himself, now in some way miraculously revealed to him, would withstand the temptations that beckoned. He stood for a moment in indecision, heard Paulette's piercing cackle peal out over the rest of the bar noise, immediately felt a recurring sense of revulsion, and turning on his heel, still more than a little damp, walked on until he found his car.

# CHAPTER 27

# Another World of Nouvelle Cuisine

"Hal, we need to relax. You've been through too much this week," Simon said, rubbing Hal's aching head and shoulders. "Let's go to that restaurant you're supposed to be reviewing for Norman tonight. It's only up in Costa Mesa. I'll call and make reservations, what do you say?"

"Yeah, let's do it, but don't stop doing that, please don't stop . . . mmm . . . . Think you can dial with one hand?"

"It always surprises me at what I can do to you with one hand," he laughed. "Just relax a minute. Where's that business card? Never mind, found it." He dialed the Urgent Desire Restaurant and Bar and made a reservation for 6:30PM. "What kind of food do you think they have at the Urgent Desire anyway?"

"No idea, but whatever it is, I've got to write up the review so that it sounds favorable. They are paying advertisers in the paper. That's how Norman keeps a roof over his head and turquoise on every appendage. He's become a master of literary disguise, and except for the restaurant owners who are taken in by his reviews—not that all of the restaurants are bad or anything—his readers know exactly what he's telling them. Now I've got to do the same thing."

"It'll take your mind off the crap at school anyway," Simon said, returning to massage Hal's back. "What did McHenry tell you when he called you back in?"

"That we're going ahead with the child abuse report. There will be a preliminary hearing on Tuesday afternoon. That's when I get to face off with Barry's parents. Whether Barry wants to or not, he will be leaving his parents' house. What people they must be! Monsters. But even the bloodthirsty Grendel in *Beowulf* had a mother; she turned out to be worse than her son. Anyway, it's done. I may be out of a job, but it's done."

"Barry turns eighteen in a few weeks, though. Then what?"

"He can live where he wants. He can also finish school. After that, who knows? I like him and I feel sorry for what he's been through, but frankly it will be good to have him out of my, rather our, hair. I found him after school and he promised not to sleep over here again with Miguel. By the way, what's up with Miguel, our other problem child?"

"We do seem to be running some sort of home for wayward people. I have no idea, but I think that Eric and Carl do. It's OK if Miguel stays here for a while, don't you think?"

"Oh sure, sure. Might as well get into trouble with the immigration service along with the police who think I'm having it on with my students. Sure, why not?"

"See why we need a night out? Now go get a shower and get ready. Hey, you know I'm here for you. I don't need to tell you that, do I? This will all blow over, Hal, you'll see."

"God how I love you, you hairy little medic. Come back here a minute."

"Nope, not a chance. I know where that goes, and we have to get on the road to Costa Mesa. Take a rain check though," Simon grinned. "Don't forget to take a pen and paper.

\* \* \* \*

The era of culinary experimentation arrived in various forms. Restaurants featuring nouvelle cuisine sought to lighten the heavy sauces found in traditional French cooking; Thai restaurants began to entice those tired of Chinese starch palaces; food from Morocco presented grand feasts of dishes hitherto untried by most Californians; Japanese hot grills enthralled the masses with feats of fast carving and serving of sizzling hot steak; and Mongolian barbecues offered tantalizing combinations of vegetables and meats, all grilled as you watched. Imaginations ran rampant among restaurateurs who were eager to cash in on the new boom in adventurous eating.

The Urgent Desire Restaurant and Bar had been converted from what looked like a country-western barbecue place that had seen rough use and hard times. The décor still consisted of knotty pine board walls plastered with rodeo posters and photographs of the anonymous dead from last century, mostly in faded sepia tones. More than a slight whiff of smoke and barbecue sauce still permeated the air. Whether or not the newly established Urgent Desire would eventually change its wall décor into something else was a question almost immediately explained by Hermie Schmits the new owner, to Hal and Simon who were seated in a booth.

"Well some of these old prints and photos are rare, it seems, and a lot of the people who come in here were customers of the old place, and they expect to see this stuff on the walls. Eventually, we'll probably phase out the country junk. We've already remodeled the restrooms," he proudly announced. "We want our theme to be much sexier and even erotic. Here, have a look at the menu."

And what a menu it was. Starters included such items as *Unzipped Chicken Logs, Aroused Lobster Barquettes, As You Like It Ham Mousse*, and *Quickie Quiche*. The list of entrees featured *Not-The-Ones-You-GotRid-Of Crabs, Bend Over Greek Chicken, Hot Beef Injection Filet Mignon*, and *Down There Tuna Steaks*.

Everything except good taste had been employed to name the items on the menu in an effort to present to the jaded restaurant customer a new and 'sexy' milieu of dining pleasure.

"Please, just let us be your hosts tonight. Our guests are usually a couple, I mean, a guy and his girlfriend, but we'll do our best. We want you to try a number of our food items, so just sit back and relax," Hermie said as he made his way toward the kitchen. A bottle of white wine appeared on the table, sporting a perfectly ordinary label.

"Guess they haven't got around to renaming the wines. Got any ideas for new names?" Simon giggled.

"I'll try to think of something when I come back," Hal said heading for the restroom. A few minutes later he returned with a combination look on his face that read as shock and outright hilarity. "You've got to go in there, Simon. Just go have a look."

Hermie was right; the restroom had been entirely remodeled to reflect the announced theme of the restaurant. The door to the men's room was not really a door, but an opening consisting of two adjoining pieces of pliable rubber that met in the middle. They were a shade of pink and dark rose that did nothing to disguise the female body part that they were intended to emulate. In order to get into the restroom, it was necessary to squeeze through the center of the opening. Once inside, the pink vagina theme continued, but with the walls covered with paintings and large photos of women in poses that would have made Peter Paul Rubens blush. Vaginas of all shapes and sizes proliferated every possible space, and standing at any of the urinals virtually forced the user's nose into a particularly juicy one.

Simon emerged in the same state of disbelief that Hal had. "My God! What do you suppose the women's restroom looks like?"

Before they could conjecture, and perhaps ask for a tour of a room that would likely have been decorated with pictures that they would have found more interesting, the food arrived. "These must be the *Aroused Lobster* things," Hal said, spearing one onto his plate. Simon helped himself to the *Unzipped Chicken Legs* which had indeed been 'unzipped' and stuffed with an aromatic breadcrumb mixture.

"I think you can say good things about the chicken, Hal," Simon said forking over some to Hal's plate. "How's the lobster?"

"Can't taste it. It's hidden under whatever this ungodly sauce is. Could be anything in there. Here, you try it."

So went dinner. The selections brought out for sampling were invariably accompanied by Hermie who wanted to find out how things were going. "Don't feel as if you have to exaggerate when you write us up, Hal. We'd rather have an honest appraisal of our menu than one that just butters us up. I'm sure you'll be fair, and I'm also sure that you have had a very fine dinner. That's how confident we are here."

Dessert had not been mentioned up to this time, and because the other courses had been heavy, the two men were hoping to avoid it altogether. But no such luck. Out came a platter of various sweets for them to sample. "You know how everybody likes Ding Dongs, Hal," Hermie said. "Well, we have a variation on them right here. Have a *Dripping Dong*!"

It was almost too much, but Hal managed a forkful of the sickly sweet chocolate dessert that was indeed shaped like you'd expect. "Yes, quite rich," he said, "but we are entirely full, Hermie. Thanks for an entertaining evening. I hope you'll like the review, but we've got to go."

"Not without a *Spanish Fly Cognac*, Hal," Hermie said, producing same. Finally, the men left and found their car.

"I'm thankful for one thing," Simon groaned as he drove toward home. "I'm glad that you have to write this place up and not me."

"It will be a challenging article, my love. And I'm glad you're driving. Get us home. And you were right about something else. I can't imagine doing anything better that could get my mind off school for a while. Hey! We never did see the women's restroom! Want to go back tomorrow night?"

# CHAPTER 28

## Gin and Moonlight

No one would ever have accused Dorothy Eakins of being a religious person; she attended no church, never had since adulthood. Her parents had baptized her as a Presbyterian, marched her off to Sunday School during her formative years, but failed to instill in the recalcitrant Dorothy any of the 'true faith'. As soon as she was old enough to make up her own mind, she never went back to church.

But that is not to say that Dorothy was devoid of any belief in the spiritual world. Her steadfast and unwavering knowledge of the existence of at least two ghosts imbued her with a similarly stanch faith in 'things seen and unseen' as the church creeds have it. She made it her business to keep tabs on her ghosts, those spirits of her long-dead relatives that she was convinced still populated the cottage behind Hal and Simon's house, not that she had really seen them since childhood. She made frequent visits to the haunted cottage with the high hopes that she would once again see the two spectral lovers in an eternal clench, dressed in period costumes. From time to time, she slunk into the back yard, took a chair, and sat in the dark to watch, fortified with a large iced gin which she always brought along. She whiled away the time by recalling her stories of murder and mayhem, handed down to her from other relatives. These night watches allowed her to sharpen those same stories, slightly embroidering them into much more colorful tales for the edification and enjoyment of her friends.

That very night she took up her vigil. She sat in her accustomed chair, hidden from view, when all of a sudden she saw a dim light pass across the windows inside the darkened cottage. The light from a candle, the unmistakable flicker of a single candle. Despite her earlier hopes of seeing a ghost or two, she began shaking, and the appearance of the moving candle made the hair on her neck rise. She was dumbstruck, glued to the spot as the candle continued to move. Then it stopped moving, and she heard faint sounds like someone panting or breathing with some effort. The quiet night brought her more of these same sounds, almost moaning, soft moaning and sighing. Should she go closer? Could she go closer? Her feet and legs felt as heavy as lead as the realization chilled her heart that her stories had been more than mere tales after all. Oh, if only Cynthia Daley were here! All those years of her pretending to believe Dorothy's stories—and Dorothy knew she had been pretending—would once and for all put Cynthia's unvoiced but obvious skepticism to flight.

The moaning from inside the cottage continued, growing in volume and intensity, going on and on. Dorothy felt that time had stopped, that she was gazing at a scene that was outside of time itself, and thus she had no idea how long she listened to the unearthly sounds from within. She gulped down the remains of her glass of gin as she sat there dumbstruck. Finally the sounds grew to a crescendo and culminated in a hair-raising shout. Her heart raced and she sat bolt upright in her chair, still too frightened to move. Then silence from the cottage. She thought she could hear the murmur of voices but nothing was certain to her astonished senses. The candle began to move once more, but then its light disappeared altogether and pitched the inside of the cottage into complete darkness.

She sat there for a few more minutes waiting for her breath to come back. The moon had risen and cast the front of the cottage into an eerie light. Dorothy stood up and heard the click of the door latch. Someone or something was coming out of the cottage. Torn between her daytime resolve to see her ghostly relatives again and the utter terror produced by the opening door, she gave into the latter and bolted toward the gate as the door to the cottage slowly swung open. Grabbing up her gin glass, she wasted no time on the way home, convinced more than ever that her ghosts still walked among the living, and from time to time came to visit the scenes of their previous life. Oh she couldn't wait to tell Cynthia about this. Just wait until tomorrow. They would have a three martini pitcher afternoon.

* * * *

"Who was that?" Barry whispered to Miguel as they left the cottage.

"I didn't see no one," Miguel replied.

"Somebody just ran out of the back yard and went through the gate over there," Barry said.

"Dunno. You imagining things. Hey, you want to stay the night? Nobody home yet. We gotta be out early though."

"Yeah, sure. Let's go eat first. We can come back. Can't let Hal catch us again, you know? I promised I wouldn't stay over here again, not after the last time. It could cause him a lot of trouble."

"No problem. I take you down home early. Just don't make no noise this time, OK?"

"It wasn't me making all of the noise, you know. Let's go."

Miguel spent his days hiding out at Eric and Carl's place, and this would be the last night he'd stay in the cottage. They were all pretty sure that the immigration people had lost interest in Miguel and that it was safe enough for him to move back in with them; besides, they missed the three-way sex he provided and they wanted him back. He knew enough to stay clear of the vengeful Denise who had reported him in the first place, a deed that had come back to plague her.

What Eric and Carl didn't know about was Miguel's secret high school boyfriend. He wasn't sure how he would tell them about Barry, or if he wanted to. He knew that he couldn't stay longer at the cottage, but it did give him and Barry a place to make out. He was always extremely neat and tidy, making sure that everything was clean any time he stayed there. He knew that they knew, or at least that Simon knew. There was always food in the fridge, always replenished no matter what he ate.

What else he knew was that he loved making love with Barry. He'd have to find a way to continue what they had together. He had to find a way.

# CHAPTER 29

# *Hear Ye, Hear Ye!*

The preliminary hearing took place in a small courtroom, thanks to the intervention of John McHenry who fervently wanted to keep the whole issue as low-key as possible, and bad publicity away from his high school. He watched Barry's parents carefully as they trooped in looking as if the hearing had interrupted a beer bust in their back yard. Barry came in behind them and sat some seats away. Dressed in sloppy, if not downright dirty clothes, they took seats and sneered at Hal Schroeder from across the room. Apparently cleanliness was not next to godliness in their brand of religion.

Everyone was sworn in and stood as Judge Thompson entered and took his seat.

"Sit down, please. We're here today to hear the grounds for the complaint made and signed by you, Mr. and Mrs. uh . . . Roadapple, against Mr. Schroeder in which you accuse him of various acts resulting in the alienation of your son Barry, is that right?"

"Right. That queer over there got to our kid," Cal Roadapple said. "He otta be kicked out of the school and not be around good kids like ours."

"Mr. Roadapple, we will do without any name calling. Do you have any evidence to support your claim that your son was molested by Mr. Schroeder?"

"Shore do. Look at these," he said producing some photos. The judge looked at them carefully.

"Where did you obtain these pictures, Mr. Roadapple?"

"Taken right outside that queer's bedroom winda. That's the kinda stuff he does all the time. Had a friend of mine take 'em one night."

"Were you aware of the existence of these photos, Mr. Schroeder?" Judge Thompson asked as he had the bailiff show Hal the pictures. Hal's face went white, and then red as the enormity of how his and Simon's privacy had been violated by this bigot. He composed himself and handed the photos back to the bailiff.

"No, Your Honor. I was unaware of them until this moment, and I would ask the court to have all copies and negatives surrendered."

"That will be ordered, Mr. Schroeder. Now, Mr. Roadapple, are you asserting that the other man in these pictures is your son, Barry?"

"First off, Barry ain't my son. Me and his ma got married two years ago and I sorta adopted the kids when I moved in."

"Yes, I know, Mr. Roadapple. That's why his last name isn't the same as yours. But you didn't answer my question. Do you think that this other man in the photos is Barry?"

"Wal, no. Ol' Willy couldn't git a picture of him and Barry, but don't them pictures prove to ya what kindova queer he is? That's the kind that's got Barry in school."

"Mr. Roadapple, do you know that it is illegal to photograph another person without their permission? And do you also know that it is a violation of the right to privacy to take photographs of a person's home without their permission?"

"Wal, no, but whut difference does that make? It's what's on them pictures that counts."

Judge Thompson turned to Barry. "Barry, you've been sworn to tell the truth here. I now want to ask you, has Mr. Schroeder in any way made any sexual advances toward you?

"No, sir."

"Has he at any time made any suggestions of a sexual nature to you?"

"No, sir."

"Has he ever invited you to his home?"

"No, sir. But I stayed in the cottage in the back of their house once. He didn't know about it. He didn't invite me, honest. He was pretty upset when he knew I'd been there that night."

"What did Mr. Schroeder tell you after that, Barry?"

"He said that he understood why I wasn't staying at home. I'd shown him the belt marks on my back, and he knew that Cal there was beating me. But he told me I couldn't stay at his place. It would look bad, make people think the wrong thing."

"What did you do then, Barry?"

"I went back home and sneaked around, just keeping out of Cal's way."

"Thank you, Barry, that's all for now. I want to show you some legally obtained photographs, Mr. Roadapple," the judge said, opening a manila folder. "These were taken of Barry by the police five days ago. I want you to tell me how Barry got these welts on his body."

"Shore I'll tell ya. Just like he said, I walloped him with a belt onct he tole his ma and me that he was a queer. Just gave him a good one all over. Teach him a lesson. Beat that queer crap out of him."

The judge sat back in his chair. "Bailiff, take Mr. Roadapple into custody.

Mrs. Roadapple, do you have other children at home?"

"Yes, Your Honor. Two girls. But they aren't in this."

"I will want to know if there has been any similar abuse perpetrated on your daughters. A case worker will be interviewing you very soon."

"Wait just a gall-durn minute here," Mr. Roadapple yelled as he was being handcuffed. "What kinda deal is this? You gonna arrest me for giving my kid a whooping that he needed?"

"Whether he needed it or not in your estimation is beside the point, Mr. Roadapple. You are under arrest for child abuse, endangering a minor, and assault. I am dismissing your complaint against Mr. Schroeder on the grounds of insufficient evidence. Further, it is ordered that all photographs and their negatives taken of Mr. Schroeder be surrendered to this court by tomorrow at 3:00 PM. Mr. Schroeder may want to press charges against you for invasion of his privacy, but that is up to him. I am further ordering that Barry be taken out of your home forthwith and placed with Child Protective Services until he becomes of age which I understand will be within a month. We're adjourned."

Another, almost hidden figure had also been admitted to the courtroom. "Judge, I'd like to say something if I could before we adjourn." Hal looked over and recognized Sid of Sid and Leonard. "I'm Barry's uncle, his mother's brother although I'm the last person she wants to recognize as such since she married Roadapple here and bought into his so-called religion. Barry needs a home for a while and I'd like to volunteer ours. He doesn't want to go into a foster home, and we can provide him a place to stay until he's an adult and wants to leave."

"We will want to investigate that possibility, Mr. . . ."

"Siddons, Your Honor."

"Mr. Siddons. It's always better to place a minor with another relative if that's feasible. As this must be decided right away, I want to meet with you and a representative from Child Protective Services in say, half an hour back here in my chambers. Right now I want to talk with Barry." With that the judge left and Barry was shown into his chambers.

Hal watched Barry's mother slump out of the courtroom, bereft of the arrogant sneer with which she had arrived. Mr. Roadapple was led off to jail; Mrs. Roadapple made her way with her head bowed toward the chamber doors. OK, he'd won, Hal had. Exonerated, but he figured that cases like this do not simply evaporate, particularly in these days and times when the likes of Senator Briggs was out to 'cleanse' the state education system of all homosexual teachers. He nevertheless felt better than he had in days, ready to face whatever else the powers of hatred might manufacture to hurl against him and others like him.

He stuck around to say something to Sid. He hadn't talked with either him or Leonard since that drunken weekend in Palm Springs when he and Simon had been invited to stay in their trailer.

"Pretty good of you to do that, Sid," Hal said. "I had no idea."

"Well, I did. I knew that you were Barry's teacher. He started coming around more lately, mostly hiding out from his step-dad, that bastard. What I didn't know was that he was sneaking into your cottage and sleeping over, not until recently, that is."

"He's got a lot to tell you about that night I caught him. We ought to have drinks at our house soon and get all of this ironed out. How's Leonard?"

"Fine, as far as I know. It's hard to pry him loose from Palm Springs, even these days as the temperature out there is hitting the high 90s. You guys didn't have a very good time out there, I think."

"We're just not that used to drinking all day," Hal said. "I noticed that you ducked out a time or two yourself."

"It's the only way to survive that crowd. Most of them never notice when I leave. Maybe you guys will come out again some time. I can guarantee you that you'll have a better time."

"Thanks. But what about Barry? Think he'll agree to stay with you?"

"I know he will. And his mother won't say anything about it either. She wasn't always the way she is nowadays, just since she married that redneck Roadapple. Well, it's time for me to meet with the judge. I'll let you know what happens. Say hello to Simon for me." "Will do," Hal said, shaking Sid's hand.

John McHenry had been waiting to talk to Hal too. "We won, Hal. No more complaints from that bunch. We can go back to business as usual."

"Can we? This is just starting, John. This Briggs Initiative menace is the next thing. We're raising money for the campaign to fight it."

"Maybe you haven't heard the latest. You've got an unexpected ally who came out against the proposition, and he's a very powerful ally, someone you probably would never expect to be on our side."

"We can certainly use all the friends we can get. Want to tell me?" "None other than Jimmy Carter."

*****

*Another unnoticed figure had slipped out of the courtroom just as the judge had rendered his decision. So he got away with his faggy stuff this time. Doesn't mean he's off the hook. We'll get that queer, one way or another, the figure thought to himself. Good thing Willy's not around to get into trouble. The queer could get him for taking those pictures. Gotta do something else to make this work.*

# CHAPTER 30
## *In Vino Veritas*

"I'm telling you that I never in my life heard such creepy moaning and groaning. And then that awful scream! That's when I hightailed it out of that back yard."

"But Dorothy, that was your big chance to actually see them again. Why didn't you stay for at least a peek?" Cynthia asked. The usual martini afternoon had been expanded to include two more of the local ladies who attended either out of curiosity or skepticism or just for the martinis. Dorothy had promised sandwiches too. Sitting in rapt attention to Dorothy's tale of her latest ghostly encounter were Ethel Declamber, Hazel McKenna, and Cynthia. The sandwiches had almost been dispatched, and a new pitcher of martinis made the rounds of empty glasses.

The ladies were arrayed around Dorothy's garden, ensconced on comfortably padded chairs, martini glasses close at hand.

"When I heard that door creaking open, I wasn't about to stick around. Who knows what they would have done to me if they had seen me there? No siree-bob. I just got right out and headed home. Pass that pitcher over to Ethel, will you Cynthia?"

"It's odd, isn't it? Have Hal or Simon mentioned anything about hearing the ghosts?" Ethel asked as her martini glass was refilled. "I mean, they live there. Surely they must have heard something if there was really anything to hear." Ethel was naturally a skeptic, a pragmatic woman who had learned late in life not to trust much of anything. Her disappointing affair, if that's what it could be called, with that bounder Gaston Plimpton a few years back had left her permanently scarred, with a mind that was not easily swayed by anything so highly dubious as a ghost sighting. "What I mean is, couldn't they have simply been having guests over?"

"Guests that move candles back and forth in the windows? Guests that moan and groan like souls in agony? No, guests would have turned on the lights for one thing. Oh it was the dead come to visit where they had died, no doubt about it."

"Have you told Hal or Simon about what you heard?" Hazel asked. "They would certainly want to know, I'm sure."

No, Dorothy had not told them for the simple reason that she didn't want them to know that she sat up in their back yard at night. They might think that she was spying on them; besides, she was a bit embarrassed by her obsession about the ghosts except among her friends, and regarded her activities among the dead as pretty much her own business. But of course she could not resist telling a good story to the girls, particularly when the story was so well oiled by hefty supplies of gin martinis. "I'm not so sure they want to know. I told them when I started working for them that there were ghosts in the cottage, but even as they nodded at me, I could see they didn't believe it. I'll let them find out for themselves. They will, believe me, they will."

"Well, it certainly is strange, Dorothy. But Hazel," Ethel said changing the subject, "are you singing in anything at the moment?" She knew full well that Hazel was not singing anywhere except in the alto section of St Mary's Episcopal Church choir. Hazel's last appearance on stage had been in the ill-fated opera that Ethel had subsidized, *The Plains of Windy Troy* that had brought Bertrand Lebland to fame.

"Oh dear me, no," Hazel said. "Not since Gaston's opera." Like everyone else in town, she knew that Ethel had not only paid for the opera, but had also paid for its composer who had summarily been found out to have other sexual interests. Knowing Ethel's nefarious intent in asking about her singing, she could not resist hurling a few things back. "What a lovely man he was, that Gaston. Oh I know he had his faults, but which of us doesn't? We had such lovely tête-à-têtes over my role as Aphrodite. He was such a good influence on my instrument."

The gin was working wonders on Ethel's sharpening tongue. "Your instrument? Is that what you call it? If you mean that hoarse croak that you call a voice, I'd say it needed some influence. What exactly did that bastard do for you, Hazel?"

"Oh dear, I seem to have stuck a nerve," Hazel said smiling. "What did he do for me? He massaged my throat for one thing. Ah, he made me feel young again, as if I were really the goddess of love. More than that I will not tell."

"Well, if he went any further south than your throat, he must have discovered that you've got more under that ugly dress than the rest of us have if that's what you're hinting went on. I caught him in bed with my pool boy, my dear, and if you think that we're ready to believe that he was having it on with an old trout like you, then we're also ready to believe in Dorothy's ghosts," Ethel spat back.

"Now just a minute," Dorothy said. "What do you mean making a crack like that? You're just a disappointed old lady who got taken to the cleaners, Ethel. Just because Plimpton didn't want to climb into bed with you is no reason to take it out on us."

"Now girls, girls! Let's not get bitchy. She didn't mean that, Hazel. Did you, Ethel? Let's have another drink and drop this silly fight," Cynthia said coming around with the pitcher.

"Not get bitchy? Ha! She's just jealous because Gaston paid more attention to me than he did to her even though she was putting him up and paying his bills. So he never did get around to seeing what was under *your* skirts, did he?" Hazel was on a roll, and her long dormant feelings about the pretentious Ethel bubbled to the surface aided by the gin. "And when he moved to the hotel, there you were, parked out front at all hours, and reliable sources saw you sitting down the hall outside his door, mooning for what you never got. What did you hear behind closed doors? The same kind of moaning and groaning that Dorothy heard the other night?"

Suddenly a light bulb came on. "But that's it! That's exactly what Dorothy must have heard. Two people having sex in the guest cottage. Did either voice sound like a woman's voice?" Ethel asked.

"Aha! So you did hear what was going on in Gaston's hotel room, huh? You pathetic old hen. Bet you really got an ear full," Hazel was relishing this.

It took Dorothy a minute or two to think about what she actually did hear, the martinis helping to keep things a bit foggy in her memory. "I can't say. But who knows what kinds of voices ghosts might have after being dead for so long?"

"And that shout at the end. Climax, probably. Pooh! All that business about moving candles. Whoever they were wanted to keep the lights out so nobody in the main house would notice them, that's what that was about."

"But who? Hal and Simon weren't home at all. I know that for a fact. No, you won't convince me that what I heard was anything but the two dead ones come back to haunt us," Dorothy concluded, sinking once more into the lassitude provided by the gin, and unwilling to give up her stories.

"Oh pooh!" Ethel said. She stood up and moved toward the table where the pitcher was, and on the way, spilled half a glass of her drink on the hapless Hazel. "Oh dear! Excuse me."

"You did that on purpose, you evil old bag," Hazel yelled, rising unsteadily to her feet. "I'll fix you, you pretentious sow." She lunged at Ethel who deftly moved aside as Hazel propelled herself into the shrubbery.

"Enough! Both of you, stop this! Acting like silly teenagers!" Cynthia said, keeping the two combatants apart. "Now sit back down and cool off."

"I wouldn't sit down with that one for all the martinis in town," Ethel said, gathering up her purse and walking unsteadily toward the garden gate. "I'm going home. Thank you for an entertaining afternoon, Dorothy. I hope that your ghosts come to visit you right here so you won't have so far to walk." And with that she managed to get to her car. A screech of tires a few minutes later, a slight crash, another screech and they heard her drive off.

"Well, she certainly can throw cold water on a good party," Dorothy said, reaching for the nearly empty pitcher. "We should make some more of these. Sit down, Hazel. Have another. Did I ever tell you how the ghosts got to be there in the first place?"

More groaning, this time not from ghosts. Glasses were refilled from the replenished pitcher.

Yes, Dorothy had told them. Many, many times.

# CHAPTER 31
## *Gaudeamus Igitur*

High school graduation ceremonies required the diligence of every faculty member, all of whom were obliged to attend, along with more than a few uniformed police, and a number of undercover cops scattered among the crowd of spectators, all in an effort to forestall shenanigans and improper tricks that the graduating seniors thought would be fun to add to the program of dull speeches, marching band numbers, and diploma presentations. The participating seniors were lined up and herded through an inspection team comprised of school officials and teachers who searched under graduation gowns for illegal items such as water balloons, noise makers, fireworks, cans of beer, and of course marijuana. Clothing was scrutinized. No nude graduates covered merely by a gown allowed.

Despite these draconian measures, the spirit of the day was one of joy and celebration, the causes for elation depending on each grad's experience in high school. Some saw the day as the culmination of their efforts to get into college and university; others regarded graduation as a final fling to celebrate no more school. Still others plotted ways to thwart the efforts of the administration to preserve the day as one of dignity and decorum by figuring out where firecrackers could be hidden and set off at what they considered would be particularly appropriate times. Parents and relatives joined the ceremonies with visions of sugarplums dancing in their heads that took the more pragmatic hope of their beloved offspring finally leaving the nest.

Barry viewed the day differently, and felt he had some unique events to celebrate. He had turned eighteen one week before, was out of his parents' house and living with his Uncle Sid in Laguna, had found Miguel whom he adored, and finally would have a diploma. Life looked good to him as he made his way through the inspection line and onto the staging area where his classmates waited in strict alphabetical order. Once seated, he turned to scan the grandstands where a wild and cheering horde of parents made more noise than the seniors did. He looked around for Hal Schroeder, and saw his face among the faculty. He's a friend, Barry thought, and I love him like that. He realized that his affection for Hal had been born from his need to be loved, and he also realized to what extent he had jeopardized his teacher's career. He was sorry, but now that things had turned out so well, he was sure that Hal would forgive him.

He scanned the crowd and there, right there in the middle he saw the handsome brown face he'd been searching for. Miguel, despite the distance, saw him looking and beamed back at him. That was all Barry needed. He searched no further. None of the Roadapples had bothered to attend; Barry figured they wouldn't, and so he didn't bother trying to find them in the throng of parents.

The school band struck up a Sousa march to entertain everyone until the actual ceremonies would begin, but succeeded instead in becoming a third group that made a lot of noise, combining their oompahs and trumpet blasts with the roar from the spectators and the ongoing screams and shrieks provided by the senior class. Isolated by his own thoughts from the din, Barry sat quietly. What would he do? He'd have to find a job. He needed a car. How long could he stay at Uncle Sid's? Should he try to get into college? Could he pay for it? His grades weren't the best; in fact, he had just barely passed everything he needed in order to graduate. He felt slightly scared. Who would take care of him? Did he want anyone to take care of him? What would happen with him and Miguel? One thing rose as a certainty in his mind; he would never go back to live with the Roadapples, no matter what.

The graduation ceremony moved quickly forward, the National Anthem signaling that things were beginning, bringing everyone to their feet. Loud cheers and whistles accompanied its conclusion, carefully timed and cropped speeches began, the principal's speech delivered, some boring school board member rose in self-importance to the podium, the diplomas began to be given out, and with a great sigh of relief from the administration, another graduation concluded, this one without serious incident. The vice-principal gathered up several trash bags full of contraband seized from beneath graduation gowns, and wearily plodded toward the main building.

Barry turned in his cap and gown, said goodbye to a few friends, and went in search of Miguel. He would not be staying for 'Grad Night Las

Vegas', a huge, all-night party set up in tents on campus and given by parents where the grads could have a night of fun without getting into trouble with the police. No alcohol—well, hardly any—no drugs—well, hardly any—just good clean American fun replete with gambling on what was considered a safe scale. Barry had other plans that put fake Las Vegas in the shade.

A hand came out of the departing crowd and touched his shoulder. Miguel propelled him to his car, drove them off the school grounds, made a turn into a residential area, turned off the motor, took Barry in his arms, and kissed him. Things would have got hot and heavy right there had not a neighbor walked by. The boys quickly parted, and Miguel started his car. They could wait until they got home. They thought they could, anyway. Barry looked over at the handsome Miguel and figured that he couldn't have had a more perfect graduation day.

* * * *

"You see what one queer teacher can do? There's that Barry, up and admitted to his folks that he's an out-and-out fag. They told everybody at church what he said to them. Don't tell me that the older ones don't recruit the young guys. Now he's living over in Fagtown too, with that fag uncle of his. Well, this Briggs thing on the ballot will fix a lot of the trouble. It'll pass too, Willy, you can bet on that. Lots of us around who hate the whole bunch of them."

"Listen Dick, I'm getting tired of this. I got more to do than trail around, trying to take pictures of these guys. Who the hell cares anyway? I don't, not anymore. I'm done. Find yourself another photographer to sit around and wait. I haven't been paid for those last pictures."

"Willy, you can't leave now. Who would I get to do this? Besides, if Hal the fag ever figures out who took those pictures through his bedroom window, you're in big trouble."

"You mean you'd tell him if I quit? Why, you asshole. I thought we were friends. How about all those camping trips we took together? Remember that night we had to sleep in the same . . ."

"You said you'd never mention that again! It was a mistake, that's all. Just because two guys beat off together doesn't mean anything."

"Doesn't mean anything, huh? If that's all we did, it probably wouldn't, but that's not all we did and you know it. You've been pissed off about it ever since. That's when you started this hate campaign, wasn't it?"

"Hey, we were pretty drunk that night. I don't remember anything else."

"Well, I do. I remember waking up with you sitting on top of me and my dick up your ass, that's what I remember. How'd that get there, I wonder? Drunk my ass."

"That's a lie and you know it! We never did any such thing! Me on top of you?"

"Yeah, and me inside you until I came and you came. Some jack-off session, huh?"

"Didn't mean anything. Think you're queer just because of that? Think I am? Well, I'm not. I hate those bastards and everything they do. So quit if you want to, go ahead. In fact, I wish you would. Don't want you around bringing up drunken nights to fling in my face anyway. You can fuck off, Willy. Just drive me home. And don't call me, you hear?"

"Me call you? Ha! You're the one who'll be calling me, next time you want what I got here, ready to go right up there where you got that itchy, empty feeling. Want to give it a goodbye ride? Here, I got it out for you. Here it is, sweetheart, right here, big and hard and ready for you. Yeah, you know you want it. Ahhhh . . . right, that's right. Put your other hand on my big thick cock, Dickie, yeah, both hands. Mmm . . . yeah, feel my balls. Yeah you like it, don't you Dickie? You know it's all yours. Easy, easy man. I'm ready to pop. There's only one place I want to come, and you know where that is. Now get in the back seat."

# CHAPTER 32

# *The Kindness of Strangers*

"Of course, it's not the work, you know that. It's just that I'm not sure about a party right away. Especially one that combines what you seem to think are victories and milestones," Hal said.

"You're just being sheepish," Simon replied. "You won in court, didn't you? You're off the hook with those awful people. Besides, if it weren't for you, Barry would have had to stay with them instead of getting out from under their hatred. And nobody celebrated his birthday, Hal. He's a man now, and we ought to validate that. Come on, he needs to know that he has friends."

"Oh, I wouldn't say that nobody celebrated his birthday. I suspect that he and Miguel did all right. Any more positive reasons up your sleeve for having this shindig right away?"

"Plenty, but I'm saving them for your next wet blanket attack."

"OK, OK, you won't need to get out the big guns. You win. You know I can never say no to you anyway. Let's have a look at the calendar. Hey, why don't we have a Fourth of July party? That's only a couple of weeks away, and we can combine a lot of things at once."

"I can think of about four things right off the bat. Barry's birthday and graduation, Bertrand's play opening on June 28th, we can celebrate the end of school and beginning of summer, and the outcome of your court appearance. A real Independence Day. It'll be perfect. Now for the guest list," Simon said triumphantly.

The two or three weeks between the making of these plans and the party itself gave Hal and Simon some much needed relaxation and time merely to enjoy living quietly. The summer had brought on a welcome lull in the anxious days before school closed. Now the mild days in the coastal town seemed to yawn lazily, stretching themselves into languid evenings that held the delicious prospect of easy dinners and good times with friends.

The next week saw the opening of *A Streetcar Named Desire* to which Hal and Simon had front row seats. "We'll be seeing more of Bertrand on stage tonight than we have around the neighborhood lately. George says he's been entirely focused on the play, hardly sees him either—at least not anywhere but in bed—and reports that he had no idea what a perfectionist Bertrand is. Where is George, I wonder. Probably backstage with the star himself," Simon said.

Tim Calloway had finally managed to get his vision of Williams' play onto the stage, generally ignoring Bertrand's frequent suggestions during early rehearsals. Tim had been determined to revive the play but not in a way that merely aped the famous film with Vivian Leigh and Marlon Brando. He well understood that comparisons would invariably be made, but he also had strong ideas about how his players could come to their own unique style of portraying the famous roles. It worked beautifully. Brett Harrison, who played Stanley Kowalski, not only had muscles, he also had acting talent. In the scene between him and Blanche, he portrayed another side of Stanley, showing just the edge of compassion for his ill-fated sisterin-law, a character trait that even Brando either chose not to display, or didn't find to be a part of the Stanley he wanted to reveal. Brett didn't overdo the compassion angle, but gave a glimpse of it, betraying a more human side of the normally predictable character of the tough Pole. It brought the audience to a deeper sense of the tragedy that unfolded before it, and some of its members openly wept.

It was a chastened and very different Bertrand portraying Mitch on opening night, a much changed Bertrand from the obnoxious martinet who had made a nuisance of himself at the beginning of the play's rehearsals. The transformed Bertrand, still a bit mystified by his beach experience that fateful night, proved himself to be a true showman and consummate actor. He played the smitten Mitch Mitchell with grace and appropriate ardor, and was equal to the portrayal of disappointment and anger that ensues when he learns of Blanche's shady past. He neither upstaged anyone nor tried to steal any of the scenes in which he appeared.

Six curtain calls for the entire cast, finally two for Stanley and Blanche who took the stage for a last bow. In the wings stood George, waiting for Bertrand and beaming as if he were Gypsy Rose Lee's mother on her opening night. When Bertrand walked off stage from the last curtain call, George hugged him and kissed him squarely on the mouth. He didn't care who was watching. No one seemed particularly surprised except for Bertrand who at first bristled at the open display of such affection, but then wrapped his arms around George and kissed him back. There was another round of applause from the cast and crew backstage for this unexpected performance.

"You were the best, Bertrand. I'm so proud of you that, that, well, I don't know what to say. This is going to get you a lot of work, you know that don't you? There were important people in the audience tonight, people in show business, people who produce other plays."

"I heard that the LA Times reviewer was going to be here. I wonder what he thought. Guess we'll find out in the paper soon enough. Let's go find Hal and Simon. Time for drinks at our house. Some of the cast will be coming over too," Bertrand said, breathing in the thrill of having made a good performance. "I'll meet you out front after I get changed and get this makeup off of me, OK?

As he sat for a moment in front of his dressing room mirror, he saw a new person staring back at him. In the past, he would have taken a critical inventory of incoming wrinkles or blemishes, but the reflected face he saw wore the look of calm confident happiness. That night on the beach when his life changed provided him with a reservoir of peace, and the ongoing contentment that his life was finally moving in a more than satisfying way. He didn't need to grandstand any longer; that's what he'd done at The Blue Cove all those years, ruining his voice for the drunks who hung out there, accepting their hollow praise as genuine, eagerly soaking up their attention.

Looking at him was the face of a man who knew for a fact that he had real talent, had indisputable ability as an actor, and with that realization came a kind of humility. He thought of George for a moment. It was undeniable that his talent lay within himself, but he could not discount the fact that George's faith in him had in many ways lit that spark.

He hastily finished cleaning up and changing, and was about to leave to find George when Brett Harrison came into the dressing room. "Hey Brett.

Don't you feel great? It was a powerful performance tonight. Brando couldn't have done better."

Brett said nothing as he walked over to Bertrand, his powerful arms pulling him up out of his chair. His strong embrace took Bertrand's breath away as Brett gave him the second kiss he had that night, fully on the mouth.

"I guess you liked my performance too, huh?" Again, nothing from Brett as he peeled off his t-shirt and enclosing Bertrand again in his muscular arms. Bertrand reached around Brett and felt his powerful back muscles, beautifully formed and descending to a perfect V-shape at Brett's belt. Brett loosened his belt and Bertrand felt his hands moving down over the two flawless orbs inside Brett's underwear. Then Brett's pants and briefs fell away and he stood before the astonished Bertrand, entirely naked.

Brett began to unbutton Bertrand's shirt, kissing his neck and face as he exposed Bertrand's chest. "Wait, wait! Brett, we have to stop. People are waiting for me outside. George is waiting!"

"Let 'em wait. I've been waiting for you too. A long time, every rehearsal, every scene. You want this and I want this." Brett went back to kissing Bertrand's neck.

"What about Linda? I thought you two were an item, getting married and everything?"

"She's nothing to me. You're everything to me. We are going places, you know that? You and me, Los Angeles where they really do theater. You and me," he said. He buried his face in Bertrand's chest.

# CHAPTER 33
# Pageantry and High Art

Even in a climate like Southern California's, which many who do not live there wrongly believe to be one of eternal summer, the advent of July brings about a general change in attitude and perspective as far as day-to-day living is concerned. Perhaps the cessation of school terms leads the mind set of the local population into a more languid and relaxed mode of living. Whatever it is that changes things is up for conjecture, but there is a noticeable movement toward taking things easier that pervades coastal towns like Laguna Beach.

The reality is that the town is hardly ever busier. The annual Pageant of the Masters begins, and crowds of tourists throng to its portrayals of *tableaux vivants*.

This particular year saw the Pageant committee hire a new director whom they thought might inject more life, so to speak, into what had become to many the same old thing, year after year. Mr. Armand Debustier arrived from New York to take charge, and take charge he did. First of all, he revamped the program and reinstated the actual name of what was being done on stage, and in the original French. For reasons no one could remember, the words *tableaux vivants* had been avoided in advertisements for the annual show, but Armand insisted that programs and everything pertaining to the Pageant of the Masters include them.

By March of that year as in all years past, the program had been decided on, the paintings to be portrayed chosen, and a general call to the townspeople published in search of participants. There was no dearth of hopefuls who swarmed the Pageant stage that spring day. A certain nervousness swept the crowd, punctuated by desultory conversations. "It was probably omitted because the publicity people couldn't spell it, that French stuff I mean," said Hazel McKenna who had lined up along with the other townspeople who had for years been assigned parts in various of the *tableaux*. "I for one, think it gives the Pageant some class."

"It could use some class. It's become a source of ridicule among people who think they know about art. Some smart-ass critics only come to see it to laugh at it," Ed Benson said. He had for many years been cast as Jesus in the recreation of Leonardo da Vinci's *Last Supper*, and he fully expected to be seated in the middle of the holy table once again this year. "I don't know what there is to laugh at. Every scene is always put together with great accuracy and care. Some people just don't know when they are in the presence of great art."

If anybody looked like what most people think Jesus looked like, it was Ed Benson. One year when the Pageant had portrayed a 19th century painting called *Behold I Stand At the Door and Knock*, Ed was given that role as Jesus as well. Had he decided to wear the robes and sandals usually associated with Jesus of Nazareth around town, he doubtless could have attracted a following of disciples. Yes, he had every expectation of being appointed to his annual role as the Savior of the world, sitting among the twelve and instituting that most central rite of the Christian faith. Just the thought of being Jesus elevated his mind to higher spiritual climes, and he waited with the other try-outs with the assurance that he was born for the part.

He was not chosen, nor was Hazel McKenna for whom no role in any of the selected *tableaux* could be found. Instead of Ed Benson, a much younger man received the role of Jesus, a man whom no one knew, an out-of-towner. Ed's disappointment quickly moved to anger as he ruminated over all the reasons why he should have been retained for the role he had so long portrayed. "That's what comes of hiring outsiders," he fumed. "Who does this new director think he is? The Pageant was always put on by the people of Laguna, not by people dragged in from God knows where. He's ruining the Pageant this way. The spirit of the whole thing is gone."

"I could very easily have been portrayed in that Vermeer painting," Hazel said. They were now drinking scotch at a nearby bar and trying to heal their wounds. "Too old is what he meant when he said 'We'll need a fresh face, Mrs. McKenna. Sorry!' Bull. That girl he got instead doesn't look anything like what Vermeer painted. I even have the pearl earring." A second round of double scotches arrived, and as the afternoon drew on into the evening, Hazel emerged unsteadily from the bar somewhat mollified and resigned to her being left out of this year's cast, but Ed was anything but pacific about his fate. He wasn't sure what he would or could do about it, but he was far from letting the whole thing drop. He ordered another scotch and mulled it over.

But now it was July and the Pageant of the Masters' opening night had sold out as it always did. The show went flawlessly, accompanied by orchestra and the stentorian tones of an announcer who for years had been the voice of Tony the Tiger for a cereal advertisement on TV. As each *tableau* was viewed for five minutes or so by the ooing and awing audience, the next *tableau* was being set up on the back side of the revolving stage. A curtain descended before the stage revolved; the curtain then rose, revealing the next scene. Tradition dictated that the last scene of all would be *The Last Supper,* always the highlight and most admired of all the *tableaux*.

The stage manager who got everyone on and off the various sets was about to mount the table around which were ranged the twelve disciples with Jesus in the middle. The cast dutifully awaited his cue which he announced: "Jesus, party of thirteen, your table's ready." It's an old joke now, but at the time created chuckles among the holy band, and the quip particularly affected Jesus himself whose tittering moved on to giggling as he took his place at the center of Leonardo's table. He couldn't stop. He tried to stop, but the more he tried, the funnier it seemed, and the more he giggled. Suddenly the stage was revolving into its place to face the audience. He was still giggling, trying desperately to contain himself. The curtain rose to expose the scene, and Jesus broke out in a great gaffaw. There he was with the head of the beloved disciple on his chest, roaring with laughter.

There were those among the audience who joined right in; in fact, quite a few of them did. The solemnity and reverence that the scene was supposed to produce were replaced by out-and-out hilarity, and even a few of the disciples found themselves caught up in the unexpected conviviality of the supper.

Armand was furious, and ordered the curtain brought down early. The audience began to clap, and Armand was unsure whether or not he should walk on stage to acknowledge their applause. Would they know that the whole thing had gone horribly wrong, or would they think that's the way he had planned it? He decided that he would have to face whatever they thought and walked out on stage to a mixture of hearty applause from parts of the audience, and hefty booing from another sector who felt that some sort of sacrilege had been performed before their very eyes.

The hilarity that swept through the audience, enjoying a lightened view of Jesus, also infected the cast while simultaneously re-igniting a theological argument that had captivated the best minds of the medieval church for over 1000 years: namely, Did Jesus laugh? The Pageant dressing room divided into proponents of the possibility that Jesus must have laughed, and those opposed to such an idea.

Proponents who had even a modicum of biblical knowledge admitted that the Gospels were silent on the issue; nevertheless, they advanced the fact that as Jesus was truly human, he must have laughed at some time. After all what human doesn't? They cited instances when he very well might have been induced to laugh—the marriage at Cana was exampled—as well as numerous other times when he must have felt great joy over curing lepers and restoring sight to the blind. Scripture tells us that Jesus wept; therefore, if he displayed that emotion, he could easily have given vent to its opposite one.

The opposition to the idea of Jesus laughing rested its case on two evidentiary foundations. First the lack of scriptural testimony seemed solid enough in and of itself to provide a solid 'no'. Second, if Jesus did ever laugh, was he likely to have been all that merry at the dinner held on the eve of his execution? No, they thought not.

The debate rolled along until all of the *Last Supper* cast had changed out of their costumes, stowed their wigs and beards, and removed their makeup. None of the debate mattered in the least to Armand.

Armand hadn't stayed long on stage. He marched to the dressing room, listened to what he considered a ridiculous discussion, and summarily fired Jesus on the spot, an eventuality that ended his earlier levity. The stage manager barely escaped the same fate, but got off with a warning about promoting inappropriate humor on pain of dismissal.

The next day, Ed Benson was summoned to meet with the director who graciously asked him if there was any chance that he might assume the role of Jesus for the rest of the season. "No, not for only one season, Armand," Ed replied. "I would want your assurance that the role is mine for at least the next five years, and I want it in writing." He got it, and the Pageant's *Last Supper* was served up henceforth with the veneration and respect that Leonardo da Vinci's masterpiece deserved.

*Lagunatics*

Down the street from the festival grounds, Denise Lebouche was raking in the cash at Le Bleu each night from two full seatings of diners who were either headed for the Pageant or had just come from it. She had taken Roger's advice and hired Paul, a capable head waiter and manager, a man whom she still resented paying the salary that Roger also came up with. She had to admit that everything was running well at the restaurant and bar, and that her stock of cash in the bank was satisfactorily growing. What did she need with Eric and his boyfriend? She was doing quite well without either of them, and despite a few times when she felt very much alone in her gloomy house, she generally was aware that everything had turned out in her favor. Even the increase in her rent for the restaurant was forgotten at the end of each night when the waiters' accounting made her ever richer.

During the run of *A Streetcar Named Desire*, she noticed on the reservation list the name of Bertrand Lebland, party of two, for 7:30, Wednesday evening, that very night. Although she never attended plays or concerts, she was very much up to date about people who performed in them, and considering herself a part of the upper echelons of celebrity as a famous restaurateur, she was always happy to rub elbows with those she deemed to be top drawer.

Bertrand arrived with his co-star Brett, and with much cooing and deference, the ebullient Denise ushered them to a table. "Ah Monsieur Lebland, Ay ave not had time in zees busy season to see your play, but Ay ear zat eet ees a great success." As she had not really heard of Brett Harrison who had somehow escaped her notice as she combed the review of performances, she ignored him. As soon as Bertrand and Brett were seated, two champagne cocktails arrived, followed by Denise who announced that they were 'compliments of the house'. Then she stayed, beaming at her illustrious customer who wished nothing more than that she should go away.

"This is Brett Harrison, Mrs. Lebouche. He's also in the play and really one of the two major stars in the production." Denise turned what passed for a pleasant look in Brett's direction, now understanding that he too was a celebrity although he looked to her more like some kind of a thug. He extended a hand to her.

"Ay am so glad you come to Le Bleu tonight," she said. Then she stood there, seemingly awaiting some sort of rejoinder or conversational continuation.

"Thank you. We came to have dinner and discuss some business," Bertrand said, hoping that she would take the hint and go away. She didn't.

"Ah, zee business is all Ay ever talk about. Eet ees always interesting to see ow tings will go zees days. Ay tink eet ees different for zee play," and she rattled on and on. Bertrand fully expected that at any moment she would be pulling up a chair and joining them. Finally, something in the kitchen required her attention and Paul came to get her.

"Whew! Maybe she won't come back for a while," Brett said. "We should have just gone to Denny's."

"Yeah, but Eliot Drake isn't likely to show up at Denny's. He's in the bar. Did you see him as we came in?"

"Yep, and he saw us too. What luck, Bertrand! Eliot Drake in our audience for the best performance we gave. He's only the most successful producer in Hollywood today, and to think that he wants to talk to us! God, this is just the best!"

Eliot Drake's appearance at their table occasioned a reentry of the redoubtable Denise who had no idea who Eliot Drake was, but her unerring instinct told her that he was somebody famous. Over she came. "Oooo and will this gentleman be joining you, Mr. Lebland?" The gentleman would, another place setting was produced, and a glass of champagne was poured for him. "Ay ope you weel enjoy zees leetle token of my pleasure zat you ave come to dine at my umble restaurant," she gushed as she refilled the other two flutes with Schramsberg Blanc de Noir. Then as she had before, she stood there as if she were one of the party. When conversation did not resume and a none too subtle silence fell on the table, even Denise got the hint and finally withdrew.

"She's either eccentric or just has bad taste," Eliot said once Denise was out of earshot. "I haven't seen a get-up like that since that ungodly Egyptian epic that starred Joan Collins. Even the busty Joan couldn't make up for those costumes. Who is she anyway? The owner, I take it?"

"Very much the owner as well as supreme ruler. My neighbor once worked for her right here, and his stories are many and hilarious, not only about her wardrobe—he says she never wears the same thing twice—but also about how she runs this place. From what he's told me, we're indeed blessed to be getting free champagne from her, but then again, we haven't seen the final tab. Anyway, we can hope that she won't be back for a while."

Brett tried to control his anticipation of what Eliot Drake wanted to talk about; he tried not to fidget, not to look too eager. He spilled his champagne.

"Truth is, I don't have time for dinner tonight, must drive back to Los Angeles right away, but I wanted to tell you what the studio and I have in mind. I'll be sending you more details later." Brett was by now nearly peeing himself. This was exactly what he had dreamed of, had yearned for, had worked for with every word he spoke on a stage, and with every minute he spent at the gym and in front of a mirror. Finally, a top-name producer was offering him a role in Hollywood! "There is one requirement for this particular job," Drake said. "We would need both of you."

# CHAPTER 34
## Where the Heart Is

The Fourth of July fell on a Tuesday, and festivities were planned either for the weekend prior to the national holiday, or for some, the following weekend. The long-awaited party at Hal and Simon's on Myrtle Street was scheduled for Saturday, July 8 after a discussion that yielded the wisdom that more friends might be available then than on the previous weekend. Invitations went out and party preparations began.

Hal bustled around the kitchen for days beforehand, entirely in his element. All the cares and anxiety of the past weeks and months dissolved as he planned menus, wrote out shopping lists, and started the prep work. He hummed as he anticipated spending some days with his boys and their partners, all shared with Simon, and on Saturday, with many other friends. The house gleamed, the lawns and gardens had been tended, and it seemed to Hal as if the air itself sparkled and crackled with excitement. None of his almost palpable eagerness was lost on Edward.

Far from being skittish about large crowds as many cats are, Edward seemed to sense that there was something in the offing that he was going to enjoy. By Friday he hung around the front door more than usual, awaiting the arrival of what he perceived were members of his fan club. "He acts as if we ignore him and that he's starved for affection," Hal remarked as he watched Edward's frenetic behavior. "He carried on all morning until I had brushed him twice. He really is a queen."

"Can't think where he gets such notions, can you?" Simon laughed. "Hey, here come the boys. Two of them anyway." Parking their car and getting bags out of it were Tom and Mark.

"Hey! How was the drive up?" Simon called to them as they began to bring their gear up the sidewalk to the front porch.

"Hey yourself," Tom said, giving him a kiss. "Not bad at all. Except for packing the car. Mark's brought enough stuff for an African safari. What you see here is only the first load. Do we get the cottage? We'll need it." "Never mind him," Mark said also planting a kiss on Simon. "You won't be surprised to find out how much of this is his."

"God, you two really are a married couple, aren't you?" Hal said, hugging them both. "Yep, you've got the cottage if you want it. It's been cleared of ghosties and ghoulies, long-leggity beasties, and things that go bump in the night."

"You might have to put up with Edward, though," Simon said. "He's been waiting for you."

"Come here, you old ruffian," Tom said, scooping Edward up and cradling him upside down. "Nobody loves you here anymore, huh?" Edward launched into appreciative purring interspersed with cat talk. "When do you expect Mike and John?"

"Any time now. They're driving in too. It'll be just the six of us tonight for dinner, just the family," Hal said. "We have a lot to talk with you about. It's been quite a remarkable past few months. Go get yourself settled in and come back for drinks." The boys headed off for the cottage, followed by Edward.

"Don't they look great? Healthy and happy and together," Hal said, putting an arm around Simon. "Makes you feel like a proud parent, huh?" Before Simon could answer, a car horn announced the arrival of the other two, fresh in from San Jose. "Perfect! Let's go help them."

Mike and John got out of their car and stretched. It had been a long drive down to Laguna, and they had caught some afternoon stop-and-go traffic through Los Angeles. "I kept telling John that your cooking would be worth sitting on the I-5 and smelling fumes for a solid hour," Mike said, hugging Hal and kissing him. "So, Mommy, you'd better not let me down."

"Cooking? You think I've been cooking? You're looking at an old lady schoolmarm on vacation here, sonny. We've ordered pizzas," Hal teased.

"Yeah, right," Mike said, craning his neck to peer into the kitchen. "Hey, that's Tom's car out front. They're here already?"

"Yep, and got dibs on the cottage. Hope you don't mind the guest room."

"Well, I think we can get all the stuff that John packed into the car into the guest room. I was sort of counting on the cottage, though."

"Didn't we just hear this conversation about fifteen minutes ago," Simon asked. "Maybe we should have bought a bigger house." He grinned at the two handsome men who were unloading their bags in the front hall. "Let me help you guys in with these."

It felt like Christmas, but then family reunions always made Hal think of Christmas. His midwestern family had traditions that he remembered as a small boy, and the savor of them pervaded every occasion when Tom and Mike and their partners arrived for long weekends. "Hey, who all's coming on Saturday?" This from Tom who had returned from the cottage. "That's Mike's car out there! They're here!" He raced toward the guest room to find his former partner, a man whom he regarded as a brother. They emerged, arms wrapped around each other, laughing like idiots. "Look! He's getting thin on top. Now who would have ever predicted that back when we met up and lived on Shadow Lane? All that thick black hair that used to drive the girls, and not a few of the boys, nuts on the beach is going south."

"Yeah, well this blond mop doesn't quite look as full as it used to either," Tom said, giving Mike a knuckle rub. "And what's this? Chest hair? About time, I'd say," Tom said, pulling on a tuft that bushed up from Mike's tshirt. "Pretty sexy, huh?."

"Goes all the way down to the floor," Mark said, joining in the kidding contest. "Where's John?"

"Edward's got him outside. Come on out," Tom said. "Anything we can do in the kitchen?—I always ask, and there never is," he piped up so Hal could hear him.

Simon produced a tray of mimosas and led the procession out to the patio. "We've had some trouble with ghosts in the cottage, did Hal tell you?" he said.

"Yep, there was a high school ghost and his Mexican boyfriend ghost, or something like that. Wasn't that it?" Tom asked.

"Right. But we still don't know exactly who was getting in through the fence behind it. It's all been quiet for a few weeks, so I don't think you need to worry," Simon said. He smiled a bit wistfully.

"Maybe we don't need to worry about ghosts, but there's something else, isn't there?" John asked as he judged the look on Simon's face.

"It's this Briggs horror," Simon said. "It's not over with by a long shot. What do you hear in San Diego, Tom?"

"Most people I talk to think it's all crap, that it won't pass, and that it would start a witch hunt if it did. Besides, most Republicans I know are against it. But I think some people are still afraid. They certainly are in my school. Anything that threatens us like this is worrisome."

"Now, now kids. This is a weekend of parties and celebrations," Hal said, joining everyone on the patio. "No gloomy political stuff, OK?"

The six of them settled down to chatting and catching up. News about jobs and promotions. Tom and Mark were looking at a house to buy in San Diego. Mike and John thought they'd wait for a while until San Jose's downtown redevelopment was complete. Hal sank back into his chaise longue and listened to their banter with the satisfied air of a patriarch whose family members provided him with the perfectly ordinary but most welcome news that their lives were going well, that they were happy and prosperous, healthy and still in love with each other.

Hal carefully preserved the memories of what the boys liked to eat, and he cooked accordingly. Tonight would be steaks au poive, potatoes Anna, and apple pie.

Later at dinner Tom looked at Mike across the table. "He's done it again. Do you remember this dinner?"

"The same one we had on the night we decided to stay in Laguna together, isn't it?" He beamed at Hal.

"It was one of the happiest nights of my life," Hal said, "second only to one other night when I was too busy to cook anything."

"Oh we remember that night too, and I'd say that you and Simon were cooking pretty well from what we could hear though the doors," Mike said. "And you should have seen naked Simon tritzing through the hall the next morning, trying not to attract attention on his way to the bathroom. Remember that?"

"Yes indeed. We offered him a pillow to sit on at breakfast, as I recall," Tom grinned.

"All right you two, now leave Simon alone so his face can return to a normal shade," Hal kidded.

"I don't need the pillow anymore, you'll be happy to know," Simon volunteered. Gales of laughter just as the phone rang.

"I'll get it," Hal said, heading for the kitchen.

"Hello? Who's this? You'll have to speak up, I can't hear you," he said into the mouthpiece.

"Hal, I need your help. I didn't know who else I could call," the muted voice said. "It's Dick Palmer. Hal, I'm in jail in Santa Ana."

"Dick? I'm sorry you're in jail but why did you call me?"

"I . . . I . . . can't say right now. But if you could come bail me out. I'll pay you back right away. They won't let me pay the bail. Gotta be somebody else to do it. Please, Hal, I didn't have anybody else I could call."

"Well, I guess I could. Sort of having a family get-together right now though."

"Please Hal, I can't stay here another night. I've already been here one night and tomorrow is Saturday and I don't know if they'll let me out. Oh I don't know anything right now except I need your help. Please, please."

Hal thought for a minute. Why wouldn't Dick Palmer call one of his cronies from his church to get him out of jail? During that minute's hesitation, the plaintive voice began pleading again. "Hal, please. It won't take long and you'll be home again soon. My car's in Laguna. Please . . ." and the voice broke down into sobbing.

"OK, Dick, hang on. I'll come up. Just tell them I'll be there as soon as I can. How much is it?"

"$500," his voice croaked out. "They'll take a check, they said. Oh thank you Hal, thank you. Please come soon." And the line went dead.

Hal signaled to Simon to whom he related the phone call. "Want me to go with you?" Simon asked.

"Yes, if you wouldn't mind. There's something very strange about this and I don't want to be alone with Dick Palmer. The boys will be all right."

They explained their errand: "A man I work with is in jail, and we're going up to bail him out. Shouldn't take long." "In jail for what?" Tom asked.

"He didn't say, but he sounded pretty bad on the phone. Right now, you know as much as we do. Let's go, Doc." Hal grabbed his checkbook, and they were out the door and headed for Santa Ana.

"The good Samaritan, that's our mommy," Mike said as he heard Hal's car leave.

* * * *

"Public nudity and lewd behavior, that's what's on the arrest warrant," the desk sergeant told Hal and Simon as Hal wrote a check and signed the release papers for Richard Palmer. "He'll be down here in a few minutes, and he'll come right through that door. You can wait over there." They sat down and watched. The door had no bars on it but through its window, they could see another door across the next room that did. A smell, not exactly antiseptic and not otherwise identifiable pervaded the waiting room which had been painted a warm beige and given fairly comfortable chairs for visitors.

"Lewd behavior? Dick Palmer?" Hal said. "No wonder he didn't call up one of his church people to get him out. He's not about to let them know that he's been arrested for this kind of what they would denounce as sin."

"And his church is the same one that Barry's parents go to?"

"The very one. Chock full of haters, bigots, and judgmental jerks who are intolerant of everybody's behavior that appears the least bit 'sinful'. It will be very interesting to find out the kind of lewd behavior that Palmer got caught doing."

"Well one thing's for certain. He didn't get into trouble with a student. If he had, the charges would have been different, and he probably wouldn't be getting out on low bail," Simon said.

The door opened and a bedraggled and very haggard Dick Palmer emerged. His wallet and other property had been restored to him, and now he looked at Hal with red eyes that bespoke a night of pain and tears. His presence changed the air in the room. He smelled bad and he knew it. "Hal! Oh God, thank you, thank you for getting me out. I don't want to get too close. It's been hell all night in this place." He looked like he was about to collapse as he staggered toward them. "Could we leave, please?"

"Sure. This is Simon, my partner. Just a couple of conditions. First of all we're going to find you some newspapers to sit on in the back seat of my car. The second is your story about how this all happened. Where's your car anyway?"

"In Laguna. I'll show you." He went ahead of them toward the exit, revealing the back of his pants which were heavily stained. "They pushed me down onto the toilet that was filthy. Animals! Those animals I was locked up with made me sit in that filth!" his voice rising in fury as he recalled the night he had just spent. As they passed a restroom in the corridor, Dick said, "Hey, let me see if I can clean up a little in there, OK?" He came back out in ten minutes, his pants now wet from his attempt at cleaning them. They bought a newspaper from a rack outside, spread it on the back seat of the car, got in and drove off with the windows down.

"Now for the story," Hal said, turning onto the southbound freeway.

Silence at first, then sobbing came from the darkened back seat. "It wasn't my fault," Dick stammered between sobs. "I swear it wasn't." "What wasn't? Come on, Dick. Let's have it all," Hal said.

More hesitation from the back seat, and then, "It was all a mistake. I just went down to the beach to watch the surf. This guy came up to me, started talking, very polite and nice. We talked for a little while. It was dark and I couldn't see his face very well but he seemed like a nice guy. We went up the steps toward some rocks where we could sit and talk some more. And then there were the police, shining flashlights on us and telling us that we were under arrest."

"For nudity and lewd behavior, according to the desk sergeant," Hal said. "I think you left out a few details here, Dick."

Silence again from the back seat.

"Want to tell me why you called me and not one of your close friends from your church? That church that you're always throwing up to everybody

*Lagunatics*

at school as the paragon of caring communities? You must have a few pals there whom you could have called." More silence, broken only by what began to sound like suppressed sobbing.

"And another question. How come you waited a whole day to call? Weren't you arrested last night? What time was that, exactly?"

"About 10:00PM," Dick said, between sobs. "Ever been arrested? It's . . . it's . . . horrifying, terrible. They treat you like a criminal, as if you're already guilty of something . . . awful." His voice trailed off and he buried his face in his hands.

"What happened to the other guy, that nice man you were uh . . . talking with?"

"Got out early today. Somebody bailed him out," the weak voice said.

"I'd guess you still have a court date pending over this, huh?" Hal asked.

"Yeah, next week," and Dick dissolved into open sobbing. "You aren't going to let this get around, are you Hal? I mean it's vacation and school's out for the summer, but this could still get out."

"But you're innocent, Dick. What have you got to worry about? Let me get this all straight. You went down to the beach in Laguna, not your own beach in San Clemente, to look at the surf just after dark. You met a man there and the two of you went up into the secluded rocks just to talk. And while you were just talking, the police arrived and arrested you for no reason. Sounds perfectly logical to me, don't you think so too, Simon?"

Hal had a much better idea of what had gone on in the rocks above the beach, and that idea both delighted and infuriated him. In his back seat sat the man who had been among Hal's sworn enemies, a man who fulminated against queers in the classroom, a man whose church supported the hated Briggs Initiative. That part of what he now suspected angered him when he thought of the weeks in which he had been falsely accused of molesting Barry, weeks of feeling as if everyone in his school had it in for him, hated him, nights of lost sleep when he worried whether he'd have a job at all.

The part that elated him was that this same man, this homophobic asshole who couldn't say and do enough against gay people, this self-hating queer now sobbing in his back seat was having to face up to the fact that he was a queer himself. At least that's what Hal thought as he drove on through the dark, down Laguna Canyon Road, and finally to Coast Highway.

"Where's your car, Dick?"

"Bottom of Mountain Road," he murmured. Aha, Hal thought, almost gloating. The stairs down from the infamous Boom-Boom Room crossed over numerous rock crevices that had for years been the trysting place of choice for men wanting a quickie with other men. Anyone who frequented either of the nearby bars knew to stay away from the rocks now that the police had begun patrolling that part of the beach access, but people like Dick Palmer, and presumably his beach friend for the evening, would not have been equipped with this information. They were therefore easy prey for the vigilant cops.

They pulled up beside Dick's car. "Just a minute. One more piece of the story before you leave, Dick. Who was sucking whose cock when the police cast an unwelcome spotlight on your exciting show? Naked, the complaint said. So I'd guess you had your pants down. How about your buddy? Were you going down on him, or he on you?"

Dick Palmer lurched from the back seat of Hal's car without answering. "I'll give you the money on Monday," he said, darting into his own car, starting it up, and hurrying away into the night.

"You were a little hard on him, don't you think?" Simon asked as he and Hal drove back to Myrtle Street.

"Yeah, maybe. You certainly don't believe that cock and bull story, do you?"

"Not for a minute, well, at least I don't believe there was a bull involved," Simon said with a chuckle.

"Ha! Right you are. It makes me so god-damned mad about jerks like him. He hates himself because he's homosexual, and then takes that internalized hatred out on people like me, and you, for that matter. He might think I won't get this around, but I certainly will. If there is anything I can do to drop a scandal in the middle of that nest of vipers he calls a church, believe me, I'll do it. I know about his cohorts, particularly that Willy he runs around with, the guy who so nicely shot photos of us in bed, and before next week is out, everybody who knows the fake Dick Palmer will know about the real one. Now, let's get back to our boys, and our life."

"I'm glad I went with you to get him out, Hal. He seems sort of desperate to me, and this whole thing might entirely unhinge him. I think you might want to go easy, let things come out on their own. After all, there will be a public court date. Why don't you make sure that his church people know about it, and in the spirit of their idea of charity, they might want to be there to support him. They will have to find out what really happened at that, don't you think?"

"That's a great idea, my love. You're just the best, Simon. You always think things out better than I do, know the better way to deal with everything," Hal said, taking Simon's hand and kissing it as he drove toward Myrtle Street. "It's a perfect plan."

# CHAPTER 35
## Party Conversations

The summer party began early the next day with guests arriving by around noon with a number of items to celebrate: the end of school for Hal and Barry; the success of *Streetcar* for Bertrand and George; Ken and Roger's anniversary; the holiday itself, and as far as Hal and Simon and their boys were concerned, a family reunion. Hal had outdone himself; patés, terrines, baked meats of several kinds, sandwiches, salads, and several desserts crowded the buffet table. "The old girl's done it again," Tom said to Mike as he surveyed the goodies.

"You're going to give him a complex, you know. I don't need to remind you that Hal is barely ten years older than we are, and, I might add, he's not losing his hair," Mike said, forking up some ham onto his plate while looking up at Tom's receding hairline.

"Would you have still picked me up if you'd known then that I'd be going bald?" he asked, smiling over his glass of wine.

"Who picked up whom back then? Weren't you the one who wanted to surf naked that time?"

"Yeah, I admit it. God you were so cute. Course I thought you were really a girl," Tom laughed.

"Right. A girl in Speedos with a hard-on. We did have a great summer, didn't we?"

"The best. Things end, though, huh? You're happy, aren't you?"

"Very. I think it was painful for Hal and Simon when you and I parted company, but they're OK with how things went. Think we might have stayed together if it hadn't been for graduate school pulling us in different directions?" Mike asked.

"Who knows? I don't think we had any problems, did we? And you're still my best friend. Then you met John and that was that."

"Didn't take you long to find Mark. What's this house like that you guys are looking at?"

---

Roger and Ken chatted with Eric and Carl on the patio. "Then what appears at our door but these two old farts from upstairs, loaded down with things they assumed that we would be delighted to have in our place," Ken said. "And what trash it is. They cleaned out their voluminous closets full of crap and made us a 'gift', or at least that's how we were supposed to regard this junk."

"Lucky for us our former landlady is notoriously stingy," Eric said, referring of course to Denise. "Not a chance she'd part with a single item from her treasures that she keeps locked up in the dark tower. You heard about her burglary, didn't you? Now you couldn't get into the place with dynamite. What all did Hans and Gerald give you?"

"Well, let's see. There was a lamp that looks like a modified stove pipe except that it's red and flexible—very trendy in the 50s probably, a carved wooden armadillo missing one ear, two plastic and chrome folding chairs, a collection of things that are supposed to look good on the tops of tables . . ."

"And the fake Christmas tree, don't forget that," Roger piped up."

"Right, along with some of the ugliest purple ornaments ever made."

"What are you going to do with all of it?" Carl asked.

"Uh . . . that's where we got into a bit of trouble," Roger said. "Ken waited all of one day and then took the whole kit and kaboodle down to the Salvation Army thrift store. Who knew that Gerald was a thrift store junkie? Imagine his surprise when he recognized all of his 'gifts' right there for sale at thrift store prices."

"Probably where he got that junk in the first place," Ken said. "As soon as we saw that beaten up wooden armadillo back in our lobby, we knew we'd been busted. Serves them right. The nerve they have thinking that we'd be glad to take their old discards off their hands and be thrilled to have them in our place. Well, the upshot is that they aren't speaking to us. Frankly, it's a blessing as far as I'm concerned."

"Speaking of Denise," Roger said, "what do you think's happening at Le Bleu these days?"

"Haven't a clue," Eric replied. "She's paying the rent, that's all I know and all I care to know. I'm sort of surprised she hasn't shown up here today. She's never been shy about inviting herself to parties, anybody's parties. If she gets a whiff of the fact that Bertrand Lebland is here . . ."

---

Bertrand was indeed there along with George who was trying to figure out his partner's subdued mood. The play is going very well, he thought to himself, sold out at every performance. His voice is back. Maybe it's because he can't sing, but I haven't heard him talk about that lately. He won't go near the bar. When I suggested we go out for a drink there, he refused. It's not like him; it used to be his favorite haunt. He just seems to be in a constant funk. I wonder if he's tired of me.

"No, it's not you, George," Bertrand had said when George asked him about why he was so down lately. But George was not entirely convinced. He knew about Bertrand's history of ex-partners, knew that the longevity for anyone in Bertrand's life could be measured in weeks or at best, a few months. If that pattern continued, his time with Bertrand was nearly up. On the other hand, if they were winding down as a partnership, the quality of their lovemaking did not indicate anything like an end to them as a couple.

Bertrand was busy accepting congratulations and accolades for his role in *Streetcar*, moving among the party guests and chatting half-heartedly about the play. George moved off, deciding to give Bertrand as much space as he wanted, and he found himself in the kitchen talking to Hal who was replenishing a platter of cold roast beef. "Not sure I'll be your neighbor for long," he said.

Hal stopped slicing beef. "Why? What's wrong?"

"I wish I knew. He's not distant exactly, but he seems so preoccupied somehow. I guess I should expect some sort of moodiness from an actor, but it's hard to figure out what to do, how to respond. I'm worried, that's all. Never had to deal with this with Marty who was as predictable as a clock.

Got used to that, probably took it for granted. One thing I can't do with Bertrand is take him for granted," George said picking up a slice of beef. "Maybe it's just the pressures of the play. When's the run over, in two weeks? Why not ride it out until then and see how things are?"

"You're probably right. Everything else is OK, if you know what I mean."

"Uh . . . yeah, from what we can hear through two sets of windows, I'd be the first to agree there."

"That's all you two have going on over here, listening to us?" George laughed.

"It's more like trying NOT to listen," Hal said. "Here, take this platter out for me will you? And quit worrying!"

No sooner had George left through the dining room doorway with the platter than Bertrand came into the kitchen from the patio. They have their exits and their entrances, Hal thought. "Hal, could I talk with you sometime soon?" he asked. "Maybe tomorrow?"

"Sure. Are you enjoying the party? I don't usually ask guests that, but you seem to be the center of it with everyone wanting to talk about the play."

"Yes, thanks. It's nice of everybody," he replied. The preoccupation that George mentioned clouded Bertrand's handsome features.

"Something's wrong, isn't there," Hal asked, stopping his work and looking deeply at Bertrand. "You've got George worried, you know."

"I know, and I'm agonizing over that. It's not him, it's not about us either. Please Hal, let's talk just you and I, OK?"

"Of course, but you need to know that I keep nothing from Simon."

"Then the three of us. Tomorrow afternoon, OK?"

"Don't want to include George, huh?"

"No, I can't, not right now."

―――

The front door had been left purposefully open to admit guests without Hal or Simon's having to answer the bell, but the bell went off anyway. Who else? Denise of course, announcing her arrival. As Eric predicted, and as she was wont to do, she had invited herself to the party, having heard that it was really a fete for the triumphant Bertrand whose play she had still not bothered to attend. How she found out about the party from her astonishing grapevine of sycophantic informants, none of whom could be remotely considered friends, was always a mystery, but here she was, dressed for the occasion in high movie star mode in a pink sheath dress that Mae West might have worn while on the make. This remarkable form-fitting garment would have accentuated body curves on the voluptuous Mae, but had the effect of wall paper on Denise who had the body shape of an oversized cereal box. Had she turned up with a pompom parasol and poodle, no one would have been more surprised than the gaping guests who now watched her clomping entrance.

Simon greeted her. "Denise! What a surprise. Hal hadn't told me . . . that is . . . we didn't expect . . . please, come in."

Entirely unabashed, she barged in, barely acknowledging Simon. "Yas, Ay ear zat you have zee beeg party for my fren Bertrand (pronounced in the French manner) and Ay would not lak heem to tink zat Ay ignore heem. Where ee ees?"

"Actually Denise, the party is to celebrate a number of events, but come with me and we will find your 'fren' for you," Simon said, ushering her and her pink wonder of a dress into the living room. They worked their way through the partiers toward the patio; there they found Bertrand. "Here's a friend of yours, Bertrand," Simon announced as Denise hove into view. Damn, Bertrand thought, just what I need. He had not told George, who had had a school function to attend that night, about the recent dinner at Le Bleu with Brett, nor about the conversation with the Hollywood producer. Now here was the voluble Denise, likely ready to blab everything. He decided to play dumb, as if he had never met her.

"Ah Monsieur Lebland," Denise shrilled, extending her hand for a European kiss. Bertrand looked at her as if she were something out of a bad burlesque—he wasn't the only one who regarded Madame Lebouche in this way—and took her hand. "Ay deed want to congratulate you on your performance (she hadn't seen it) in zat play you do ere in zee teater."

"Thank you, but could you tell me your name?"

*Lagunatics*

"Ah monsieur, you tease me," Denise said letting out a coquettish giggle. "You ave come to my restaurant last week, you know you deed, you and zat udder star from zee show." All of this at top volume. "Ay ope ee ees ere at zee party too," she cooed.

Across the patio, George took in all of Denise's effusive greeting, and his face darkened as he began to put some things together. Bertrand looked in his direction and watched as George rose and went in the house. "Uh no, Madame, he is not here. Will you excuse me a moment?" Bertrand said as he abruptly headed for the house. Inside, George was not to be found.

---

Barry and Miguel arrived late to the party, owing to Miguel's undependable car. They thought their tardiness might not be noticed, but Hal had been getting concerned about their whereabouts; one of the reasons for the party was, after all, to celebrate Barry's birthday and graduation. They came in through the back gate, there to encounter Denise who had watched Bertrand's disappearance with dismay. She had begun to scan the party to see if a suitable celebrity might substitute for him when what to her wondering eyes should appear but the very man whom she had reported to the police as having stolen her jewelry. "Zo, you are ere! Ay tot you are een jail, you teef!"

Miguel shied away just as Hal arrived. "Enough, Denise. As we all know by now, Miguel had nothing to do with the disappearance of your jewelry."

"Ay know zat he could get into my ouse when he want. Ay don't care what the police tink," she said, her voice rising. "What you do wees my diamonds, zats what Ay want to know?"

"Do you mean that ugly crystal golf ball that you once lost down a drain at the restaurant, Denise?" Roger asked, coming between her and Miguel. "I'd have thought you had that insured for millions and would have collected on it by now."

"Yes, don't we all remember that night," Hal said as he moved into place to complete the wall between Denise and her prey. "But nothing would have flushed that thing down, more's the pity." Miguel and Barry took this opportunity to disappear among the other guests. Once Hal was sure that the coast was clear, he turned on the furious Denise.

"Isn't enough that you have arrived wearing that pink horror?" Hal asked, earnestly wishing that he had been able to let her have it in French. "You weren't invited here in the first place, and I won't have you insulting my guests now that you barged in here anyway. So either shut up and behave yourself or take yourself and that ugly dress out of my house. Got it?" he said, also raising his voice.

She got it all right, and glaring at Hal, moved across the patio. Her arrival at the other side found her among other guests who were not her friends either. She had already encountered Roger with whom she believed to have mended fences, but the truth was that, despite his recommending a manager for Le Bleu to her, he had done nothing else to encourage the renewal of warmer relations between them. Even she sensed through her notoriously thick skin that Roger was more than cool toward her. Now there stood Eric and Carl, grinning at her. Not smiling, grinning. She decided that a friendly reception did not lie in their direction, and she turned toward a clump of other guests unknown to her with a view toward making an impression. No fear; she always made an impression.

---

A last minute addition to the guest list had been Martha and Dana, fresh from the rarified air of Hollywood where Martha had become the doyen of fashion among the minor deities of show business. Dressed in Nordstrom's latest for the well turned-out gay gentleman, Martha held court in one corner of the patio while Dana went off in search of Bertrand. "Yes, Dana has a role in that new TV series?" he informed what he assessed as an adoring group of provincials here in the outback of Orange County. "We've had a busy time, you know?" Martha's annoying habit of ending sentences as if they were questions had not abated, and if anything, had got worse.

The provincials feigned attention but failed to ask for the exact details of the 'busy time'. "Directors, producers, other stars, in and out of our house constantly?" Martha went on, grandly failing to mention precise names of any of the Hollywood guests just alluded to.

"Oh, who exactly has been over?" Barry asked.

"Well, it wouldn't be good to name names, but a recent visitor used to play a famous lawyer for years? His new series is the one Dana's in?" Martha replied, looking conspiratorial.

Martha's crowd of the once interested began to dissipate, looking in the direction of Martha's well-known partner Dana who was combing the party for his friend Bertrand. Finally Martha was left alone with only one auditor, Augustus the friendly dog from next door.

Dana came back from his search. "I can't find Bertrand. I'll go to his house to see if he's there. You'll be OK, won't you?"

"Well I hope you won't leave me here alone for very long? I can already tell that this party is a drag?"

"I'll be right back," Dana said, giving Martha a reassuring peck on the cheek.

---

"You didn't need to keep that dinner a secret, you know," George said once Bertrand had found him in their kitchen. "Have I given you some reason for you to think that I don't trust you?"

"No never. I'm sorry. I should have told you about having dinner with Brett that night, but there's more than just dinner that I am having trouble telling you about."

"You know that I'm not the jealous type, Bertrand. If you wanted to go to bed with Brett, all you had to do was say so. We agreed on that, didn't we? I've always known that you might have trouble staying with just one man. Don't you think I would have understood if you wanted a fling with all those muscles?"

"It's not that, and it wasn't that. Oh yes, he came on to me after the opening night in my dressing room, but we didn't . . . I couldn't . . . I didn't want to . . . George, there's something else," Bertrand said, reaching for George's hand and pulling him into a chair beside him. "I have to ask you something first. Have you noticed a difference in me lately, I mean over the past few weeks?"

"Yes, of course. But I thought you were being a little moody lately worrying about the play."

"Something's happened to me, something I don't completely understand. I've changed somehow. My whole way of thinking is different from the way it was only a few weeks ago." Bertrand tried to relate his experience on the beach that night that had resulted in his contempt for The Blue Cove and everything it had meant to him. "It was as if some outside force came into me. I sat there for quite a while just stunned. When I passed the bar on the way home, I could hardly look in its direction."

"And that's what's been bothering you?"

"No, not exactly. I didn't know at first how to tell you about what happened, mostly because I wasn't sure of what had happened myself. All I knew was that my life with you was the most important thing, that what we have together made the only sense. Does that sound hokey?"

George leaned over to hug him. "If it does sound hokey, it's music to my ears."

"I envisioned my new life with you right here, in this house, living together making a life together. I'd get a few parts in some plays, and you'd teach school. A few weeks ago, that would have sounded as dull as hen shit to me, but right now, it feels like heaven."

They sat holding each other in their quiet kitchen with the sounds of the party next door going on. Finally, "There is something else, though. Brett and I have a chance to go to Hollywood to be in a TV series. Here, look at this." He produced a letter from Eliot Drake which spelled out the proposed series and the parts that he and Brett would very likely be suited for after passing screen tests and whatever else.

"But that's what you want, isn't it, what you've always wanted? This could be a great opportunity, a big chance for you," George said, suddenly brightening. "Why would you think that you couldn't tell me something this important?"

"You think that this is great news? Yes, I suppose it is. Don't you see what this could mean to us? That's what's been worrying me."

"Hey, lots of people live here and work in LA. Why not you? It's not as if it's Mars, you know."

"I'd have to be up there quite a lot. Eliot wants us both, you notice. And then there's Brett who seems to think that he and I are the new hot couple."

"What's really worrying you, Bertrand? Down deep, I mean? You can handle Brett, and you know you can. What is it really?"

The answer was hard to articulate and there was a long pause between it and the question. "If this had been offered to me before I met you, I'd have taken it in a heartbeat. But now I'm afraid," Bertrand said. "Scared shitless."

"Of what? It's not stage fright. I've seen you and you're a natural up there."

"Do you hear that party going on next door? That party represents more than just people showing up on the Fourth of July, George. Hal and Simon have friends, real friends. And more than that, they have family. I want that, and maybe that's what I've always wanted. I never had much of a family, and early on, figured I'd have to make my own way without one. Didn't think all this time that I needed one or wanted one."

His voice rose into a howl. "After all, I had all those old lepers down at The Blue Cove, didn't I? I had Vi Winters, and applause, and all the tricks I could handle, didn't I? I was living the high life, wasn't I?" He began to cry while George held him. When he was able to speak, he said, "Then you came along. Man, this is going to sound too smarmy, but I don't care. I love you, you big idiot. I know now that I've never loved anyone in my life before, but I love you. That's what happened to me on the beach that night. It was as if I had been handed a whole new script, right out of the dark. I knew, I knew everything that a forty-five year-old fag needs to know, that he's been wasting his life on stuff that didn't mean shit, and that suddenly he has a chance to have a real life with a man who loves him. There. Did that sound like I was acting, like I just memorized that from some play?"

Another long pause between question and answer as George beamed at his lover. Finally, "No, that didn't sound rehearsed at all, and what it sounded like was music. See? You really do sing."

"I can't let it end, can't let anything get in the way of us, not even a chance at TV, not now, not after all this time of emptiness. That's what I'm scared about. That's why the Hollywood stuff . . . oh hell, I just don't know what to do. What can we do?"

Neither of them said anything else right then. There are times inside the relationships between people that defy all forms of expression, that rise beyond each one's ability to do or say anything except to be there for each other. They had no ready answers, but Bertrand felt the transcendent lightness that he had experienced on the beach surge through him, and he hugged his lover more closely.

Watching this scene from a corner of the room, Dana thought at first that he might just duck back out noiselessly and rejoin the party next door. His attempt brought him into contact with a chair, and the scraping sound it made alerted George and Bertrand. "Who's there?"

"Just me," Dana said. "I didn't mean to eavesdrop, but once I found you in here, I couldn't comfortably leave. Besides, it's not every day that you get to tune in on high drama like this," he said as he smiled at them. "Certainly nothing on TV. I'm really sorry."

"You're just the person we need right now," Bertrand said. "I just got an idea."

―――

Sid had managed to pry Leonard away from Palm Springs, and they joined the festivities on Hal and Simon's patio. Once they had drinks—Simon apologized for not having any Bloody Marys on hand—they formed up part of a group that included the San Diego boys, Tom and Mark. "We just love it out there in the desert, don't we Sid?" Leonard enthused. "You must come out for a weekend!"

"You know, if I were still hitched up with ol' Mike there, we'd be out there in a heartbeat. But Mark has some severe problems with being in the sun. Burns like crazy in no time at all. We'd have to come out to Palm Springs on a rainy day," Tom said having heard Hal and Simon's story about their stay in the triple-wide trailer. "But thanks anyway. Hey, Barry's your nephew, Hal told me. How's he doing?"

"Fine. Certainly better than he was. Where is he anyway?" Sid asked. "We want to give him his graduation present."

"He and Miguel are keeping a low profile right now. At least while Denise's still here. They won't come out until she leaves. Probably time to get rid of her anyway. Excuse me for a minute," Tom said as he moved toward the pink horror.

"Hi Denise. Remember me? I'm the one who told you off at that party at Norman Stands a few years ago. Remember? Tom your busboy?" "Yaas, Ay remember," she said giving him a cold stare.

"Well, here we are at another party together, and you're about as welcome at this one as you were at that one. Seems like everywhere you go, people just hate to see you there," Tom said in a mock joking tone. "I just don't understand it myself. Why, you're so charming and always so interestingly dressed. I'd think that everyone would be delighted to have you crash their party. That's what you did, wasn't it? Crash the party?"

She looked at him and gave him her pretend look of not entirely comprehending what he had just said. "Crash in this case means come to a party where you weren't invited. And I hear you've already made yourself obnoxious. How long before you run out of guests to annoy, do you think? And don't pretend you don't understand what I'm telling you either." He edged her slowly but inexorably toward the gate.

"Ay understand you. You always been a rude person. Now you tell me Ay am not wanted ere? Where ees my fren Bertrand? E want me to come to zees party."

"Ah, but it isn't his party, Denise. And I watched him when you came in. He didn't know you from a bale of hay—and even in that pink dress you're wearing, there are more than a few similarities. You know, I almost feel sorry for you, Denise. No one wants you around, and you're too conceited to know it. You have the nerve to barge in wherever you want and think that everyone will be glad of your arrival. Ha! What a laugh. Well, goodbye Denise. It's been nice chatting with you again. Maybe we'll meet again at the next party you're not invited to."

He left her standing alone by the gate. She surveyed the party and either decided that Tom was right (probably not), or that she wasn't going to be schmoozing with Bertrand after all, or that she had, as Tom said, run out of people to charm. In any case, she put down her glass and left.

Had Tom been cruel? He wondered for a moment or two as he watched her go through the gate toward her car. He made his move to get rid of her on behalf of Miguel and Barry, weighing their feelings against hers. No contest. Her malignant presence at the party had be excised; as the hosts, Hal and Simon couldn't do it although Hal had come pretty close to ousting her earlier. Now that she'd gone, the party lightened. Miguel and Barry came out of the cottage where they had been staying out of her sight.

"Now for the surprise," Leonard said as the boys appeared. "Show them, Sid."

"Take it easy, Len," Sid said. "It's not that big a deal. Come on out to the street, guys." They followed him out to Myrtle Street. A minute later, the whole party heard whoops of joy, yells of pleasure. Another minute later, Barry came running back in.

"Where's Hal? Hal! Come out and see this! It's a car! My own car! What a great graduation present, Uncle Sid!" Some of the party moved out to the street. There, shining in the July sun sat a late model Toyota, not new, but in beautiful shape. Standing beside it was Sid who handed the keys over to the exuberant Barry.

---

"Well it's about time? I've been standing here alone for hours?" Martha whined as Dana, Bertrand, and George rejoined the party.

"Hi Martha," George said greeting his former partner. "How's rag selling at Nordstrom's these days?"

"No need to be snide?" Martha said. "And don't call me Martha? You know how I hate that? Nobody calls me that in LA, do they Dana?"

"Uh . . . nobody I know of, pet," Dana answered. "Listen, we've been cooking up a tremendous idea. You know that my TV series is ending and the last filming is next week. I just might have a new job if what we've been talking about works out. Isn't that great?"

"I hope it won't mean more nights away? You're always at work when I'm at home?"

"Don't you want to know what it's all about?" Dana asked. "It could mean a lot of money."

As usual, Martha was less interested in the details of any plans that did not include him directly than in the ultimate results, namely money. The three men reviewed their idea anyway to an obviously bored Martha. "It's a perfect part for me. Bertrand and I are the same age, and he's willing to give up this opportunity to me. If we can sell the idea to Eliot Drake, that's all it will take. Now come on, Marty. Let's hear some enthusiasm."

Enthusiasm over anything that did not have to do with Nordstrom's or the gossip that came from it was a difficult emotion for Martha to drum up, but finally: "Of course, I'm glad? I was wondering what you'd do after the series ended? Where do you think Hallie is? When can we leave this dreary party?"

George tried not to look supercilious, but a smirk crept over his face. He wondered how he and Martha had managed to live together all those years. He stole a glance at Bertrand who was similarly trying to control himself, and who in his turn was wondering what Martha had in his personality kit that kept Dana enthralled. Maybe more than met the eye? His question silently communicated itself to George who smiled back and quietly said, "No, it's not *that*, I can assure you." He took Bertrand's hand and communicated something else that they both very well understood. But the mystery of Martha's allure went unanswered.

# CHAPTER 36
## Aftershocks and Aftermaths

Dorothy Eakins came over next morning to help clean up party remains. The patio in particular needed her attention as she gathered up wine glasses, found plates behind shrubbery, and forks stuck into potted plants. Hal was in the kitchen dealing with leftovers; Simon had gone to work at the hospital; the boys were still in bed; Edward was curled up in the morning sun.

Suddenly, a tremor. An earthquake, that phenomenon so greatly feared by non-Californians who imagine greater catastrophe than most earth movements actually engender, shook the town. Like all of them, the movement seemed to go on for quite a while, shaking rafters and walls, rattling dishes, and crashing down pictures from walls where they had been carelessly hung.

Dorothy sat down on a lawn chair for the duration, completely calm and serene in her native knowledge that quakes happen from time to time, and that old residents simply wait them out and go on with whatever they were doing. She watched as the trellis between the main house and the guest cottage swayed and creaked, and then broke loose and fell. Hmm . . . she thought, this one is a bit stronger. She stayed where she was and thought it might have been a good time for a martini.

Inside the house, Hal watched as the accumulated glassware from yesterday's party, awaiting their turn in the dishwasher, clattered and danced, a few of them falling off the counter and breaking on the kitchen's tile floor. A couple of cabinet doors swung open but since most of the dishes were not inside, no damage obtained. He held onto the stove to keep his own balance as the tremor continued, stopped, and then gave the house and grounds an aftershock.

"Wow! A really good one!" yelled Tom as he came into the kitchen. "Any damage so far?"

"Just a couple of glasses, I think, but I wonder if Simon was driving or had already got to work," Hal said.

"I'm sure he's OK, Hal. My guess is that it wasn't that hard of a hit. If he was in the car, he probably just pulled over and waited it out." The siren of an ambulance wailed by on Coast Highway two blocks away. It was heading south. "You know he'll call right away."

The rest of the house came to the kitchen to exclaim about the quake. "Taking orders for breakfast," Hal sang. He cleared away the broken glass, moved things around on the counters, and calmed everybody down. "Coffee in five minutes."

The phone rang.

---

Back at their place, Roger and Ken were literally thrown out of bed when the quake hit. Ken headed immediately for their pride and joy, a beautiful piece of hand-blown glass that sat perched on a pedestal in the living room. He grabbed hold of it on its teetering stand and was able to steady it as the tremor shook the room. Roger had not been so successful with the contents of the bookshelves on the other wall; books tumbled around him as he valiantly tried to stop them. "Let 'em fall, Roger! Get out of the way! Get into the middle of the room!" Ken yelled at him. Too late. The shelves left the walls and covered Roger with more books and other objects that they had displayed there. He extricated himself from the jumble just before the aftershock arrived, unscathed but shaken. He helped Ken remove the art glass piece to the bed in the guest room.

The aftershock, and noise from the kitchen, the unmistakable sound of falling and breaking china and glass. A chorus of hanging pans clanged their response to the groundswell.

Voices outside in the hall, some frightened, some even terrified. Residents had rushed out in a frenzied effort to escape what they perceived was apocalyptic destruction. Among them were Hans and Gerald who were making their way downstairs. They knocked on Roger and Ken's door. Ken opened it with some difficulty now that it had been slightly torqued by the tremor. "Are you guys OK?" he asked.

"Yes, we're fine, but we lost everything. Our place is a wasteland of broken glass. Not a single shelf survived," Gerald said while he quelled sobs. Ken had the uncharitable thought that their place was something of a wasteland anyway, especially when their vast collection of arty glass was still in tact, but he said nothing and instead invited them in.

"We didn't have too much breakage it seems," Roger said, trying to tidy up the pile of spilled books. "Come in and have a glass of wine with us. I think I can find a bottle and some glasses among the ruins. Oh, but you don't drink. I'll see if I can make coffee."

Theirs was an older building whose foundations seemed to communicate the earth's movements quite easily and with greater force than other, more newly constructed buildings would have done. The top floors felt the tremor more than the bottom ones did, and consequently sustained greater damage. In a very short time, the news stations reported that the quake had been a relatively minor one, registering 3.8 on the Richter Scale, and had been centered some miles inland. That information did little to calm the nerves of those whose dwellings had, for one reason or another, taken a heavy hit from the quake. Most of the town came through with little or no damage, no one was without electricity or water, and as people began putting things back up on shelves and realigning pictures on their walls, life resumed as if nothing much had happened.

Hans and Gerald went back upstairs to assess the damage, followed by Roger and Ken. The door opened onto a scene of inconceivable destruction. The furniture lay covered in shattered glass; pictures either hung askew or had plummeted to the floor; every display case was broken and on its side, one of them still lighted up what remained of its plate shelves. Gone, entirely gone was their immense collection of translucent glass objects; only a scant few pieces had escaped demolition. Here and there, items that had been framed in gold—a few small boxes—sat among the shards of the vases, candlesticks, bowls, and plates that now provided a glittering carpet of broken glass. "I told you that you needed to secure those etageres. They should have been fastened to the walls, every one of them," Hans said, turning on his partner as if everything were his fault.

"Oh fuck off. Isn't enough that we have this mess to deal with? I suppose you think I planned the earthquake too," Gerald shot back. "You just had to have this penthouse on the top of the building that rocked like a cradle. If we lived downstairs, we wouldn't have lost it all."

"So it's my fault, is it? And who had to start buying all this stuff in the first place?"

"We both did and you know it. You can't stay out of thrift stores and junk shops," Gerald yelled back.

The mention of a thrift store was, as far as Ken and Roger were concerned, dangerous territory. But it seemed that their donating the 'gifts' that they had received from Hans and Gerald to the local thrift store and having been caught at it, was a minor issue in view of what the earthquake had done. Nevertheless, as the argument between the two escalated, Roger and Ken thought that a silent retreat back downstairs to their own condo a wise move. As they closed their door, they heard the continuing fight upstairs, now reaching epic proportions as more and more accusatory jabs were flung back and forth.

"Let's just clean up here and go see what else has happened in town," Ken suggested. They spent the next hour or so putting their place back in order, figured out that their loss from breakage was minimal, and headed to Myrtle Street. Once in the hall, they got an earful of the continuing war being waged in the penthouse whose door remained open.

Events like earthquakes, wildfires, and floods find random victims, often leaving disastrous results beside unscathed and untouched neighbors. The extent of damage to the town and its residents appeared more concentrated as Hal and the boys neared the hospital. There were a number of cars askew along the highway, some abandoned, some had run into each other, their stunned owners now sorting out insurance questions. The police kept the highway clear for emergency vehicles, and a line of ambulances arrived at the emergency entrance to the hospital to unload their injured cargoes.

They parked in Simon's spot in the parking lot and hurried into the lobby. "We're here to see about Dr. Simon York," Hal announced to the receptionist.

"Are you his family," she asked.

"No, uh . . . yes. I got a call from his colleague that he'd been injured and had been taken here," Hal said.

"I'm sorry, but if you're not his family, I can't give you any information about him."

"We're all the family he has out here," Hal said trying to keep his composure. "He's from the Midwest. We live in the same house. He must have had his colleague call me. Isn't there a note about that somewhere?" The receptionist looked through a stack of memos and notes. There was a line behind Hal trying to get in to see their own injured kin."

"No, I don't see anything here," she said. "Who was it who phoned you?"

"A Doctor Simmons, I think. I was so rattled that I didn't pay that much attention. We just raced right over here."

She picked up her in-house phone and paged Doctor Simmons. "Now if you'll just step aside, I'll let you know when he answers. Just write your name here. Next, please!"

Hal and the boys moved away, but there was little room in the crowded reception area where they could stand. Hal was starting to panic. How bad were Simon's injuries? What exactly happened? They had seen his car on their way over; its driver's door had been crashed into. How had they got Simon out of it, he wondered.

"Mr. Schroeder!" the receptionist called over to him. "Dr. Simmons will be down in a few minutes."

The few minutes turned into twenty minutes, then half an hour, then nearly an hour. What could he do but wait? If he were Simon's blood relative or his spouse, he would have been already ushered into the ward where the injured were being treated. He was furious at not being able to see his lover, his Simon, his partner. What right had this place to deny him going to Simon? Over an hour and still no Dr. Simmons. Probably busy with emergency room cases.

"Look, you guys. Stay here will you and wait for Simmons? I've got an idea. I know how to get into Simon's office and station. If I can find his nurse . . . I've got to find her. I've got to see him."

"Go, Hal. We'll wait right here. If Simmons gets here, we'll tell him where you are. Get going," Tom said.

Hal slipped out the front door and headed for the doctors' entrance at the rear of the building. As he rounded the corner, he happily noticed that there was nobody in sight. He made it to the door. Locked. Damn, he thought. No keys, no way to get in. Then, he saw someone approaching from inside. He ducked behind a shrub and watched as the door opened and the man left. He quickly darted for the door, catching it just before it closed again. He was inside.

Out in the adjacent hall, something like controlled pandemonium reigned. Injured people were being triaged on gurneys for everything from minor wounds to broken bones. He made his way past the moans and groans toward Simon's office. How to find Karen, Simon's nurse, that would be the next challenge. If she were on duty, she would no doubt be helping in the ER. He looked into filled hospital rooms, hoping that one of them was where Simon might be. No luck. Room after room, and nothing.

Then he saw her. Karen. He headed in her direction as she scurried away carrying an IV. "Karen!" he yelled after her, but the general roar in the place prevented her from hearing him. He ran after her, and when he turned the same corner that she had, once more lost sight of her. He went on, searching every room, looking at every gurney. Finally he caught up with her. "Karen! It's me, Hal! Where's Simon, do you know?"

"How did you get in here, Hal? You can't be in here."

"But I am here, and I want to see Simon. Where did they take him?" Hal asked, his panic fighting with his impatience.

"He's in surgery, Hal. He has a broken pelvis and possibly some internal injuries. He's on the fourth floor right now. Dr. Bradford's the best surgeon here and he's doing the operation. He was conscious when they brought him in but he was in a lot of pain, and we had to sedate him."

Hal barely heard her last sentence as he headed for the elevator and the fourth floor. He raced up the stairs and reached the waiting room where there was yet another desk with another receptionist, a jolly-faced older lady with a sweet smile. "May I help you?"

"I'd like to check on the condition of Dr. Simon York. I was told he went into surgery a while ago. Is he out yet?"

"Are you a relative?" the sweet face asked. Here we go again, Hal thought.

"Yes, I am his next of kin."

"Well, then Mr. York, let me check for you." She went to a card file. "We update these constantly, you know. Let me see . . . Simon York . . . yes, here it is. He's in recovery right now, Mr. York. I could let the surgeon know you're here if you like."

"Oh could you do that, please?" Hal asked, his lie to this sweet faced lady dying in his throat. She picked up a phone.

Within five minutes, a tall gray-headed man emerged from the depths of the operating rooms. "Mr. York?" he said toward Hal. "I'm Dr. Bradford.

You're here about Dr. York?"

"Yes, how is he?"

"Let's talk over here, please," Dr. Bradford said, guiding Hal to a corner of the waiting room. "Please, sit down."

"Oh God, is it bad? Is he seriously hurt? Will he be all right?" Hal asked trying to stay calm.

"Yes, he's all right. We stopped some internal bleeding, but he has a fractured pelvis that will take some time to heal. He's very lucky that his spleen didn't rupture. But that's not why I brought you over here to talk without being overheard. You aren't 'Mr York' and I know it. You're Hal Schroeder, Simon's partner. He told me as he was being sedated. He said you'd be here to find him and that they wouldn't let you in because you aren't a relative. He also said that you'd figure out a way to get in here," Dr. Bradford said with a sympathetic smile.

"You're right, you're right. Thanks for understanding. We've been together for over five years now. He's my life, Dr. Bradford," Hal said, welling up. "This crap about only relatives seeing people they love . . . that's got to change. It will change one day."

"There are ways around the law without sneaking in, you know. My partner and I adopted each other. Legally I can see 'my son' and he can see 'his son' no matter what. Took some money and some legal shenanigans, but we did it. If I were lying in recovery right now, my partner could be there too.

And you know what, that's where you're going, into recovery to see Simon. He won't be awake yet, but you'll get to see him. Come on."

A stunned Hal got to his feet and followed Dr. Bradford through swinging doors, down a corridor and into the recovery room. There lay Simon, covered up and sleeping like a baby. Hal longed to crawl into bed with him, to cradle him, to help him wake up. "You can hold his hand if you want," Dr. Bradford said, "but not for long. He'll be awake in an hour or so."

"And then what? When will he be able to come home? Will I be able to take care of him when he does?"

"He'll have to give the minor fracture in his pelvis time to heal, I'd say a good month or so, but he can very likely go home in another day, right after we do some tests."

Hal sat down beside Simon's bed and took his hand. He felt as if he would cry, not because there seemed to be anything wrong with Simon that he could see, but just from the joy of knowing that he'd be all right. "You said he'll wake up in an hour or so? Couldn't I stay here until he does? Please?"

"Well, it's against the rules here, but everything's a bit out of order today anyway. Sure, go ahead."

"I've got some friends waiting for me in the ER reception room. They'll want to know. But I could come right back."

"Take the rear corridor down to the elevator. And take this with you," Dr. Bradford said as he wrote something on a pad. "This will get you back in here without having to break and enter."

"Thanks, I'll be back in no time."

Hal found the boys patiently, well . . . impatiently, waiting where he'd left them. "He's OK. I found him, and he's OK. The doc's going to let me stay with him until he wakes up from the anesthesia. You guys can go on home if you want. I'll call you when Simon's awake." Hal filled them in on Simon's injuries. "I don't know how it happened. I'd guess somebody lost control of their car and broadsided Simon during the earthquake. But he's going to be OK. So go on home, and I'll see you later." Hal headed back to Recovery.

He took up his vigil beside his lover, and once more held his hand. "You're going to be OK, my love. God, there was a moment when I didn't know anything that happened. I thought I might lose you, that you would be taken away from me, that you might already be gone," he spoke softly to the sleeping Simon. "What would I have done if you had gone, my Simon? What would I do?" Then the tears came. He didn't care. He leaned over and kissed the inside of Simon's hand, wetting it with his tears. "We've got to take care of each other, make as sure as we can that we're safe. This was too close, too close."

As Dr. Bradford said, Simon began to move and stir after about an hour. He opened his eyes to find Hal peering into them. Groggy as he felt, and as unsteady as his voice was, he said, "I knew you'd be here. I think you've been here for quite a while, huh?"

"Not long, about an hour. Had to sneak in the back way. We're not relatives, you know. What the hell were they waiting for, do you think? For your mother to show up? Idiots! Had to lie to that nice woman in ER. Karen told me you were up here. Oh god, I'm glad you're OK." And the tears started again.

"I don't feel OK except for you being here. Look under the blanket." Hal lifted the blanket and found the catheter. "Damned uncomfortable. They'll take it out now that I'm awake. Want to call somebody?"

Hal went to fetch a nurse and Dr. Bradford. "OK Hal, you get to leave for a few minutes while we test some reflexes," the doctor said. "Nurse, take out the catheter now."

Simon came home to Myrtle Street three days later. His accident had been the result of panic from the driver who broadsided his car, a woman who felt the road tremble beneath her as she drove, causing her to become confused and to make a sharp right turn into Simon's door. She emerged from the wreckage without injury apart from being shaken up.

Now ensconced in their bedroom with Hal in full nursing mode, Simon was allowed visitors, the numbers of them carefully monitored by Hal. "Any damage at your place?" he asked Bertrand and George.

"Not much, a couple of glasses. Strange that some people got hit hard. Did you hear about Roger and Ken?" George asked.

"Yes, Hal told me. Worse was what happened to their upstairs neighbors. Glass everywhere, I hear."

The inventory of friends and acquaintances and how they weathered the quake wound its way through town with tales, some ordinary, some strange, until Hal arrived with a tray of lunch. "Visiting hours are about over, you two. He needs rest and right after he eats, he's going to get some."

"Listen Nurse Ratchet, I spent the entire morning asleep, and I can't sleep anymore today," Simon said as he chewed into a sandwich. "You'd think he's the doctor here, bossing everybody around. Want some lunch? You'll notice that as usual, nursie has brought enough for four field hands."

"You need to build up your strength," Hal said straightening Simon's pillows.

"If I ate everything you bring in here, you'd soon have to build up *your* strength just to move me around," Simon said. "Now please, you guys, help me out here. Hal, sit down and quit fussing. Eat a sandwich."

"Just a minute," Hal said. He headed for the kitchen and returned with a greater supply of sandwiches, mugs of soup, and iced tea for the four of them. "Might as well make him happy."

"Anything new on the political front?" Bertrand asked. "George tells me that things are pretty quiet as far as he knows now that school's out."

"Things are probably not quiet; it's just that we are out of earshot right now," Hal said, pouring tea. "The haters won't be giving up regardless of who's against the initiative. They're up to something, no doubt about that."

# CHAPTER 37

## *Heavenly Treasures*

The Christ Almighty Church of God met on Sunday mornings in an abandoned store that had once sold sporting goods, situated in a strip mall in San Clemente. Pastor G. D. Torrents tended his flock there in what he had labeled a tabernacle, where he also routinely fleeced the membership after regaling them with fire and brimstone orations that stirred the rams and the ewes to dig deeper into their already strained pocketbooks. Money, he never failed to remind the recalcitrant, was the root of all evil, and they were better off giving it over to him to be spent against the forces of evil as he saw them made manifest in the homosexual agenda. "What ye have seen this week is God's own judgment, God's own condemnation, God's own punishment on the evil-doers in Laguna Beach," he railed. "God has spared us from destruction in these latter days to do His work!"

Bertha Peoples sat in the front row of the tabernacle, waiting for the end of the pastor's exhortation to give more money. She wondered how she might have displeased God last week when the earthquake struck and did a great deal of damage to her house. She certainly hadn't been spared from the destruction that G. D. Torrents said had been aimed at the sinners in Laguna. Besides, she knew a couple of neighbors who had houses full of broken items. True, she thought, they aren't members of our church, but she had thought they were pretty good people. Well, God only knows how they came into the wrath of God himself. She'd have to ask the pastor. She had something else to ask him too.

"And so we who are pure and holy have been charged with wiping out the abomination that we find around us. Let us pray," intoned Pastor Torrents, whereupon he launched into a prayer that was nearly as long as his talk had been, a prayer that reiterated much of what he had said in his oration, a prayer that, Bertha noticed, had only one or two things to say: namely, the intolerable presence of sin that attacked the Christ Almighty Church of God, and of course, the fervent hope—nay, demand—for more money to come into the church coffers.

Pastor Torrents waited outside for Bertha. He noticed that she had passed the collection plate without contributing anything, and he wanted to talk with her. "Well Bertha, I wonder how you're getting along."

"Not so well, Pastor. My house was nearly destroyed in the quake, you know. It's going to take a lot to fix it up, and the insurance won't help much. I wasn't able to get earthquake insurance. That's what I wanted to talk with you about."

"Oh, I'm sure it won't be that bad, Bertha. God provides, you know."

"Well, I wish he'd provide me with the money to at least get the back wall put back up," she said. "I can't use my own kitchen."

"Now we mustn't question God, Bertha. God will take care of you, O ye of little faith."

"I was wondering if I might be able to get some help from the church here, Pastor. I'm on a fixed income, you know, and if I get any insurance money, it won't be for quite a while."

"Now Bertha, you know that we don't have the sort of funds here to just fork out money for everybody. We have to pay rent, and we have our campaign to run, now don't we?"

"Yes, I suppose we do, but Betty there in your office told me that we take in quite a lot of money every week. I wouldn't need that much, just a few hundred dollars to tide me over for a while."

"Betty's mistaken there, Bertha. But I'll see what I can do. Now you run along home and I'll be in touch," G. D. said as he edged away from her and toward a young man who was quickly handing out fliers to the departing congregation. "Remember, pray and God answers prayers!"

Whoever it was with the fliers disappeared before he could be identified, but everyone standing in the parking lot had a notice that read:

Trial Date Set

Your fellow parishioner, Richard Palmer, needs your compassionate help and care. He will be called into court on next Thursday at

10:00AM to answer charges. He is accused of public indecency. Now is the time to exercise your Christianity in his behalf. He needs your support at trial.

Superior Court, Santa Ana, California

G. D. Torrents read the flier, and then looked around at his flock. He had wondered where Dick Palmer was and why he hadn't been at services. "What's this mean, Pastor?" several people asked. "Where's Dick? What's this mean 'public indecency' do you think? Why he's my kid's math teacher."

"I'm sure it's some mistake," G. D. Torrents said as he walked back into the storefront, closing the doors behind him.

"Well, I'll be there," said several voices almost in unison. "Me too," said a number of others. A delegation got itself together and organized carpools to Santa Ana. After all, it was their Christian duty.

Inside the storefront tabernacle of the Christ Almighty Church of God, G. D. Torrents sat down to count up the day's take. Not bad for the fifty or so attendees this morning, nearly $900. He pocketed the offering money, opened the door to the parking lot to find the place deserted, and walked to his car. The church's cash was kept at his house where the church's office had a desk, and where from time to time, Betty the secretary typed and ran off bulletins and did the mailing. How she managed to surmise the amounts in the treasury, he couldn't figure out. He kept her away from the church's cash, just as he kept the entire congregation in the dark as to its fluid assets. Now that she was spreading the word that the church coffers held more than G. D. wanted known, he might have to find a replacement for Betty.

He looked once more at the flier. Who had handed them out, he wondered. He drove home, there to open the safe that contained the church's cash, depositing the day's offering inside. He entered the amount into a ledger he kept there, and added it to the total. A cool $155,787.00. All in cash.

What the pastor did not notice as he looked lovingly into the safe where bundles of money lay in perfect order, was a shadow at the window, nor did he hear the clicks of a camera taking photos. It was Willy. He hadn't been paid for his photo job at Hal and Simon's those weeks ago, and his appeal to the pastor for money owed him had been met with evasions and promises to pay in the future. Today Willy had followed him home to demand payment.

What he got was the added benefit of some compelling photos of his own. There should be no problem with the pastor once these were developed if he didn't get what he came for.

---

"I can tell you this, Bertha," Mrs. Roadapple said over the phone, "he didn't help one bit when they took my husband to jail. He's out now, but Torrents never lifted a finger. You didn't see me at church today, did you? Well, I'm through with that bunch, that's what."

"He expected me to give more money today," Bertha replied, "broke as I am. Wouldn't even hear me when I asked him for some help. What kind of trouble do you think Dick Palmer's in?"

"No idea, but if he waits around for Torrents to help him out, he'll wait a long time. What did that flier say?" Bertha read the announcement to her. "Public indecency? This otta be good. Let's you and me go up there on Thursday."

# CHAPTER 38

## 'Once to every man and nation...'

The delegation from the Christ Almighty Church of God that drove up to Santa Ana on Thursday did so without its pastor who elected to distance himself from the proceedings, which, he rightly surmised, would embarrass him and his congregation by their association with the accused. Nearly thirty of the flock strode into Courtroom B just before 10:00AM, there to witness a row of arraigned malefactors sitting on a front row bench, awaiting the presence of the judge. Third in line was Dick Palmer.

In the back of the courtroom sat Hal, George, and several other men who had recently formed up an anti-Briggs Initiative committee. Another man sat some seats away, a man Hal slightly recognized but did not know.

"All rise!" the bailiff announced as the judge came into court and took his seat. Once everyone was reseated, the proceedings began with the first of the accused. Petty theft. Plead guilty. Six months in county jail and restitution. The second was a shoplifter who received similar sentencing. Then it was Dick Palmer's turn. He hadn't looked around at the audience, but when he was told to stand to hear the charge against him, he glanced back to see the multitude of his church peers who had arrived . . . for what purpose, he wondered. He couldn't think of any one of them who would automatically be on his side, would defend him, would extend him any sort of compassion. Using the example of the crowd before Pontius Pilate in ancient Jerusalem, he surmised that they were here to condemn him, to crucify him. He'd show them. He'd plead not guilty. If they were here for a show, he wouldn't be providing one.

The bailiff read out the indictment: "Public nudity and lewd behavior."

"How do you plead?"

"Not guilty, Your Honor," Dick Palmer stammered.

"That is of course your right, Mr. Palmer. You have the chance to clear this whole thing up here and now as well. Or your case can be continued pending trial. It is also your right to explain and defend yourself here, or by means of a lawyer. Which would you like to do?"

"I . . . I'd like to explain . . ." Dick said.

"Go ahead."

Dick told the same story he had told Hal and Simon the night that they went to bail him out of jail, how he was innocently walking along the beach, how he began talking with a man whom he didn't know there, how what happened was misconstrued by the police who arrested them.

"It says here in the police report that both you and the man you met were undressed and were engaging in sexual activity. Are you disputing this report, Mr. Palmer?" the judge asked.

A long pause.

"Mr. Palmer?"

"Yes, I am."

"Is the arresting officer present?" the judge asked the bailiff.

"No, Your Honor."

"Then we have to take Mr. Palmer's statement as fact and dismiss the charges against him."

"No, you don't have to, Your Honor," said a voice from the back of the courtroom. The unidentified man. "I was the other man." Quite a roar throughout the audience.

"Please come forward sir. Do you want to testify in this case?"

"I do. My name is Bill Richards."

"Swear him in, Bailiff." That done, the judge asked, "What can you tell us about the events in question?"

A very different story emerged, one in which Dick Palmer had not only been complicit in sex on the beach, but had suggested it in the first place.

"It didn't take long to figure out what we both wanted, Your Honor. When a man puts his hand on your crotch and feels what's there, that's a pretty good indication where things are going," Bill Richards said.

"He's lying. It's all lies!" Dick Palmer said. "We never did anything. I've never seen this man before!"

"No, not lies, Dick. And if you hadn't sold me out that night, I wouldn't be here today. You lied to the cops, said I propositioned you. Got me an additional charge of soliciting sex. Then I find out you belong to the fundie church down in San Clemente that wants to root out queers everywhere."

"Let's come back to the question before us, gentlemen," the judge said. "What evidence do you have, Mr. Richards, beyond your story that you think varies from Mr. Palmer's?"

"Do you mean how can I prove we were having sex? Well, they caught us naked, didn't they? And that was in the dark, under the porch floor of a house. Before that, we were in the light, saw each other very clearly, if you know what I mean."

"Without being too explicit, Mr. Richards, tell the court what you mean."

"Dick here has some unusual things down there. First, he's uncircumcised, not that that's unusual, but he also has a birthmark that covers about half of his penis. Now how would I know that if we hadn't been uh . . . exploring each other with the help of the street light before we ducked under that house?" Dick Palmer visibly paled.

"Is this accurate, Mr. Palmer? Do you have the physical aspects that Mr. Richards has described?"

There was no denying that he had. He hung his head and murmured, "Guilty."

The fine amounted to $500 with no jail time. Probation for one year.

The stunned congregation of the Christ Almighty Church of God filed out of the courtroom. "I'da never thought it of Dick Palmer," one of them said, shaking his head. "That queer'll never be welcome back at church. We'll run him off if he tries."

"Nah, he'll never come back. He knows what'd happen to him if he did," said another compassionate follower of the Reverend G. D. Torrents.

Bertha and Mrs. Roadapple left together. "See? I told ya Torrents wouldn't be here. I feel kinda sorry for Mr. Palmer. You know I've got a gay brother, don't ya? That's where Barry's stayin' right now. He's better up there than he was livin' with me and my man."

Their chat took them to the parking lot where their dispirited cohorts were getting into cars. Hal watched with something like triumph as the somber church members drove off. It was, after all, a war that they had begun, had waged, and had escalated against him and others like him. The war was not over, but he felt that this battle had been won, even at the expense of his own sense of well-being. He drove George and the other men back to Laguna and reported everything to Simon.

"I count this as victory number two. First, that mess with the Roadapples that came out in my favor, and now this. A stunning blow to the bigots, Simon."

"I suppose it was," Simon replied. "But somehow it seems a hollow victory to me."

"Come on! These people are our enemies! They are out to destroy us. That so-called church down there is nothing more than a spewing lava bed of hatred. Look what it almost did to Barry. We've got to fight back and win where we can," Hal said.

"You're right, of course. The institution itself fosters exactly what basic Christianity preaches against. My church back in Iowa may have been in the dark about a lot of issues, but we were taught to think about other people. I can't help thinking what kind of hell Dick Palmer's been through."

"On the brutal and rocky road to self-discovery, you mean? Yeah, you may have a point."

"If we're ever going to win the war of equality with the society in general, it's not going to be because of court decisions or even legislation. It's going to be through one-on-one contact. The way I see it, it's the only way that will work on the long term. You can't legislate respect for other people."

"No, but you can set up laws that protect everyone from being harmed by the unreasonable hatred of bigots," Hal said. "We have no such protections right now. We have to fight for those at least."

"I couldn't agree more, my love. But I'm talking about how we deal with individual men like Dick Palmer, men who have so much self-hatred that they vent it on others. What they need is compassion, not punishment. He's one of us, Hal. Think about that. Whether he wants to admit it right now or not, he's one of us."

Hal did think about it. He thought about what had happened to Bertrand once he saw what a gay extended family looked like and how it operated, how Bertrand's whole attitude toward himself had changed once he coupled up with George and began a new life. He thought quite a lot about what Simon said, and he took stock of what they had together.

Then he phoned Dick Palmer.

# CHAPTER 39

## 'Comes the moment to decide . . .'

Saturday morning breakfast on Myrtle Street and the usual suspects had been rounded up. "I'm speechless," Norman Stands said as he buttered a hot scone.

"Now there's a hyperbole. You? Speechless? This is not our Norman; this person is an imposter," Ken laughed.

"Not with all that silver and turquoise loot on, it isn't," George giggled. "Gotta be the real thing."

"You know what I mean, you bitches," Norman sniffed. "I go away for a month and the whole town goes to ruin. And I don't mean that little tremor that everyone got their panties in a knot over, either."

"Any damage at your place?"

"None to speak of. But everybody seems to have changed partners. I figured you two might keep on humping next door, but who would have thought that Martha would ever leave Laguna and move on up into the higher ethers of Hollywood? And with Dana, no less! Did you hear that Brett has moved in with them too? God only knows what that's about."

"There's more, old dear," Hal said, pouring more coffee. "Anyone want eggs?"

"More? Well, let's have it. What else?"

Roger piped up. "Miguel and Barry. Miguel's legal for a change. Got a green card and he's working for me at the hotel. That is, the two of them are, at least until fall when Barry's going to start school."

"Too nice, honey. Isn't there some real dirt anywhere? What's been happening at The Cove? Doesn't anybody have the decency to frequent our holy shrine anymore? Vi Winters must be desolate now that she has to sing her entire gig by herself. I hear you're not part of the act anymore, Bertrand."

"Too busy. After we had to replace Brett in *Streetcar*, we had a lot of work to do to get Stanley Kowalski believable again. Extra rehearsals, for one thing. But the show's on its feet and doing well. You should come see it. You'll probably like it better than you liked *Oklahoma!*" Bertrand said. Norman's scathing review was still a sore topic, but the scars were healing.

"Yes, well, I was perhaps a bit too severe back then. But Europe has mellowed me; I'm not the hard-hearted crank I once was. My, my, my . . . those Italians . . ." he said as he gazed off into middle distance, lost in reminiscence.

"I'm sure there are tales he could, and not doubt *will* tell," Hal said.

"Let's just say that many Italian men tend to be respectful of older gentlemen," Norman said as he returned from his mini reverie.

A knock at the kitchen door.

"You said I could come by. Is now still OK? Oh, I see you have company. I'll come back later."

"No, no, I wanted you to come over for breakfast. Come in, and meet some friends," Hal said as he ushered the surprise guest into the dining room. "Everyone, this is Richard Palmer, formerly Dick Palmer. Introduce yourselves. Let me get you some coffee, Richard. Sit right down."

\* \* \* \*

Richard Palmer's arrival was the result of two long phone conversations between him and Hal, and then a face-to-face meeting. Hal had never imagined himself as a psychological mentor, but he found himself during that meeting with a tearful man whose self-loathing, coupled with anguish and remorse, had almost brought him to nervous collapse.

"Lucky it's summer, Hal. I couldn't work right now. The thought of getting up in front of kids and teaching math scares the shit out of me. I don't know who I am anymore. I can't sleep, and I'm not eating much," he said as he broke down in sobs.

Hal waited for this bout of weeping to subside, and he put his hand on Richard's arm. Richard turned to Hal and wrapped himself into his arms, laying his head on his shoulder. "Oh God, what am I going to do?"

Hal held him for some time while Richard managed to collect himself. "One thing you're going to do is stop lying to yourself," Hal said. "Now, let's talk about how you can start. So now, it's Richard, huh? What's that about?"

"Think about it. After all my friends found out everything about me, my nickname became a joke. Might as well have been Cock Feeler. Anyway, Richard's my given name and it sounds better, don't you think?" "Sure. Tell me what else is going on," Hal said.

"They kicked me out of the church, you know. As soon as they found out what happened on the beach and at the trial, a couple of them told me that I wasn't welcome there anymore."

"And that surprised you? You were their henchman, their hit man against queers. You didn't for a minute think that they would tolerate your being one, did you? So much for Christian charity and compassion. Doesn't their action toward you tell you something about their mindset? I wouldn't call myself a churchgoer, but I do know what the Founder of the Faith said about forgiveness. You're better than that, Richard, and you deserve better. Don't you see now that hatred is what keeps them going?"

"Yeah, when I started to think about all the stuff that Torrents spouts every chance he gets, and how there isn't much of what you'd call community there. Just money giving and diatribes against fags, uh . . . homosexuals," Richard said.

"And you are one. That's the truth you have to come to, Richard. You are gay. Now that piece of illumination didn't need you to be struck down from a bright light from heaven, did it? Frankly I don't give a damn about that so-called church, but I do care about how you're going to come out of all of this," Hal said.

"But there's so much to deal with. My parents for one thing. My friends from high school. They all live nearby. I can't hide out like you can," Richard said.

"None of us can hide any longer, Richard. We're all too much in the public notice. No, you've been hiding out long enough. And you're right. It will take some courage to live an honest life as a gay man. But you know what? Chances are that your folks and your friends, that is your *real* friends, will be OK with you, no matter what."

"I've got a lot of confessing to do, starting with you. I was the one who was sneaking into your guest cottage through that loose board in the fence. Willy and me." His face saddened when he mentioned Willy.

"And you guys took those pictures of Simon and me? That was pretty low, Richard, but they didn't do the harm that that asshole Torrents and his minion Roadapple hoped they would. I'd be lying if I said that those pictures didn't worry me; they did, and I was upset about what might happen to Simon too."

"Can you forgive me, Hal?"

"Yes, I can. It took a while for me to come to that, but you've got Simon to thank for helping me past a real hatred toward you for threatening us. Simon's the peacemaker in our family, the one of us who sees consequences better, and who thinks about other people better. And I know what made you do it. It's hard sometimes for me to think about the kind of hatred that gets good people to do bad things in its behalf, but I'm getting lessons on how that works. That church you went to is a hotbed of that kind of hatred, and knowing what it has done to harm others helps me understand what it did to you. But now tell me about Willy. What was that look on your face when you remembered him just now?

Richard looked away. After a long pause, "I . . . I'm . . . God I can't say it! Yes, I can. I'm in love with him. We used to get it on, pretending that we were just two straight guys who needed to get a load off. Now I know different. When we had sex, it was like a dream. I didn't want it to end. One time afterwards we just lay naked together and started kissing. We'd never done that before. I didn't want to admit it then, but I was in love with him. We made fun of what we did, just so we wouldn't think of ourselves as fags. But I knew deep down that I wanted him, and that he wanted me." "What about now?" Hal asked.

"I sent him away. Told him I didn't want to see him again. That was a lie, of course. As soon as I said it, we got into the back seat of his car and had sex. Then the loneliness set in and that's how I wound up down on the beach that night. We haven't seen each other since the trial mess. Now I don't know if he wants to see me, but I want to see him."

"Go with it, Richard. Call him. See him if he'll see you. Even if it ends there. It's a stop you can take along the way toward telling the truth."

"Yeah, you're right. I will."

"Richard, you've got a lot of work ahead of you, and if you need me to be your friend, I'm here for you. We're both here for you, Simon and me. Come by the house and spend some time with us. You need to see that fags —and yes, it's an OK term if you are one—can lead a happy life once they come to terms with who they are. Will you come over?"

"Sure. This time through one of the proper doors," he laughed.

"Hey, you're feeling better, huh?"

"Yeah, much. Thanks for being a friend, even after I've treated you so badly, Hal. I'm so very sorry," he said, starting to break down.

"It's OK, and don't go getting weepy on me again, OK? You'll be fine. Just take it a day at a time." Hal hugged him, and Richard kissed him on the neck.

* * * *

Breakfast resumed, introductions all around, with a few side-long glances about what this guy was doing here. Everyone present except for Norman knew who Richard Palmer was, what he had been up to, and what damage he tried to do. And now here he sat among Hal and Simon's closest friends, drinking coffee. It was a baptism by fire, not only for them, but especially for Richard.

He tried to be as calm and sociable as he could be, surrounded as he was by the bizarre and wonderful company of gay men. He looked around thinking, I'm one of them, I'm one of them! And it feels pretty good if only they would stop staring at me as if I were from Mars. Well, I guess I am from Mars, certainly an alien. He turned toward Bertrand. "I saw your play the other night. I don't go to plays much, but I really liked it. You were great in it." It was the perfect ice breaker.

"Why, thank you! You might want to pass on your good vibes to the man with all the jewelry across the table. Meet Norman Stands, the restaurant critic for the newspaper. He hasn't seen the production yet, but since they aren't serving food at it, he might write something nice," Bertrand said as he winked at Norman.

"Never mind that aging actress, Richard. He's got a real mean streak. Now what all are you doing over summer break?"

And so the conversation went on, enveloping the new convert into it. "You'll get used to gender pronouns being switched around, Richard," Simon said, noticing the slight confusion on his face. "It's just a way a speaking. Fortunately, it's a habit that seems to be going away."

"Hal told me about your accident. You look like things are healing fine," Richard said.

"Better than we expected. Had a really good nurse here," he said, reaching over for Hal's hand.

"Uh . . . Hal," Richard said, "could I see you in the kitchen?" Once there, he said, "I've got something of a surprise."

"What? Another one? You showing up and staying with this bunch was a good one already. What's up?"

"Willy. I called him last week like you suggested. We got together, Hal. He wants to meet you and Simon. He's five minutes away. Think it would be all right if he came over now?"

"My God! You don't mean that you'd subject him to this group, do you? Are you sure? I'm not at all worried about them, or you for that matter, but how do you think Willy will take a morning of gay chat around scones and coffee?"

"That's why I had to test the waters first. I think he'll be OK; in fact, I know he will. He told me some things about where he's been that I never suspected. Should I call him?"

Simon was consulted, consent given, and Willy dutifully showed up ten minutes later. "Another surprise, everyone. This is Willy Barnes, Richard's friend," Hal announced. More room made around the table as Willy nonchalantly said hello to the ever-increasing crowd, now numbering nine.

Hal surveyed his table of chatting, happy friends, new and old. He kept the food coming, the coffee flowing, and the conversation fed itself. We could have made an enemy of this man, he thought as he looked over at Richard. We had every right to get even, to ruin his life even further than he already had. But we didn't. Now look at him, smiling and talking with my Simon. This is the best, no matter what else happens. To think that it all started on Shadow Lane, all those years ago.

# CHAPTER 40
## 'For the good or evil side'

The summer roared on with the Pageant of the Masters in full swing, the town crowded with tourists, the gay bars bustling with new arrivals, and perhaps best of all, the current polls showing that the Briggs Initiative was losing. By mid-August, a number of editorials in several major newspapers had condemned the initiative as either a blatant violation of civil rights, or an affront to constitutional freedom. Most political pundits foresaw its being shot down at the state supreme court level. Nevertheless, right-wing churches like the Christ Almighty Church of God continued their campaigns against what they saw as creeping immorality making its way into society and undermining all notions of decency.

The orations from the likes of G. D. Torrents managed to hold a core of the faithful in thrall as he held forth in his storefront tabernacle while brandishing a well worn version of the King James Bible. The truth is that his congregation had shrunk over the last few weeks, and among the defectors were Bertha Peoples and Mrs. Roadapple. "I told Cal that I wasn't settin' foot in that church again," she said to Bertha on the phone. "He can go if he wants to, but there's something fishy about that Torrents."

The Reverend Torrents finished his Sunday talk, said goodbye to his scant flock, and went back inside to count the day's take. Barely $200. Probably the hot summer weather, he thought. He was just pocketing the money as a man came in. "Reverend Torrents?"

"Yes, what can I do for you? You're a bit too late for services today."

"I'm here from the Internal Revenue Service, Reverend. I don't usually make business calls on Sunday, but you are a difficult man to find," the agent said handing Torrents his card and showing him his credentials. "We have been trying to locate your office and your secretary for some time now."

"Well, we've never had what you'd call a church office. This is the only place we have. Betty doesn't work for us as of a month ago."

"Who keeps your records, sir?"

"She did keep them, of course, but now I have had to take on that task. Are you a believer in the Gospels, Mr. uh . . . Belden?" Reverend Torrents asked as he scanned the agent's business card.

Without answering, Agent Belden produced another piece of paper. "This is a summons for an audit of your books, Mr. Torrents. If you look here, you'll see that you are required to bring your records and income statements to the Internal Revenue Office one week from tomorrow. The address is right there. I hope that you have a pleasant Sunday afternoon. Goodbye."

G. D. Torrents, far from being frightened by the audit summons, sat quietly alone in his storefront sanctuary. Then he gathered up his Bible, walked out and locked the door behind him.

\* \* \* \*

It was probably easier for Saul of Tarsus to convince the early Christians of his newfound conversion and become the apostle Paul than it was for Dick Palmer to come out to everyone in his life whom he needed to tell. But he did it, and as he came to accept himself and his new life, he decided to use his real name. He would be Richard, no longer Dick. His mother had always called him Richard, but he had favored the nickname, thinking that it sounded more masculine; now it no longer did.

For some reason his parents had not been any the wiser about his hidden sexuality, and although he figured that they would find out about his trial and the revelations that it provided, he was wrong. While it was a monumental event for him, it had after all been a relatively minor one in the history of local jurisprudence. His mother, who had been waiting with increasing impatience for him to marry and have children, proved the more difficult of his parents to talk to.

"I don't believe it! I simply won't believe it! What about that girl you got into trouble in high school, the one who had to have the abortion?"

"That was a lie, Mom. I took the rap for Benny Simms. I wanted to look good, like a big stud in front of my friends. And you and Dad."

"And that nice girl from college that you dated. We really thought you'd stick with her . . ." his mother said as she began to break down. She began the usual questioning in her mind about where she and her husband had gone wrong, what they had done to produce a gay son. Had she been too doting; had Richard's father been too distant? She vocalized her regrets and blames while choking on tears.

"Mom, it's nothing you did or Dad did. What's important now is who I'll be from here on out. I want and need your support more than ever. I've got new friends, good friends, people that I was once trying to expose as gay. A couple of them are teachers like me. I know this is a shock, but think how I felt when I admitted it to myself."

"I'm worried, Richard. These aren't good times for gays. That Briggs Initiative is going to pass, you mark my words, and then where will you be? You don't intend to tell your school about this, do you?"

"It's not going to pass, Mom, and some of us are working hard to make sure that it doesn't. We need your help."

"My help! You don't think that I'm going to be spreading it around to all of our friends that our son is a qu . . . is gay, do you? We'd be kicked out of the Newport Country Club if they knew. John Wayne's a member there too, even though he's not in very good health these days. He'd be appalled."

Richard stood up and leaned over to kiss his mother goodbye. "You do what you need to do, Mom," he said gently as he left.

Hal turned out to be right about Richard's friends. The beer-drinking crowd that he used to hang out with in Dana Point had mixed reactions to what they had heard about his court appearance. When Richard arrived at the Ship's Anchor Bar, he overheard (he was meant to) one of his 'pals' say, "Here comes the queer." He knew he was in for it.

"Wanna tell us about that night on the beach, Dickie boy? I mean, if you were passing out blow jobs, how come you didn't let us know? I'da been first in line," said Jake Southey. "I've got a lot you could work on right here, honey."

"Buzz off Jake," Richard said.

"You got a lot of nerve comin' in here, you know that? You fucking queer. And all this time you had us going on your anti-fag crap. You make me sick."

Richard walked past the half-drunken Jake and found a seat at the far end of the bar where he ordered a beer. The bartender hesitated and then brought the beer, collected the money for it, and disappeared. Richard sipped his beer, ignoring the taunts that continued from Jake and his cronies. When that died down and serious drinking began in earnest, Richard looked around to see if he had any friends left at all. One set of eyes had watched him all the while, and then they came closer as if to pass by on the way to the rest room. "You could have told me, you know," the owner of the eyes said. "I'd have understood. I thought we were friends."

"I'm having a little trouble figuring out just who my friends are right now, Randy," Richard said. Randy looked askance. "Are you my friend?" "Not in that way, I'm not," Randy replied.

"Didn't ask you to go that far."

"We can't talk in here. And I don't want to leave with you, if you don't mind. Meet me at that coffee shop across the harbor in twenty minutes." With that, Randy left the bar. Richard finished his beer and left by a side door, avoiding walking past Jake. When he got to the coffee shop, he saw Randy sitting in a booth in the back.

"You're not the first gay guy I've ever known, you know," Randy said as Richard sat down across from him. "My best friend in high school kept his secret from me just like you did. Turned out he had the hots for me for years, since eighth grade. Never told me. Must have been hell for him, too. We did everything together, once we even jacked off together like about every other guy does at some time or other. But you know what pissed me off? That he didn't think our friendship was strong enough to let me know how he felt, how he was."

"Do you ever see him anymore?"

"Not much. He moved to San Francisco after college. He and his partner bought a shop on Castro Street. No, I don't see him very often. Our lives have gone in different ways. But you know what? I miss him. He and I were like that," Randy said, putting two of his fingers together. "If I'd have been gay, we'd be together right now, I'm sure of that."

"You and I haven't been that close as friends, Randy. How come you're pissed at me?"

"I thought that we were good enough friends that you could tell me anything, but maybe I was wrong."

"You got to understand that I wasn't even telling *myself* about my own life. Every time I'd get some urge to be with another guy, I'd hate myself even more. Then along came Willy."

"Willy! Willy's gay?"

"Gay as a box of birds as some of my new acquaintances like to say. He'd been in and out of the gay scene in San Diego for years before he moved up here. The first time he and I got it on—hey if this embarrasses you, tell me, OK?" Richard said.

"No, I'm fine. Go on."

"Well, at first it was just playing around, but not for me," Richard said as he tried to explain his feelings for Willy and what he did about them. "I pretended that it didn't happen, but all I could think about was being with Willy. And now I am."

"What? You guys are a couple? God, things move fast. When did all this happen?"

"Last week. Found an apartment in Laguna, nice top floor place. We moved in right after it was cleared of broken glass from that quake we had a few weeks ago. Two older guys had it, but now it's ours."

"Well I'll be damned. What's next?"

"A lot of things are next. There's a lot of work to be done against this Briggs threat. Some guys in Laguna have organized a committee to fight against it. Even though some leading Republicans said that they wouldn't support Briggs, we're not taking any chances. They're raising money to put ads on TV. There's a rally in Santa Ana next weekend, and I'm going to be there. In fact, the committee has asked me to speak as a gay teacher whose job is threatened, and as somebody who has seen the light."

"Santa Ana, huh? Sounds dangerous to me. Lots of rednecks and rightwingers up there."

"The police will be there too. It's a peaceful rally. You should come up to hear my debut as a fag speaker," Richard smiled. The two men chatted on about other topics, sports mainly, and finally got up to leave.

"Listen, keep me in the loop, OK? I am your friend, and so is my wife," Randy said. "Donna and I want you and Willy to come down sometime for dinner."

"Fine with me, and thanks. I'll talk to Willy about it and let you know."

# CHAPTER 41
## Duty and Action

It was almost time to return to school, and Hal had to admit he was less than enthusiastic about the fall term starting again. Every other year, he'd been eager to get back to work after two months off, but the current atmosphere, polluted as it was by the uncertainty of the Briggs Initiative, returned a kind of gloom to his mind. The summer had evolved into weeks of nearly carefree times, and Hal was a bit loathe to leave the sanctuary of his home and once more to deal with the doubts that he had left behind at the close of school in June.

Nevertheless he filed into the initial teacher meetings, generally big time wasters, and he surveyed the auditorium. Familiar faces in various attitudes ranging from boredom to complacent gazed languidly back at him. A few smiles of greeting, a couple of waves from across the room. Richard, he noticed, sat with his colleagues in the math department, chatting amiably with one of his neighbors. Hal caught his eye and got a broad smile in return.

Principal McHenry got up to welcome everyone back, gave out the usual state of the school address, talked about what building improvements had been made over the summer, and then launched into a more interesting topic. "We are faced with a great social problem, one that has important consequences for all of us. I am talking about the upcoming election and the Briggs Initiative. As you all know, this ballot measure, under the guise of protecting our students, seeks to root out gay teachers from our midst, presuming that they are inappropriate influences on the youth of the state. There is, of course, no proof of inappropriate influence, no evidence whatever that a gay teacher is anything but a teacher, just like everyone else.

"This initiative is a misguided, hate-inspired, and harmful attempt to undermine the entire educational system. If passed by the voters and approved by the courts, this measure would usher in another witch hunt that would make the one in the 1950s seem puny by comparison. Whatever your personal feelings about gay people may be, I appeal to your sense of common decency and the rights of privacy that we all expect to have, and vote against this initiative. More than that, I encourage your help throughout the community to work for its defeat. There will be a rally at the courthouse in Santa Ana next week, one that I plan to attend, against the Briggs Initiative, and I hope that many of you will be there as well."

He concluded with a few more nuts and bolts issues necessary to begin school, and sat down. At first, nobody moved, but then Richard Palmer got to his feet. "I'll be going to that rally. Anyone who needs a ride can go along with me." His math colleagues looked at him as if he were an alien. They couldn't have been more stunned, remembering as they did that only two months ago, Dick Palmer was in the forefront of the pro-Briggs campaign. His sudden change of course was the same as his coming out, and it didn't take long for that possibility to dawn on the minds of his coworkers.

Richard looked over at Hal and smiled. Hal smiled back and followed suit. "Same here. I'll be driving up there with my partner, but we have room in the car for more people. Just let me know." More stunned looks. What did he mean by 'partner'? Certainly word about the trouble with the Roadapples had leaked out and was known by most of the faculty, but they had been content to lay that issue to rest and be quiet about it. They expected Hal to be quiet about it too, and now here he was proclaiming a partner?

A general muttering began among the assembly, then the French teacher got to her feet and offered her car as well. Then two of the gym teachers, and a couple of people from social science. A total of twenty or so teachers stood ready to attend the rally and provide rides for others. It wasn't a general coming-out party—certainly not all of the volunteers were gay—but it was a show of support that Hal had never thought to see. Not all of the faculty rose to their feet in support; in fact, about half of them sat while Hal and the others against the initiative left.

Richard caught up with him outside. "Better than I thought it would be. This is going to be a great rally," he said as he clapped Hal on the back.

"I'll bet you scared the hell out of the math department, Richard my man. Most of them looked like you just peed on their feet."

"Yeah, well they might as well get used to it," he said, heading for his classroom. "See you later."

Since Senator Briggs represented much of Orange County, he commanded a large following for Proposition 6. The county seat, Santa Ana, had long been known as a smoldering pit of right-wing notions, and to have a peaceful rally against Prop 6 right in the middle of the city seemed to many a foolhardy idea. The conservative element there sat smugly expecting the initiative to pass easily. But they had underestimated the reactions that an outraged group of citizens might exhibit.

> "Gay men and lesbians came out to their families and their neighbors and their coworkers, spoke in their churches and community centers, sent letters to their local editors, and otherwise revealed to the general population that gay people really were "everywhere" and included people they already knew and cared about. In the beginning of September, the ballot measure was ahead in public-opinion polls, with about 61% of voters supporting it while 31% opposed it. The movement against it initially succeeded little in shifting public opinion, even though major organizations and ecclesiastical groups opposed it. By the end of the month, however, the balance of the polls shifted to 45% in favor of the initiative, 43% opposed, and 12% undecided.
>
> "Some gay Republicans also became organized against the initiative on a grassroots level. The most prominent of these, the Log Cabin Republicans, was founded in 1977 in California, as a rallying point for Republicans opposed to the Briggs Initiative. The Log Cabin Club then lobbied Republican officials to oppose the measure."
>
> —Rimmerman, Craig. "From Identity to Politics: The Lesbian and Gay Movements in the United States" Temple University Press.

So it was with great optimism that the Saturday rally formed on the front lawn of the Santa Ana Courthouse that September. All seemed peaceful as cars began to unload passengers, banners appeared, and organizers started moving the increasing crowd toward a makeshift podium where several speakers were to address the rally.

Several mayors from the coast towns and cities spoke, some eloquently, others not, but all opposed the passing of Proposition 6. Hal and Simon, along with a large group of friends from Laguna applauded and cheered these salutary speeches, most of which were short and to the point. Vendors of soft drinks and sandwiches appeared among the crowd, and the rally became a picnic, filled with conviviality and the heartening feeling that exudes from a like-minded crowd that is having a good time while assuring themselves that their cause is just and right. The September sun filtered in through the trees, and supported by a gentle breeze, provided just enough shade to keep things comfortable.

Along the perimeter of the rally, the police kept a lookout for any possible trouble. No sign of the pro-Briggs contingent. After a number of speakers had finished, the police began to relax. The rally was scheduled to last only two hours, and nearly one of those was over. Surely nothing would happen now. A few of the police began availing themselves of sandwiches, some even mingling with the crowd.

More speakers came forward, and soon it was Richard Palmer's turn at the microphone. "Three months ago, I spearheaded the Yes on Prop 6 Campaign in south Orange County. I worked through a church there to promote the Briggs Initiative because I believed in it. I believed that we had to protect our kids from the influence of gay and lesbian teachers, and my efforts were tireless, underhanded, sneaky, offensive to basic American liberties, and downright evil. What I didn't recognize, or refused to own up to, was that I am a gay man, and not only a gay man but a gay teacher. I will not go into the events that have moved me from my former life of lies and deceit, and into my current life of being an openly gay man. The fact that I am standing before this huge crowd and admitting who I really am is testimony to the truth I want to speak to you now. That truth is that the Briggs Initiative represents the worst sort of misguided Americanism, the kind that denies citizens the basic rights of freedom and the pursuit of happiness, guaranteed by the Constitution of the United States. It personifies the bigotry and unreasoned hatred against a large part of the population, and it proclaims to the world how depraved and degraded some politicians can be in the name of America."

Much applause from the appreciative gathering.

At first, it didn't sound like a shot. The noise from the crowd masked it. But it was a shot, and Richard Palmer fell backwards into the row of other speakers, his head half blown away.

# CHAPTER 42

## *By the light of burning martyrs*

For many among the gay community, the threat posed by the Briggs Initiative had seemed merely political, out of their particular range of interest, and something that did not pertain to them. But that attitude changed after the murder of Richard Palmer. One of their own had been killed, and it took very little imagination, even among the most indifferent, to see how closely such attacks might be aimed directly at them. An outpouring of grief at first accompanied Richard's death, but after that came a surge of popular support for his cause, not only from gay men, but from formerly unsuspected allies. More and more people also saw the dangers inherent in arming the conservative right wing with an approved ballot measure.

Money began to pour into a central campaign that had been organized to fight against Proposition 6, editorials in even the most conservative newspapers started to question it, and speeches around the state denouncing such a travesty to individual freedoms brought furious listeners to their feet in protest against the Briggs Initiative. Banners of all kinds advocated its defeat, and campaign buttons that declared the wearer's opposition stated NO on PROP 6.

Hal and Simon continued to sponsor fundraisers by selling dinners at their house at $50 per plate. The kitchen was in constant operation as night after night of diners came and went. "We're over $3000," Hal said after the last six diners had left. "At this rate, we might make $5000."

"If you don't die of exhaustion first," Simon said. He sank down on the sofa beside Hal and rubbed his lover's head.

"I'm OK, but my schoolwork is suffering a bit. I'm behind in grading for one thing. But it's only for another few weeks. The kids understand; in fact, the kids have been great. They've started their own fundraiser, did I tell you that? They handed me over $100 in change the other day. I'm very proud of them."

"Not all of them are contributing, I'm sure. There is still that idiot fringe down there, spearheaded by Torrents and his gang of hoodlums. Who would have thought that Roadapple would take it upon himself to shoot Richard Palmer?"

"Yeah, well we're all still grieving his death down there. And frankly, nothing that Roadapple would get up to surprises me. At least he's in jail. Can't wait for *that* trial."

"He's on his own, I hear," Simon said. "Even The Christ Almighty Church of God has disavowed any connection with him or the shooting. How's Willy doing?"

"OK I think. After two weeks alone in that top floor place that he rented with Richard, he moved out and went back to San Diego. Last I heard he was working against Prop 6 down there." They fell silent as they remembered the day of the shooting, how Willy had leapt onto the podium to see to Richard, taking him into his arms. Richard was already dead, but Willy stayed there until paramedics took the body from him. They remembered the shock and horror as the reality of the murder found its way into everyone's consciousness. They remembered the cries of dismay and grief, and then the arrest of Cal Roadapple who had tried to make a getaway, but who got tackled by some enraged rally attendees.

"Come on. We've got dishes to do," Hal said as he broke free from those terrible memories. "We never dreamed that anyone would become a martyr for us, but we have one now. I wonder what the popularity polls are saying now?"

Richard Palmer's funeral was not held at the Christ Almighty Church of God; instead, his mother arranged a service at her church in Newport Beach. It was a dignified service, attended by a large number of gay men whose outpouring of sympathy and grief greatly impressed her.

There were two reasons why the Christ Almighty Church of God had distanced itself from the murder. First, Richard had been expelled from its Christian embrace because he was gay. The second was that things at the church were in disarray now that the Rev. G. D. Torrents had absconded with its funds.

After the IRS agent had visited the good reverend that Sunday and presented him with a summons to an audit of the church's books, he searched his conscience for the best course of action. He could appear at the audit and try to explain the church's finances, but that would mean a quick manufacture of books and records which, apart from the single ledger that he kept, did not exist. However he could rely on his powers of persuasion, so often demonstrated from the pulpit, to explain the church's mission and goals as well as its fight against the forces of evil. But he wondered how receptive to his message a cold-blooded auditor might be.

His other path toward relieving his brush with an unfeeling bureaucracy was to bolt and run. That's what he did.

When on the subsequent Sunday morning the faithful of the congregation gathered in front of the storefront tabernacle, they found it locked. Once a key was found and they were inside, there was no sign of Reverend Torrents. Nothing else either. Even the Bibles were gone. A delegation made its way to his residence where a similarly locked door greeted them. Now suspicions arose, and one of the flock climbed through a window. Empty safe, empty closets.

"He's gone! Just up and left!" said Fred Ovine. "And so's the money!" The dispirited flock returned to the tabernacle to announce the news.

Two weeks before the election and still no word from Ronald Reagan, the former governor of California. There had been some rumors, mostly promulgated by gay Republicans, that he would make a statement about the Briggs Initiative, but the rumors did not go so far as to say which side he might take. Tensions mounted as the pro and con campaigns neared November. Finally on November 1, the Los Angeles Times printed his opinion:

*"Whatever else it is, homosexuality is not a contagious disease like the measles. Prevailing scientific opinion is that an individual's sexuality is determined at a very early age and that a child's teachers do not really influence this."*

And that sounded the death knell for Proposition 6, the Briggs Initiative. It was defeated by over 58% of the voters on November 7, just six days after Reagan's op-ed piece appeared.

Naturally a great deal of rejoicing went on after the election, along with a general and almost palpable sigh of relief. This defeat was the first one against the forces of bigotry that had been stirred to action the previous year in Florida, and it gave hope to a segment of the population that some modicum of rightness and justice could prevail after all.

Parties and more parties celebrated the victory; The Blue Cove held one of the largest of them, giving out free drinks for an entire afternoon, and free food that night. Hal and Simon had kept track of everyone who had contributed at one of their dinners, and issued them all an invitation to come over on Saturday for drinks. "My God! I didn't think they would all show up," Norman Stands said as he surveyed the multitude of joyous gay men who crowded the rooms and lawns of the house on Myrtle Street. "Maybe you should have invited them in batches."

"Maybe. Some of them seem to be getting a little frisky," Hal said as he looked skeptically down the hall toward the closed door of their bedroom. "Just got that white bedspread cleaned . . ." he said.

"If I know who went in there, and I do," Norman said, "You'll probably have to get it cleaned again. But don't worry if the stains don't come out, dear. Tie-die patterns are back in fashion."

"Cold comfort, you old queen. Now, who is this young thing you brought with you?"

"That would be the lovely Danny, and he's not all that young, you nasty cow. He's all of forty-one."

"Relative to you, that's chicken. But where did you find him? Is he a dealer in turquoise jewelry? Has he found you that special ring you've been wanting?"

"He has no interest in jewelry except when I wear it. And I'm not telling you anything else."

"Ha! By the time this party's over, everything about him will be public knowledge. I've got to find Simon. I think he was being buttonholed by Martha. Mix and mingle, dearie."

* * * *

"And who should be coming up our walk but none other than . . . well, I can't say? But he's a blond heartthrob? We used to see him here in town?

And now here he was coming to our house for cocktails?" Martha had indeed cornered Simon as well as Roger—literally cornered them. Martha had learned by now that keeping the attention of an audience was beyond her conversational skills, and that blocking a victim's possibility of escape gave her a better chance to dispense her news. "And what a beautiful boyfriend he brought with him? His name's Brett and he said he got his start right here in Laguna in some dreary play with what's his name next door? Yaaas, Bertrand, that's the one?"

"Bertrand's been in two plays since then," Roger volunteered as soon as there was the slightest detectable break in Martha's monologue.

"Well the things that handsome Brett told us that went on between him and Bertrand? I wouldn't stand that from Dana, and you know how every man in Hollywood wants him? I can't imagine how George puts up with it?" Martha's inclination toward making up news had elevated to the level of grocery store tabloids.

Simon began edging away, pushing Roger ahead of him. "Well Marty, I have to mingle. I'm one of the hosts, you know. You really should write down all those fascinating tales of Hollywood. Keep a diary. You know what Mae West said, don't you? 'Always keep a diary, deary, and someday it'll keep you.' Now that's good advice."

Noticing their successful escape, Martha began looking around for her next victim. "Mae who?"

Although billed as an afternoon party, the revelers showed little interest in leaving even after the sun went down. People came and went, drank gallons of alcohol, ate the house bare, and still they stayed. Hal had decided that he and Simon would not be the kitchen slaves to this shindig, and when the food and liquor ran out, that would end the party. But nothing ran out. As other people arrived, they brought food and bottles of whatever they were drinking. Miguel and Barry kept the overflow of trash down in the kitchen by carting bags of it out the alley. It was a party worthy of any thrown by the fabled Auntie Mame.

At last the numbers began to dwindle at around 11:00PM, and the extent of the devastation could more clearly be estimated. Norman had left hours ago with the winsome Danny, Dana and Martha had decamped first to The

Cove and then to their hotel, Ken and Roger were asleep in the guestroom, and Hal and Simon propped each other up on the living room sofa. "What news from the Western Front?" Hal slurred.

"If you mean the back yard, things look like hell. Means it was a great party, huh? Know where Edward went? He holed up in our bedroom closet once somebody stepped on his tail. I saw him in there fast asleep."

"He'll be the only one in the house without a hangover tomorrow," Hal said as he tried unsuccessfully to get up. "How about sleeping right here?"

"Not a chance. On three. One, two, three! There, that wasn't so bad," Simon said as he swayed back into Hal's arms. "It's off to bed with you, old man. And don't even think about trying to tickle me!"

## CHAPTER 43
# *It's Always Something*

"How many do you think we have in our family these days?" Hal asked as he began making a list for Thanksgiving. "Remember when it was just the four of us, back on Shadow Lane? Now we've got Barry and Miguel, the two boys and their partners, and Ken and Roger, just for starters. Who else?"

"That sounds like enough to me," Simon said sounding preoccupied, "but we can't leave Bertrand and George out, can we?"

"No, we can't. What are you reading that's got you so interested?"

"Not anything good, I can tell you. New reports of a strange disease starting up in parts of Africa and Haiti. It's not another influenza but it kills quickly. One of the symptoms is that cancer that Wilbur Initson has, or I should say, had. He went to Mayo Clinic for it. They couldn't do anything either. Did I tell you that he died?"

"Sorry to hear that, but Haiti's a long way from here; so's Africa. What are you so worried about?"

"Mostly about the fact that nobody knows what causes the disease. Or how it is spread. We'll keep an eye on it." Simon said as he returned to his medical journal.

"I'm more concerned right now with what the right wing will hit us with next. You don't think for a minute that they've given up, do you?"

The campaign against the Briggs Initiative had left a gay population greatly changed from its blithe attitude before the threat of political, and possibly legal, forces were launched against it. Ad hoc committees that had formed to stop the Briggs terror now stood ready to solidify into permanent organizations to combat any future incursion into the rights of gay people, and they aimed to become the watchdogs over the political aspirations of the conservatives. Movements began in search of further enfranchisement, the first of which was legal marriage for same-sex couples. Hal's trouble in getting into the hospital to visit Simon when he was injured was only one instance that underscored the need for a revision of the current laws.

In general, life in Laguna settled in for the holidays. Bertrand was involved in a revival of Dickens' *A Christmas Carol* and happily took the role of Scrooge. "It will take quite a lot of makeup to get you looking like an old miser," George said. "You'll be the handsomest Scrooge ever."

"In lots of ways, I understand him, Scrooge I mean," Bertrand said. "He was a man who had lost his way, who lived for the accumulation of money instead of realizing what had happened to him over the years, and what was really important. I was like that—well, not about money—but I got calloused by life too, and like Scrooge, I got back into real living. It didn't take three ghosts to do it either."

"You're talking about that night on the beach, aren't you?" George asked.

"I've never been able to figure out exactly what happened that night, but it did happen and it changed me as surely as that Christmas Eve changed old Ebenezer. The difference is that he didn't have you to come home to."

It is likely that all couples have secrets kept locked up in the deepest vaults of memory. George had long thought about his secret, namely that he was glad that Bertrand no longer sang, or tried to sing, and that he was not making a fool of himself and being laughed at behind his back. George knew the sound of that laughter; it hadn't been all that well hidden from him in the early days of his and Bertrand's relationship, and it was a great relief when Bertrand's minor surgery took care of the problem. There were times since then that some impulse of honesty, some inclination to reveal how he had felt back then arose in his mind. Shouldn't couples be entirely truthful with each other? Shouldn't each person be able to tell the other even the deepest things dwelling in the farthest reaches of the mind? Somehow, some instinct told him that coming clean on this topic would not do anything toward further cementing their relationship, and he had remained quiet.

And it was for the better. Bertrand had found himself as an actor, and more importantly to George, as a partner. He looked at Bertrand now and knew that the best Christmas present would be his silence. He watched Bertrand going over the lines he would speak as Ebenezer Scrooge, and he loved him.

"Know what? This is going to be a great Christmas. I want to do it all. I want to see all the smarmy Christmas movies, go to lots of parties, sing all the carols, maybe even go to church! What do you think about that?"

"I sort of draw the line at church," Bertrand said, "but everything else sounds great. But on second thought, maybe that service at St. Mary's Episcopal wouldn't be bad, huh? I used to sing in their choir you know, back when I could sing. Yeah, let's do that too."

\* \* \* \*

Carl's visit wasn't exactly a surprise, but Hal and Simon had seen less of him and Eric over the last few months. They had been to the victory party, but had left early. "Come on in, Carl," Hal said, greeting his old friend. He's less of a friend than he used to be, Hal thought, now that he and Eric have got into the real estate business. "How's everything with you? Simon's still at work."

Carl looked drawn and tired. Hal was always a bit astonished at how quickly he seemed to be aging. Back in 1964 when they had first met in the Navy, Carl had a shock of blond hair, and now only fourteen years later, he had lost most of it. What was left was stringy and combed over Carl's pate in an unsuccessful effort to hide his rapidly encroaching baldness. More than that, wrinkles had begun to be prominent around his eyes and on his forehead. He's younger than I am by three years, Hal thought as he led Carl into the kitchen, but he looks ten years older.

"He's gone, Hal."

"Who's gone?"

"Eric. He's gone. I have no clear idea where, but he's not too far away. I got home last night from looking in on a property we have in Santa Ana, and he was gone. All of his clothes, everything."

"Here, take this," Hal said offering him a beer. "Now tell what's been happening. You're sure? Yes, of course, you're sure. It's just that I'm so surprised."

"No more surprised than I am. Oh hell, maybe I'm not surprised. Things have cooled down a lot between us over the past couple of months. We're both so damned busy with all these properties. Sometimes we wouldn't see each other for more than few minutes for several days at a time. When we did, it was all business, rents, leases, sales, escrows, stuff like that."

"But you have no idea where he might be?"

"The only place I'm certain he wouldn't be is Denise's mausoleum. He bought a house in Newport that he didn't think I knew about, and he might be up there. He's always liked being mysterious, Hal, you know that. I've never felt that he told me everything about himself. I've been content with what I did know, with what we built together."

"Wow, so where does this leave you if he has taken himself out of the picture?"

"I'm fine. We've done some amazing real estate deals during the last year. At first they were all in his name, and then I figured that I could get into the game too. Now I own a few places of my own."

Hal looked at him for a minute. "You'll pardon my saying so, but you don't seem all that upset about this. I mean, I'm not sure why you wanted to come tell me. I'm more surprised than you, I think."

"I don't know how I feel right now. Maybe I'm just numb, but you may be right. I can't reach my feelings about Eric. And that's part of the news. Hal, I don't think I'm cut out to be a gay man. I've met a woman and I think I want to marry her."

"Oh wow, here we go again. If you're looking for another rescue from me from a horrid marriage, I'm out of the loop this time around. What do you mean you *think* you want to marry her? You've been down this road twice before, Carl, and both times it was a disaster at the end of it."

"I know, but that was then. I've moved on since those days, matured more. No, you won't have to rescue me this time."

"When did you plan to tell Eric about your upcoming nuptials?"

"After New Year's. But he's made it easier for me by leaving."

"Maybe he found out on his own. Does he know your new beloved?"

"See Hal, it's that tone, that gay tone that you're using right now that I can't stand. So cynical and demeaning."

"Right, right. Sorry. Just a habit. But you've got to admit that your track record with women might lead anybody to be a bit dubious."

"Really? Do you think so? One of the irritants about gay life is every gay man's insistence that once you're gay, you're gay and that's it. Well that's not it. People change. Didn't Richard Palmer change, come to a better realization of himself? And my conversations with your neighbor George lead me to think that Bertrand has changed. Have you changed? Yes, you have. From the depressed, and I might add, depressing hermit you used to be to who you are right now, somebody who's worth liking and living with."

"Yeah, you're right. We're only just beginning to learn that Kinsey was right, that we aren't necessarily all one thing or another. As far as Richard's history goes, he probably always was gay; it took him years to see that. But I get your point. But what now?"

"I'd like to stay friends with you and Simon, be a part of your circle, and I'd like you to meet Lenore. That's all. I don't want this gay-or-not-gay thinking to get in the way of our friendship. I know that we haven't been that close lately, but when you think about it, you and I have known each other longer than anyone. You've always been there for me, Hal, and I love you like a brother."

Hal chuckled. "Once you loved me a little more strongly than that, remember?"

"Yeah, I do, way back in Pennsylvania the night before my first, but aborted, wedding. That was quite a night, escaping as we did to New York.

My mother is still grateful."

"How about bringing Lenore to Thanksgiving dinner here?"

"I hadn't planned on doing anything until after January 1, but I'll ask her."

Where was Eric? That was the lingering question.

# CHAPTER 44
## *Family Values*

Thanksgiving, that most American of holidays, supposedly celebrated by members of families who foregather, presumably to renew ties and the bonds of kinship. But like many other holidays, Thanksgiving's original significance as a day reserved for prayerful gratitude to divine providence for the blessings of life has given way to eating vast amounts of food and watching any number of available football games in TV. Whether or not this is as it should be, that the puritanical spirit that originated the holiday has been comfortably retired to history, and that American families can do what they like without incurring the wrath of theocratic rulers, is an opinion that must be left to individuals and their families. Generally a perfunctory nod toward giving thanks might happen. Some give no thanks at all, and generally regard the holiday as a waste of time with people with whom they have nothing in common, and whom they were just as happy to continue avoiding in the first place.

Hal thought back on Thanksgivings at his grandparents' farm many years ago, attended by aunts and uncles and cousins. The meal itself was a major production for such a crowd, but was ably provided by his grandmother whose culinary skills were equal to a hotel caterer's. After the dinner, served around 3:00PM, there began the inevitable discussion among his aunts that brought up differences of opinion, and which always ended up with hurt feelings. Hal's sister rightly called Thanksgiving on the farm the Annual Plate Throwing Contest. Family members angrily left with hurt feelings until time would heal whatever wounds had been inflicted, and usually just in time for round two at the next Thanksgiving Day showdown.

It occurred to him that members of his new family not only didn't start fights, but instead seemed genuinely glad to see each other. Simon called it the Peaceable Kingdom, and he was right. Oh it was true that some members came and went, changed partners, committed acts of dubious integrity from time to time, but that said, the men and one woman gathered this day at Hal and Simon's house were pleasant, cheerful, and of a mind to spend a happy day in each other's company.

"Things are going so well that I wonder if Denise won't show up to spread her venom around," Ken said.

"She's ill, didn't you hear? I still have a spy at the restaurant who told me she hasn't been in for a few days. He wasn't sure what's wrong with her, but if she's not showing up for the evening shift, it must be serious," Roger said.

"Simon probably knows, but confidentiality laws won't let him say," Hal said having overheard them. "He won't even tell me, even after I've tickled him until he screams."

"You are a sadist, Hal Schroeder, and I can't figure out why that lovely man has put up with you all this time," Roger said.

Hal smiled and said, "There are other compensations."

Tom and Mark had come up from San Diego; Mike and John had arrived from San Jose. "Nobody in his right mind would miss this dinner. I even learned to like mincemeat pie years ago," Tom said. "Really good to see you two. When are you coming to America's Finest City to visit? You can't be doing much surfing up there in that landlocked burb you live in. We'll take you to Ocean Beach and supply the boards."

"Burb, huh? I'll have you know that it's not a 'burb' of San Francisco if that's what you mean, you ninny," Mike kidded back. "But we'll take you up on the surfing offer if you come up so we can take you to San Francisco so you can rub off some of that rural rust you've accumulated."

"Aha! So you agree that you have to go to SF to find a real city up there!"

"No, it's just that I don't want to be embarrassed by my rube brother in the city where I live and have to hold my head up. San Francisco provides a suitable gay anonymity," Mike said, keeping up the ribbing.

"My, my, hasn't he gotten hoity-toity now? And using such big words, too!" Tom said, grabbing his former partner and nearly wrestling him to the floor.

"Hey, you two!" Hal shouted. "Wrestle outside, please. What's a parent to do, I ask you? Think they'll ever grow up?"

Their respective partners, Mark and John, stood by looking amused. "Sometimes we just feel like stand-ins to this soap opera," John said as he poured more champagne for them both. Hmm . . . Hal thought he detected some irony in that remark. "They always act like this when they get together, those two. We're used to it, aren't we Mark?"

"We might as well be. I don't see anything changing," he replied. "Let's leave them to their wrestling match and have a stroll around the garden."

Despite his best efforts to create a Thanksgiving dinner that was less caloric and dietetically deadly than its traditional predecessors, Hal couldn't give up presenting most of the favorites everyone expected to see. He did manage to do away with the yams with marshmallow topping (a dish he loathed) banning it over Simon's objections. "It's possible to have yams without all that goo as you will shortly see," he said. Nevertheless, the turkey arrived accompanied by everything else that American families admire and can't wait to dive into.

Fourteen at dinner: Roger and Ken, Bertrand and George, Norman Stands and Danny, the four boys, Hal and Simon made up the first dozen. "Well, your Danny seems to have staying power. Think he's after the crown jewels?"

"If he is, he's curiously averse to wearing any of them. I've offered him a few baubles which he has steadfastly said no to. So it has to be my overwhelming charm, you spiteful bitch."

"Maybe he just likes older men, not that you really *are* an older man," Hal quickly said with a wry smile.

"When you get to be my age, my dear, you'll be grateful for younger men who prefer us more mature gentlemen who know how to treat them. Now what's that ungodly stuff you're dispensing there?"

At the other end of the table sat Carl with his fiancé Lenore filling out the expected fourteen. She chatted amiably with everyone, and Hal became more won over as to why Carl was in love with her. Bertrand and George were utterly enthralled. She was a handsome, stately woman, probably around thirty-five or so, with a regal bearing and impeccably dressed. Her dress did not shout out wealth, but instead spoke of good taste and breeding.

She made a hit with Edward who curled up on her lap while she ate dinner. "He's a nuisance, Lenore," Hal said. "Make him leave if he's annoying you."

"Not in the least. He doesn't even beg for food," she smiled back. "I think that I've got an admirer."

"He'll make a lovely bridesmaid at your wedding. When is it again?" Hal asked.

"Early next year. We haven't really set a date."

Simon came around the table and said something in Hal's ear. They went to the kitchen together, returning in a few minutes.

"We have a proposal that you two can feel free to accept or not. We'd like to have your wedding right here, unless you had in mind a church affair."

"That's a great idea!" Roger said. "And you wouldn't have to worry about catering a reception. We can work all of that out. Wow, how exciting. A real wedding in a gay household. 'The times they are a-changing' as Bob Dylan once sang."

"I'm sure it wouldn't be the first of its kind," Simon said, "but it would be a first for us. I hope you'll consider it, Lenore."

She looked pleased at the suggestion. "We'll talk it over and let you know soon. What a very nice offer. Isn't it, Carl?" Carl smiled weakly in response, and then nodded.

"Hey, you said you wanted to stay a part of this family, didn't you?" Hal reminded him. "Well, whatever you decide, you two are part of us."

After dinner, the Tom and Mike decided on a beach trek. "And we won't go swimming for a whole hour, Mommy," Tom kidded Hal.

"Fine. Just don't get lost," Hal said to their backs as they picked up surf boards and loaded them onto Tom's car. It wasn't swimming or surf that made Hal uneasy. It was that Tom and Mike had left their respective partners, Mark and John, behind as they headed for the beach. They in turn decided on a walk into town.

I wonder what that's about, Hal thought. He had watched them looking at each other before dinner and then during it, and he knew that look that gay men give each other, that look that searches, and explores, and invites. When he got Simon alone, he said, "What do you make of all that?"

"The flirting between Mark and John you mean? It's pretty obvious. They're attracted to each other. The question is whether Tom and Mike are in on this or not."

"Oh God, who can tell? Men are going to do what men are going to do, that much I've learned. Tom and Mike can't be oblivious to what's going on, can they?" Hal asked.

"I'd guess not. Maybe that's why they went off by themselves, as if it were just like old times. Gives their partners a chance to try it all out."

"We are certainly getting broad-minded, aren't we? Well, nothing we can do. Let's see who's still here," Hal said as he and Simon returned to the dining room.

Sprawling on sofas and easy chairs in the living room were the members of the dinner party, digesting dinner as best they could. Desultory conversations, a few noddings-off, all in all, a usual Thanksgiving Day afternoon. By early evening, everyone had gone home except for the out-oftowners who would be staying over.

Tom came through the back door with Mike close behind. "How was the surf?" Hal asked.

"Not bad. You're not putting all those leftovers away already, are you?"

"Wow, the bottomless pit. Take a plate and dig in, sonny." Hal wondered when Tom would notice that the door to the cottage was shut and the blinds pulled down. It didn't take long.

"They're out there, aren't they?" Tom asked. "We figured they would be, Mike and I, didn't we?"

"Yep, and we also figured that we might as well just let them get it all out of their systems," Mike said, scooping up a helping of stuffing.

"Very uh . . . open-minded of you two. No fits of jealous rage about to happen? No angry shouting? No threats of break-ups?" Simon asked.

"Ha! Nope, we're cool. Look, it's this way. Two handsome men like our partners meet up and can't keep their eyes off each other. So what? We know how they feel, don't we? And you know how it is with gay men. Might as well go with it. What should we do, try to stop things? You know that wouldn't be a good idea. Everybody would be totally pissed off about that. Mike and I decided to just let nature take its course. No harm, no foul."

Hal had been quietly listening to Tom's rationale. He wasn't so sure that he would be equally complicit should anyone make serious moves on Simon. "Makes sense, I guess," he said. "No chance those two will dump you big dummies and run off together, huh?"

"We've got more going between us than a roll in the hay can disturb," Mike said. "Don't worry, things will be fine."

Evening, and the house was quiet but still redolent of the homey aromas of dinner. Edward had reluctantly watched the beautiful Lenore leave, but in the absence of her comfortable lap, he curled up on his favorite spot on top of the stereo. What a year this has been, Hal thought as he and Simon tidied up the kitchen, stowed enormous amounts of turkey leftovers, and put the last of the dishes in the dishwasher.

He took stock of things, not only of the beauty of peace that he saw around him, but of how it had all come together. He had seen straight marriages fail, had seen gay relationships bloom and die, had seen other gay men find love with each other, had watched pompous bigots belittled, and friends come to truer realizations of themselves. He had seen tragedy and death, and the beginnings of more gay liberation movements. He had seen the effects of hatred from a misguided religion, had seen wrongs righted, and some degree of justice served. A couple of borders had been crossed, barriers broken down, and he had to admit that his own thinking about whether somebody is either gay or straight had expanded to assimilate a larger spectrum of human feelings. All in all, a great deal of life's drama had played itself before him in the space of a few months.

It was perhaps more of a tapestry than a drama, with a wide range of colors, of characters that populated the pictures that now appeared in his mind, a varied and variegated panoply of life in Laguna Beach, woven into rich cloth by an unpredictably broad assortment of the town's denizens. "Lagunatics," he said under his breath, "some lunatics, some not; some irritating and selfish, some generous and loving; some capricious, some naïve; but in their own way, all necessary to the total landscape."

He viewed the great panorama of the last year with serenity right now, here in his kitchen, here with Simon. They were in an impregnable place once more, the happiness they sought had come to them, and from that place of tranquility, they were fortified to deal with whatever might come.

Simon turned off the kitchen lights and came up behind him. "What were you just muttering, something about Lagunatics?" he asked as he curled his arms around Hal.

"Just that I wouldn't have it any other way, would you? I mean, we've been through some tough times this year, all of us, but look at us now. Oh, I think we've had to give up some of our youthful notions that we could live in the world without paying much attention to it, but I also think we're better off taking our place, even demanding our place in the world, even if that means higher visibility as gay people," Hal said.

"My, my! Pretty philosophical this evening, aren't you?" Simon said as he rubbed Hal's head. "And you're right. We're lucky to be here, to be Lagunatics, but mostly I'm feeling pretty good about us. You and me, old man. I think we're in it together for the long haul, don't you?"

"Yep, but if you quit giving me massages, I'll tickle you until the neighbors call the cops," Hal laughed as he turned for a full hug with Simon.